Liturgy and Society

The Function of the Church in the M—————— World

THE REV————
of the So————
Mis————

This book ———— ————
general reader, ———— ————
understand better the relation of the
art, the architecture and the liturgy
of the Church to the meaning of
common worship. It should also
appeal to readers interested in
ecclesiastical art. Father Hebert has
first-hand knowledge of the liturgical
movement on the Continent. His
study of this movement, and of its
implications, leads him to discussion,
in non-technical language, of the
wider problems of the relation of
the Church and the Word at the
present time.

THE BISHOP OF CHICHESTER says:
'This remarkable book throws a
flood of light on the relations between the Church with its liturgy,
and common human life. It sets out
the principles of a new spiritual
movement which goes back on pure
individualism in worship and faith,
and declares that it is the function of
the Church's liturgy to interpret and
express the life of the Christian community as the Body of Christ, and
also to exhibit the aim and meaning
of human life in the light of the
Incarnation. Those who wonder
whether the Church should do more
than provide religion for the devout,
should read this book. Those who
ask whether human society should
find its centre in man—or in God,
should read it too. It is a book for
the times—a book that is spiritual
and actual.'

With sixteen illustrations

LITURGY AND SOCIETY

I. ST. PAUL'S CATHEDRAL

LITURGY AND SOCIETY

THE FUNCTION OF THE CHURCH
IN THE MODERN WORLD

by

A. G. HEBERT

Of the Society of the Sacred Mission, Kelham

LONDON
FABER AND FABER LIMITED
24 RUSSELL SQUARE

FIRST PUBLISHED IN MAY MCMXXXV
SECOND IMPRESSION JANUARY MCMXXXVI
THIRD IMPRESSION DECEMBER MCMXXXVI
FOURTH IMPRESSION DECEMBER MCMXLII
FIFTH IMPRESSION APRIL MCMXLIV
SIXTH IMPRESSION MARCH MCMXLVI
SEVENTH IMPRESSION MARCH MCMXLIX
BY FABER & FABER LIMITED
24 RUSSELL SQUARE LONDON W.C.I
PRINTED IN GREAT BRITAIN
BY BUTLER & TANNER LIMITED
FROME AND LONDON

Fa

PREFACE

This book is an essay on the Church and her message, particularly as embodied in the actual order of the Church and her liturgy, in relation to the problem of belief and of a true social life in the confused world of today. It is addressed not only to those who are Christians, but also to those many others who look in from time to time through the church door, and wonder whether some day they will come in. That the Church, being such as she is, should inspire a certain repulsion, is intelligible enough. But she also exercises an attraction; and here I feel sure that it is not least the sacred actions and words of Christian worship that make to very many a deep appeal, and one that is not only or even chiefly aesthetic: that even when sermons are tiresome and hymns banal, the drama of the eucharistic rite and the words of the Prayer Book speak to them of a real relation of man to the Eternal, and inspire a hope that amid the disintegration of modern life, the confusion of belief, and the falling in ruins of the towers of Babel that human idealism tries to build, they may yet come to find that this sacred symbolism is an expression of reality, of the things which cannot be shaken, of the City which hath foundations, whose builder and maker is God.

I write as an Anglican. This book was originally intended to be a treatise on the principles of Christian worship, inspired to a large extent by the Liturgical Movement in the Roman Catholic Church, which, in seeking to re-introduce the Catholic laity to the treasures of the liturgy,

7

has found itself possessed of a key to unlock many doors, and engaged in an ever-widening circle of interests and activities. Thus I began to plan a book that would show how Christian dogma finds its typical expression in worship, and how Christian religion is not merely a way of piety for the individual soul, but is in the first place a participation in a common life. But the subject would not allow itself to be limited to a purely religious and ecclesiastical treatment. If Christianity is the redemption of all life, the things done and said in church must have a direct relation to the things done and said everywhere else; the sacraments and the liturgy exist in order to give to human life its true direction in relation to God, and to bind men in fellowship with one another. Therefore it became necessary to envisage the condition of modern Europe, which, having lost the common faith by which once it lived, is seeing its social life lose its cohesion and threaten to disintegrate altogether. One must ask whether the Church does not show the way, the only way, to the recovery of a common faith and a true social life. The book must cover a wide range of subjects, and must start with the question, 'What has the Church to give to the modern world?'

This way of approach starts from the consideration of the Church as an existing fact, and as the inheritor of a long tradition. It says, 'If you want to know what the Church is, do not ask first what the theologians say about her, but look and see what she is and what she does.' If you would see what the Church of England is, look at the services which take place in the parish churches, including in your survey all that goes to make them up, not only the actual rites and ceremonies, music and preaching, but the manner in which clergy, ministers and people take part in them. Here is the present Church of England; the picture includes much that is weak and unworthy, and

much that is noble and inspiring. But it is plain that the
rite which you are witnessing has had a long history. The
Prayer Book service has remained unchanged in essentials
since it was put into English at the Reformation nearly
400 years ago; and elsewhere, in the Roman Catholic and
the Orthodox Eastern Churches, you may witness rites
which, as far as the words of the service are concerned,
have remained unchanged in essentials for a thousand
years longer. In every case, a continual development is
taking place with regard to the outward setting and ren-
dering of the rite; but the rite itself is relatively permanent,
and it gives expression to the faith by which the Church
lives from generation to generation. It does not at all
follow that the present form of the liturgical tradition
exhibits that tradition at its best. The tradition can only
be understood in the light of its past, which throws light
upon its possibilities in the future.

When therefore one invites those who are not believing
Christians to consider the Church's liturgical life, this way
of approach points them to the Church as an existing
fact, the Church militant, the Church imperfect, yet living
from age to age by the common, Catholic, universal faith
in God's saving work, which the liturgy illustrates and
proclaims in a variety of ways—by sacraments, Bible-
lessons, Creeds, prayers, psalms, hymns, preaching. And
when the Church calls men to come in and share this
common faith and fellowship, she is calling them to
share a common life of sacrifice and service. When she
incorporates us into herself in Holy Baptism, she signs us
with the Cross in token that hereafter we shall not be
ashamed to confess the faith of Christ crucified, and man-
fully to fight under His banner against sin, the world
and the devil. There is no promise here of ready-
made solutions for difficulties of belief, of morals, or
of social life, but only of a share in a common faith

and a common conflict against evil, and of help in the conflict.

Such is the 'liturgical' way of approach; and we may best see its true bearings by contrasting it with other ways. That which the Church has to give to the world is often represented as if it were primarily a call to individual conversion, the 'soul-saving' of the Evangelical preacher, or the 'life-changing' of the Group Movement. But there are at least two main difficulties here, for the man of to-day. First: When the Wesleyan preaching, two centuries ago, swept England from end to end, it could appeal to a common belief about God and Christ and the destiny of man, which, though widely denied by the intellectuals, was still fundamentally unchallenged among the common people. But this is not the case today; in the mind of the ordinary man these common assumptions have been dissolved away into uncertainty. And second: This conception of soul-saving leaves unanswered the question what is to happen afterwards—like the novels which end when the hero and the heroine have agreed to marry one another, as if that were the end of their story and not rather its beginning. What manner of life does conversion lead up to? Will all difficulties disappear? Manifestly they will not. If by conversion the problem of the man himself has been solved, the problems of his outer life and his social relations still await solution.

Another way of approach is that which appeals to the mind rather than to the will. The writer draws out a statement of belief, and defends it against all manner of objections. He seeks to clear up the uncertainties of the modern man by offering him a series of propositions, for which he claims finality and truth, so far as that is attainable. He does not always get the range of his objective, and as a rule his book is chiefly read by those who are already converted. But however this be, the writer is compelled to demand that *his* opinions and *his* way of putting things be taken as a standard, which he hopes that the reader will accept.

But the way of approach which I have called 'liturgical is essentially an appeal *away from* personal beliefs and opinions, my own included, to the common faith of the Church, to the authority of the Church, to the dogma by which the Church lives. This common faith is summed up in the Creeds as a faith in God, the Father, Son, and Holy Spirit, centring in the historical facts of God's coming to man in Jesus Christ; it appeals to the Bible, as its norm and standard, and as the witness to the historical facts on which it rests; it is embodied in concrete form in the sacraments; set forth in the liturgies; analysed, discussed, and rationalized by the theologians; and proclaimed by the preachers. The appeal to the authority of the Church must mean at least all this.

The appeal to the authority of the Church is not therefore an appeal from individual freedom of thought to a closed theological system. This misapprehension is very common. It is assumed that the authority of the Church exists in order to guarantee a series of propositions, whether by the voice of an infallible Pope, or of semi-infallible Doctors of the Church. But in fact, on numerous points of theology and philosophy Popes have contradicted Popes, and the Doctors have disagreed. They have agreed in accepting the Church's common faith and in sharing in the Church's common life. It is indeed true, and it must be emphasized, that the Church's common faith is essentially a dogmatic faith; but it is not possible wholly to identify the dogma of the Church with the particular formulations of it made by individual theologians, even the greatest. I have discussed this thorny question in the fourth chapter of this book, on Dogma; the discussion, as will be seen, leads up to the conclusion that the confession of the common Christian faith, so far from involving any renunciation of intellectual freedom, is in reality its indispensable condition: 'the Truth shall make you free'.

It is because this book is essentially an appeal to the authority of the Church that it can rightly be allowed to cover the wide range of subjects which the Table of Contents reveals. If it were an apologetic or a personal statement of views, it would rightly be required to answer a thousand and one questions in order to vindicate itself. The questions are there to be asked; to many of them I have tried to give an answer. But the pith of the matter is, not that *I* am able to answer them, but that the members of the Church, you and I, have the duty of tackling them in common, and that it is only on the basis of the common Christian faith and within the unity of the common Christian fellowship that they can fruitfully be answered at all. 'Other foundation can no man lay than that which is laid, which is Christ.'

The present age, with its manifold divisions, confusions, and distractions, can hardly be an age of theological synthesis. There are many questions which *we* are not capable of answering satisfactorily. It is rather for us to 'take no thought of the harvest, but only of proper sowing'. Before we can tackle the questions adequately, we ourselves need to become different; we need to draw together, and find a spiritual unity. Here then is the word which this book would say to those who are not yet professing Christians: 'You can only find that spiritual unity by confessing the Christian faith in God and bringing your gifts into the Church's common life.'

But it is to Christians after all that this book is really in the first place addressed, and especially to those of the Church to which I belong. I have had three chief aims. First, I have tried to give some expression to the view of the Church as the mystical Body of Christ: that the

12

Church is not merely an organization to bring together a number of religious individuals, nor yet an institution with a quasi-legal claim to validity, but a society with an organic life, such as is best described by metaphors drawn from living things—she is the Bride of Christ, she is our Mother, she is the Body of Christ, of which He is the Head and we the members. These are things which very many of us are trying to learn how to say. And many of us are convinced that the apprehension of these things is closely connected with the recovery of the true place of the Holy Eucharist in the life of the Church; not merely as Sacrifice, not merely as Communion, but as Sacrifice consummated in Communion. When we have learnt again to celebrate the Lord's Service thus—not as a devotional service for the inner circle of the faithful in the early morning, nor as a mid-morning act of devotion with no communicants except the priest, but making the Parish Eucharist with the communion of the people the central act of worship on every Sunday—that service will teach us, by our participation in it, the meaning of the Fellowship of the Body more effectively than all our books of theology.

Secondly, there are many of us in the Church who are seeking to make good our escape from the corrupting influence of Liberalism in the theological region. We are not reactionaries, taking refuge from the dangers of the future in a romantic return to the past. We do not shirk the issues raised by modern knowledge in the criticism of the Bible and in other regions of study, or by the political and social changes of the modern world, nor advocate a return to a closed theological system or to the political order of a past age. Nor do we fail to appreciate the virtues of the Liberal theologians, their desire to be honest and open-minded and to love the truth. It is rather that we believe that their Liberalism itself prevents them from doing justice to their principles; the annual Modern Churchmen's Conference shows only too clearly how Liberalism is developing a reactionary dogmatism of its own. These pages contain a number of criticisms of Liberal Theology; but I have sought to criticize it not negatively but constructively, seeking to find a better way; and most of the opinions which I have criticized are opinions which I have myself held at one time or other, in my undergraduate days and since. The way out from Liberalism is not backwards but forwards.

Thirdly, there is the mission of the Church to the modern world. Christians are still in danger of suffering from an inferiority complex, owing very largely to our habit of regarding Christianity as a way of religion for the individual; about our personal piety we have naturally a certain shyness. But Christianity is in the first place faith in the God to whom the world belongs, and in Christ as the Saviour of all mankind. Either the Gospel which we have believed is not true, or it is a Gospel for all mankind and no men can live their lives rightly without it.

In this age above all, when the peoples of Europe have lost the common faith by which once they lived, no Christian has any right to be ashamed of being a Christian. The faith which is committed to us, and the social life which is actually, if imperfectly, realized in our church fellowship, is just that for lack of which European civilization is in danger of perishing. It is of the first importance that Christians should thoroughly learn what it means to be Christians. The Church in England is as much a missionary Church as the Church in India or Japan.

Ye are the light of the world, says our Lord to us; a city set on a hill cannot be hid even if it wants to. You are a lamp set up in a room, put there by the Master of the house in order to give light; not to be hidden away shyly under a bushel-measure or under the bed, but to stand on the lamp-stand. So your light must shine before men, not for your purposes but for His; not that men may glorify you—for any sort of self-consciousness about setting yourselves up to be better than other people must be left out of account as irrelevant—but that they may glorify Him, your Father in heaven, and come with you to believe in Him and worship Him. One thing you are to be afraid of: lest you should be as salt which has lost its savour; for there is nothing to be done with the insipid stuff but throw it away. You are in the world as salt, to purify and make wholesome, or as light, to shine; let your light therefore so shine before men (Matt. v. 13–16).

I have to thank, besides members of the Community to which I belong, two other friends in particular, who will, I am sure, be grateful to me if I do not thank them in public. Parts of Chapter IX and of Chapter V have appeared in the *S.S.M. Quarterly*. I have also to thank for permission to use quotations, the Rt. Rev. Dr. Herwegen (p. 64 and elsewhere); Dom Anselme Robeyns (pp. 131, 133); the Rev. Dr. Pius Parsch (p. 135); Mrs. Birkbeck and Messrs. Longmans, Green and Co. (p. 147); M. B. Reckitt, Esq. (p. 204); and for permission to use illustrations, Donald Maxwell, Esq., and Messrs. Skeffington (frontispiece); Fratelli Alinari, Via Nazionale 8, Florence (nos. ii, iii, iv, v, vi); Dr. Herwegen (nos. vii, viii, ix); and N. F. Cachemaille-Day, Esq., F.R.I.B.A., (nos. xiv and xvi).

A. GABRIEL HEBERT, S.S.M.

Kelham,
 Newark-on-Trent.
Jan. 1935.

CONTENTS

What has the Church to give to the modern world? Religion? This answer is commonly given, and it is assumed
that a man's religious beliefs are his private concern. Hence
social life is left without a religious basis; the results are
apparent in the disintegration of modern life. The common
faith of the nineteenth century was a belief in Progress. Liberal
theology builds on this belief. Hence (*a*) it preaches a different Gospel from that of the old Christianity; and (*b*) it has no
adequate answer to the question, 'Why should I be religious?'
Orthodox Christianity is partly under a cloud. But the witness
of the Church to the Gospel of God is given, not only by the
lives and teaching of Christians, but also by the liturgy itself.
Instances from Baptism, Eucharist, Consecration of a Bishop.
These imply that Christianity is not in the first place a religion,
but a faith. (*pages* 27–42.)

PART I: CHRISTIANITY

(i) *The Problem of the World-Religions.* If Christianity shares
with the world-religions a common ritual pattern, does it
follow that it is just one of the world-religions? The fundamental difference lies in the Christian appeal to history.
(*pages* 45–48.)

(ii) *The Fulfilment of Judaism.* Argument from the Epistle
to the Hebrews: The O.T. sacrifices were inadequate; the
answer came in an unexpected way; but when Jesus had done
His work, it was found that He had answered the question by
raising it to a higher level. (*pages* 48–51.)

(iii) *The Fulfilment of the World-Religions.* The same formula
applied to the pagan religions. (*pages* 51–58.)

CONTENTS

PART II: CHRISTIANITY AND THE MODERN WORLD

considered, because it sums up the wisdom of the past. Difficulties in accepting Christianity: summary of points raised in
the course of this book. The duty of Christians. (*pages* 251–
260.)

NOTES ON THE
ILLUSTRATIONS

I. ST. PAUL'S CATHEDRAL   *frontispiece*

Reproduced from *Famous London Churches*, by C. B. Mortlock and Donald Maxwell (1934), by permission of the publishers, Messrs. Skeffington and Sons, Ltd., Paternoster House, St. Paul's, E.C.4.

II. CHRIST THE LORD   *to face page* 49

Mosaic in the apse of the cathedral of Cefalu, Sicily, above the high altar. Photo, Alinari no. 19880. The church was built by the Norman king of Sicily, Roger II, in 1148, and decorated by Greek artists. Christ is depicted reigning in glory; the book which He holds has the words in Greek and Latin 'I am the Light of the world; he that followeth Me shall not walk in darkness, but shall have the light of life'. For other examples of the 'Pantokrator', see Diehl, *Manuel d'art byzantin* (Paris, 1926), pp. 487, 490, 507, 702, 802, 848.

III. BASILICA OF ST. CLEMENT, ROME   *to face page* 64

Photo, Alinari no. 6079. This picture has a twofold interest. First, it exhibits clearly the arrangement of the primitive basilica (see p. 75, *infra*). Behind the altar can be seen the bishop's throne and the seats for the presbyters on either side. At the altar the celebrant must face the people; beneath the altar on the near side is the *confessio* or martyrs' shrine (which in this instance contains the reputed relics of St. Clement and of St. Ignatius of Antioch). Above the altar is the canopy or *ciborium*, bearing the ancient symbol of the Anchor (Heb. vi. 19). Within the enclosure formed by the *cancelli* is the place for the *schola cantorum* or choir; here too are the *ambones* for the lections. The picture shows why in the Roman rite the Epistle is still read facing east; the reader in the *ambo* naturally turned to face the bishop. On the other side is the Gospel *ambo*, and near it the Paschal candlestick.

Secondly, there is its archaeological interest. In the course of centuries, the ground-level has risen many feet. Below this church the visitor may still see part of the wall of Servius Tullius, and of a house which in the first century belonged probably to St. Clement (according to the usual reckoning the second Bishop of Rome after St. Peter, and the writer of the Epistle to the Church of Corinth about A.D. 97), and was used for Christian worship; it is therefore one of the most ancient church-sites in the world. In the persecutions of the third century it seems to have been confiscated, and acquired for the Mithra-cult; the remains of the *Mithraeum*, in excellent preservation, can still be seen. In the fourth century the Christians bought back the site, and erected a basilica; not the present building, but one whose nave was nearly half as wide again. This lasted till the early twelfth century, when the present church was built above the old one, the ground-level having again risen. To this date the mosaics in the apse belong. But the altar, *ciborium, cancelli*, and *ambones* are proved by the ancient inscriptions which remain to have been the same which stood in the fourth-century basilica.—*Dictionnaire d'archéologie chrétienne et de liturgie*, art. 'Clément, Basilique de saint-' vol. VI, col. 1874 ff.

IV. SARCOPHAGUS FROM THE OLD BASILICA OF ST. PAUL, ROME *to face page* 67

Photo, Alinari no. 6407. This Sarcophagus, dating from the fourth century, is now in the Christian Museum of the Lateran. The subjects are: (*top row, left to right*) God (the Trinity?) creating Eve; Adam asleep on the ground—After the Fall; God gives to Adam some ears of corn, to Eve a sheep— Medallion (*centre*) with portraits (unfinished) of the departed —Christ turning the water into wine—Christ multiplying the loaves (both these are symbols of the eucharistic consecration) —Christ raising Lazarus from the dead, while Martha prays (the suitability of this subject to a funeral memorial is obvious. Note that, as nearly always in the early centuries, the figure of Christ is beardless). *Bottom row:* The adoration of the Magi (for the connexion of this with the eucharistic Offertory, see p. 244, *infra*)—Christ gives sight to the blind man—(*centre*) Daniel among the lions (a type of Christ, the victor over sin and death, see pp. 244–5, *infra*)—Christ warns Peter of his coming denial; note the cock—Peter led away to prison—Moses bringing water from the rock (symbol of Baptism and Communion, see p. 243, *infra*).—*Dict. d'arch. chr. et de lit.*, art. 'Latran', vol. XVI, cols. 1698 ff.; cf. art. 'Catacombes, Art des', vol. IV, col. 2450 ff.; and G. M. Bevan, *Early Christians of Rome* (S.P.C.K., 1927), pp. 54–84.

V. THE RESURRECTION *to face page* 78

Mosaic from St. Mark's, Venice. Photo, Alinari no. 13743. The theme is Christ triumphing over death and Satan, and rescuing Adam. See p. 72, *infra*. The date is late in the eleventh century: Diehl, *Manuel d'art byzantin* (Paris, 1926), p. 536 ff. For other examples of this subject, the 'Anastasis', see illustrations in Diehl, pp. 499, 511, 545, 574.

VI. THE HOLY FACE OF LUCCA   *to face page* 81

Photo, Alinari no. 8288. In Lucca Cathedral, Italy. The legend about this much-venerated figure is that it was carved by Nicodemus, and floated miraculously to the shores of Italy in the year 783. Dating from long before the time when realistic representations of the Crucifixion began to be made, it has for its theme Christ reigning from the tree; the posture of the feet indicates the willingness of the Passion; the robe is embroidered with figures of saints, who as members of His Body share in His passion and His triumph.

VII. THE WORD WAS MADE FLESH   *to face page* 96

This and the two following subjects are modern works, from the studios of the Benedictine Abbey of Maria Laach, near Andernach, Germany.

VIII. IMMACULATA   *to face page* 113

IX. OUR LADY OF THE LILY   *to face page* 128

X. KELHAM CHAPEL   *to face page* 177

The Chapel of the House of the Sacred Mission, Kelham, finished in 1928, is the work of the late Charles Thompson, of the firm of Currey and Thompson, Derby, whose death in 1932 has robbed English architecture of a great artist. This building is not copied from the Byzantine or any other style. Its form was dictated by the needs of its use; there must be a choir suitable for plainsong singing by a large body of voices, which must therefore be wide rather than long and narrow. The solution was found in a square central space roofed with a dome, with aisles on either side, and beyond the arch which bears the rood, a spacious sanctuary with a shallow apse. The photograph was taken by night, in the dim light given by two lamps placed in the rim of the dome to illuminate the rood.

XI. THE CHURCH OF ST. ANTONIUS, BASEL

     to face page 192

This building, a Catholic parish church in the western suburbs of Basel, Switzerland, is by Prof. Karl Moser, Zürich, and G. Doppler and Son, Basel. The date is 1927. Built of concrete, it quite evidently springs out of the same civilization as the other modern buildings of our cities; the tower, carrying its cross very much in the attitude of the crucifer in a procession, presents the challenge of the Christian faith to our age. The tower is rectangular, having on the near side a smaller rectangle carrying the staircase, and running up into the belfry.

XII.   THE CROSS AND THE ALTAR   *to face page* 209

Kelham Chapel. The photograph is taken from the gallery, some 18 feet above the floor, which leads to the organ-loft.

XIII.   THE HÖGALID CHURCH, STOCKHOLM
to face page 224

A photograph taken on the occasion of the consecration of this church, in 1923. The late Archbishop Söderblom and the Pastor Primarius of Stockholm are at the altar. This church, by Prof. Ivar Tengbom, is perhaps the finest work of modern Swedish church architecture.

XIV.   ST. NICHOLAS' CHURCH, BURNAGE,
MANCHESTER   *to face page* 241

By N. F. Cachemaille-Day, of Messrs. Welch, Cachemaille-Day and Lander. Consecrated in 1932. The plan of this church was largely dictated by the fact that it is built on a main road, and that it was necessary to have a porch on the road, and also to place the congregation as far back from the road as possible. This illustration appears, with others, in *Architecture Illustrated*, Sept. 1932. It is unfortunate that from the point of view from which it is taken, the entrance to the church appears to be blocked by the wall which flanks it.

XV.   THE ROOD AT KELHAM   *to face page* 246

By the late C. S. Jagger, A.R.A. The figures are in bronze, and were erected in 1929; plaster models were exhibited in the Royal Academy in that year. This picture may be compared with no. vi, as a modern and realistic expression of the same theme: the triumph of Christ through suffering.

XVI.   ST. SAVIOUR'S CHURCH, ELTHAM, LONDON
to face page 256

By the same architect as No. XIV; date 1933. In the same year this church was awarded by the R.I.B.A. the London Architecture Medal for the best building in the London area erected in the previous three years, now for the first time awarded to a church. The complete plan includes a hall for social activities as well as a vicarage. See *The Architect and Building News*, 30 June 1933.

THE MODERN WORLD AND CHRISTIANITY

*

What has Christianity to give to the modern world? This is the problem with which we are to deal. But let us ask first, What does the modern world think that Christianity has to give?

It is commonly believed that the Churches are organizations which provide religion for those who want it; religion of various brands. Some of them are ritualistic, offering to their devotees, no doubt, partly an aesthetic, partly a religious satisfaction in the performance of a mystery-cult. Others place in the forefront a personal appeal to the individual for the changing of his life. More liberal brands of Christianity provide sermons which are really topical discussions of the questions of the day, and seek to encourage social idealism, the love of peace, and the practice of the more amiable virtues.

It is assumed that religion is the concern of the individual; each man must make up his mind for himself on theological matters. 'About these abstruse questions there can be no certainty: the theologians disagree among themselves, and in any case the rarefied atmosphere in which their discussions are conducted makes them unintelligible to the common man. Religious belief, in short, is a matter of opinion. It is not that religious belief is harmful: on the contrary, its effect is on the whole beneficial, and those who are able to hold to a religious belief and fulfil its rather exacting demands, are to be respected for it. But the differences which exist between the various churches prove that religious belief is a matter of opinion: it is for those who are temperamentally fitted for it, and to whom it appeals. There are many who do not feel its appeal, just as there are many who do not enjoy music: these naturally leave it on one side.'

The incongruity of such an attitude is obvious: for if there is a God, His existence and His nature cannot fail to be of vital concern to all men. If He exists, He is the reality underlying all human life, and the life of the individual will only be rightly lived if he has faith in God, and social life will only be on its right basis when it is founded on a common faith. Such a common faith is seen, for instance, in the Old Testament: sins and moral failings are there in plenty, but nevertheless the whole polity and social life of Israel was based on the acknowledgement of the national God. So it was in medieval England, and till long after the Reformation the social life of England was based on a common faith in God and common assumptions about right and wrong. The gradual break-up of this common faith seems to have its beginnings in the religious divisions of the nation which became permanent after the Civil War: the beheading of King Charles I will form, if this is right, the great dividing-line in English history. Certainly from that time onwards the national Church ceased to be in the old sense the Church of England, and Englishmen had to choose whether they would be churchmen or dissenters: thus the individualism began which is now accepted as normal.

It is clear that when religious belief is regarded as the exclusive concern of the individual, social life can no longer be based on faith in God. Private theological beliefs cannot be allowed to influence industrial, commercial and political affairs.

The nineteenth-century moralists believed that a Christian standard of morals could still be upheld without the Christian faith in God. But it has now become evident that this was an illusion. The modern world has moved away from Christian morals, and has now no fixed standard of right and wrong, and no common faith that there is a right and a wrong.

What then becomes the basis on which social life is lived? For multitudes today it is material well-being, expediency, comfort, success in the world, a happy life, pleasures, motor-cars, cruises, avoidance as far as possible of physical and emotional discomfort, the attainment of an easy and happy life till the inevitable end. Aldous Huxley's *Brave New World* is a terrifying satire on modern life, just because it depicts so relentlessly the direction in which society is moving. Another illustration of the domination of expediency over social life may be found in the agreement of armament firms and pacifists in denying the reality of right and wrong. A favourite argument of the pacifist is to picture the horrors of war as destructive of prosperity and comfort, ignoring the claim that old-fashioned moralists always made, that it might be the duty of a nation to go to war for the sake of right. A director of an armament firm puts the matter thus:

'Great armament firms have no national or political prejudices . . . and the value of such abstract ideas as justice or liberty they leave to the discussion of idle and metaphysical minds, or employ the terms as convenient euphemisms by which the real objects of statesmen may be cloaked, and the energies of a people directed.'

Very shocking, no doubt: but this writer shares with the pacifist the denial of justice and right as governing considerations in international relations.

Meanwhile human society becomes more and more

economically interdependent. We install gas-cookers in our kitchen at Kelham; the result is a great gain in cleanliness and efficiency; but we now become dependent on the pipe-line from the gas-works, whereas with the old coal ranges we could have a year's supply of coal in hand, and if that were not procurable, we could have made shift with wood from the trees in the grounds. Here is a small instance of a world-wide process: the whole world is now one economic unit, an organism of incredible complexity.

But spiritually the world becomes less and less of a unity. More and more men are strangers to one another, strangers to the people in the next house. The individual and the family are lost in the crowd, strangers among millions. The organization of industrial life has little of spiritual unity corresponding to it. The factories deal with their workers as 'hands', and turn them away when they are no longer needed. Labour becomes mechanized, and becomes to an alarming extent work without honour, without interest, without skill—slave-work. The machine conquers the man. A fortunate minority have it for their business to design the wonderful machines and control the organization: others are still fortunate enough to retain the old-fashioned type of employment: but already the majority of lives are controlled by the new conditions.

With all this goes a slave-mentality. An advertisement for a daily paper shows six young men with the same mechanized faces and the same mechanized minds going to their work with the same daily paper carried unanimously under their left arm. *Punch* gives us a picture at Christmas-time of isolated groups of people in a flat listening sleepily to the same Christmas entertainment on the wireless. There is little social life in the vast suburbs of our cities. It is true that there are cricket clubs, tennis clubs, social clubs, which bring people together. But the cinemas to which vast crowds go provide no social life at all. More and more the multitudes live on the surface, in a spiritual loneliness which becomes more and more complete. It is not surprising that in such a society groups of men should form desirous of marching together in uniform. Fascism is alarming, because it betrays the breakdown of the old social structure. As in the days of ancient Rome, so now the town-dweller develops a senti-mental feeling for the countryside, whose picturesque and restful charm provides a relief from the drab ugliness of the town. But the village is doing its best to civilize itself by going to the town to buy shoddy goods and enjoy the new mechanized drama, and is losing the old com-mon faith and the old social life.

There is, however, or has been till lately, a real common faith—faith in Progress, which in the nineteenth century stepped effectively into the place of the old common faith in God. Men like T. H. Huxley expressed a naïve child like faith in the power of man to perfect himself by inven-tion and industry; Progress was going to banish the need for a future heaven by making a heaven on earth.

Dean Inge, who does not believe in Progress, quotes the following phrases from Herbert Spencer: 'Progress is not an accident but a necessity. What we call evil and immorality must disappear. It is certain that man must become perfect.' 'The ultimate development of the ideal man is certain—as certain as any conclusion in which we place the most implicit faith; for instance, that all men will die.' 'Always towards perfection is the mighty move-ment—towards a complete development and a more un-mixed good.' [1]

[1] W. R. Inge, *Outspoken Essays*, second series, 1922, Essay on 'The Idea of Progress', p. 163. But see also p. 167; Huxley could see farther. Also C. Dawson, *Progress and Religion* (Sheed and Ward, 1929) esp. pp. 17 ff., 208 ff., 239 ff.

But there has been a War, and there has been a Peace; and the majority of us no longer greet the idea of Progress with any enthusiasm. It has put too many of us out of work. It is true that on the material side the marvel continues. Year by year we know more about biology and chemistry and ancient history, we improve our loco-motives and railway-carriages, and our machines to make suits of clothes for which fifty tailors would once have been required, and our fighting aircraft and bombers and long-range guns. But all this Progress does not make life more worth living. The young motor-cyclist can satisfy his sense of power by feats of speed on our splendid arterial roads; but it is a lonely pastime that isolates him from his fellows. We live in fear of the breakdown of civilization through spiritual exhaustion; we live in fear of another war which might be the end.

'Yet here are the churches with their splendid traditions of martyrs and heroes of faith, with their proved power of generating moral force. Cannot the churches keep up the moral stamina of civilization by rousing men to ideal-ism and self-sacrifice for the common good? Cannot they give up their theological squabbles, their out-of-date ritual-ism, break down the crumbling walls which divide sect from sect, and unite their forces in a common attack on the evils of the day?[1] Cannot the churches save society?'

[1] 'He said that for churches that would make room, ample and full, for the apprehension of the Christian way in the liberal and undogmatic sense, there were going to be great days again. The new spirit was going to play havoc with denominational distinctions by the simple process of taking all meaning out of them. The question was not going to be whether you were an Anglican in the old sense, or a Presbyterian in the old sense, but whether you were a Christian in the new sense. Those who sought fellowship on that basis would find that they were drawn closer together than any sectarian bonds could draw them.'—Dr. Redfern at the Provincial Assembly of the Unitarian and Free Churches, in Essex Hall, 16 May 1934. Quoted by Bishop Henson in *Unitarianism and Historic Christi-anity* (Oxford, 1934).

A considerable effort has in fact been made to harness Christianity to the forces of progress: it is called Liberal or Modernist Christianity. It attracts to itself a certain proportion of the members of many of 'the churches', but it has not captured the churches as a whole, and the strongest minds in the churches stand definitely aloof from it.

Two things about Modernism seem quite certain. In the first place, it is a different thing from the old-fashioned Christianity: not the old gospel re-stated in new forms for a new age, but a different gospel. The Liberal theologians of the nineteenth century interpreted the Jesus of the Gospels as the great moral and religious teacher, the inspirer of the pure spiritual ideals by which they desired to live.[1] But they could not fail to see that St. Paul and

---

[1] Thus the late Dr. Rashdall wrote, in the peroration of his Bampton Lectures, delivered in the first year of the War: 'Translated into more modern language, the meaning of the Church's early creed "There is none other name given among men whereby we must be saved", will be something of this kind: "There is none other ideal given among men by which we may be saved, except the moral ideal which Christ taught by His words and illustrated by His life and death of love; and there is none other help so great in the attainment of that ideal as the belief in God as He has been supremely revealed in Him who so taught and lived and died." So understood, the self-sacrificing life which was consummated by the death upon the Cross has indeed power to take away the sins of the whole world.'—H. Rashdall, *The Idea of the Atonement in Christian Theology* (Macmillan, 1919), p. 463. Quoted with approval even by Dr. A. Nairne, *The Faith of the New Testament* (Longmans, 1920), p. 90 n.

Such a conception of the meaning of Christianity underlies some words of Mr. C. E. M. Joad, where he is describing the effects of the War on those who had gone through it: 'For four years the post-war generation had observed and participated in activities which, while directly violating every principle of the official creed of the Western world, received the blessing of its official exponents. Servants of the Prince of Peace in all countries and denominations were swept off their feet in a common enthusiasm in the service of the God of War, while the appalling sufferings of mankind during the four years and three months produced in sensitive minds the conviction either that

St. John could not be thus modernized. They drew a distinction between the clear sunny faith of the Sermon on the Mount, and the gloomy beliefs of St. Paul about sin and atonement and sacrifice: St. Paul became the Second Founder of Christianity, the man who began its degradation into Catholicism. Here was an admission that their own belief was a different thing from the traditional Christian belief.

Modern study has made it tolerably certain that the Jesus depicted in the nineteenth-century Lives of Jesus, which sprang up in Germany like mushrooms, never existed at all: that such un-modern features as belief in demons and conflict with radical evil, and the eschatological beliefs connected with what we call the Second Advent, are central and primary features in the Gospel of Jesus; and that the Gospel that was proclaimed in Galilee was just as much a doctrine of Salvation as the Gospel of St. Paul. The non-miraculous 'simple Christianity' that was so confidently affirmed to be the original teaching of Jesus was, in fact, the projection of nineteenth-century ideas into the first.

The strength of 'Modernism' was and is its desire to face facts honestly and courageously, accepting the methods and results of modern historical investigation—'By identifying the new learning with heresy, you make orthodoxy synonymous with ignorance'[1]—and its impatience with anything that looks like obtuse traditionalism or stuffy ecclesiasticism. It is to be criticized, not for being critical, but for not being critical enough, and

there was no God at all, or that if there was He had forgotten the world He had made and left it to its own devices, or—worse still—that He existed and was mindful, but malignant.'—In the *New Statesman and Nation*, 1 Dec. 1934, p. 785. See also Dawson, *Christianity and the New Age* (Essays in Order, Sheed and Ward, 1931), pp. 72–9.

[1] A saying of Erasmus, which the *Modern Churchman* takes for its motto.

for uncritically accepting the dogmas of the professors: not for being too modern, but for not being modern enough. The methods of modern historical investigation are sound. The trouble is the underlying theological pre-suppositions, which are, in fact, those of a different belief from the old Christianity. It is true that Modernism, believing itself to be the true Christianity, has often sought to 're-state' the old formulae, and has seemed to accept, for instance, the doctrine of the Incarnation. But upon examination it is found that this doctrine of the Incarnation means that Jesus is simply the most divine of men, so that in Him the highest human merges into the Divine, and He has the values of God[1]; it is not the belief of the old Christianity in a Divine Action, in something that God has done. It is recognized on both sides to be a different belief from the traditional Christian belief. In fact, the historical connexions of this Modernism and of the Ritschlianism of the nineteenth century are with the 'Enlightenment' of the eighteenth century and in general with the philosophy of the age of Humanism which is now hastening to its fall.[2] It is not Christianity, not the faith of the Bible, but an attempt to adapt Christianity to the belief in Progress—to belief not in God but in man.

In the second place, Modernism has no very definite answer to give to the question, 'Why should I believe in Christianity?' Old-fashioned orthodoxy used to be quite

[1] Professor Raven and Dean Dwelly say in their Letter to Dr. L. P. Jacks: 'We should not hesitate to say that God is Incarnate in varying degrees in the whole universe of our experience; when we speak of the Divinity of Christ we mean that in Him God is uniquely and universally revealed, that He by reason of His union with the Father has for us the values of God.' *Two Letters*, by L. P. Jacks, (Oxford, 1934), p. 7. For some orthodox comments on the phrase 'the values of God', see O. C. Quick, *The Christian Sacraments* (Nisbet, 1927), p. 59 f.

[2] See G. Aulén, *Christus Victor* (S.P.C.K., 1931), pp. 149–59.

definite: one was told that if one did not believe one would go to Hell. Liberal Christianity is too enlightened to believe in Hell. And when the modern man asks, 'Why should I come to your services, and be enthusiastic over your ideals, if I don't feel like it?'—it can preach at him, it can seek to inspire and uplift him, but it cannot command. For to command belongs to God, and the God of Liberal Christianity is a projection of human ideals, and no longer Judge. When the preacher recoils from this, and turns seriously to believe that God is the Judge of Man, and that man and civilization and human progress stand under God's judgement, he has returned to the God of the Bible, he has ceased to believe in man's power to save himself; he is no longer a Modernist in the old sense. He is now prepared to command the modern man in God's name.

But where has the old-fashioned orthodoxy been all this time? It has come in for a good deal of contempt: as a Swedish writer happily puts it, speaking of the different faculties at Upsala University at the beginning of this century, 'Theology had become accustomed to be the last coach in the train.' It is still common to hear Orthodoxy spoken of as reactionary and heresy as progressive, and that the heresy of today becomes the orthodoxy of tomorrow. In fact, these phrases date from the time when orthodox Christians themselves were identifying their belief with a static system of doctrines, and the Tractarians and their successors had taken this identification for granted. Consequently they fought tooth and nail against the theories of Darwin, which seemed to deny the truth of the Book of Genesis—though as a matter of fact the doctrine of fixity of species which Darwin had disproved had more to do with the current Aristotelianism of Oxford than with the Bible. A few, such as R. W. Church and Charles Kingsley, accepted Darwin's methods from the first, but the popular mind gained the impression that orthodoxy had received a severe blow. Similarly the popular mind, both inside and outside the organized churches, has never yet quite got over the belief that the inspiration of the Bible is interpreted by the Church in an infallibilist sense—namely, that the Bible is supposed to contain a collection of absolutely true statements: the revolution of the earth stopped for twenty-four hours while Joshua was chasing the Canaanites. The ordinary man knows nothing of the work of scholars like Lightfoot and Hort, Turner and Gore, and has a vague sense that the Higher Criticism constitutes a challenge to Christianity.

Orthodox Christians are often found labouring under something like an inferiority complex: and it would be true to say that congregations tend not infrequently to shut themselves off from the surrounding world, in a rather esoteric devotionalism: a life of piety, often very intense, which concerns itself in the first place with the salvation and sanctification of the individual soul. This is far from being universally the case: in very many respects, with which we cannot deal in detail here, the Church is bravely tackling the problems of modern life and winning respect. One notes, for instance, that Harold Laski in the *Daily Herald* in May 1934 writes a very respectful account of the Archbishop of Canterbury, and that at Christmastide and Passiontide *The Times* has for some years made a practice of giving as its first leader a very strong and orthodox statement of the Christian faith in the Incarnation and the Resurrection.

Yet the majority of the population do not go to church. A town parish thinks it is doing moderately well if out of 10,000 people it has 500 communicants: one out of twenty. The fact is that the Church is definitely opposed to the increasingly secular drift of civilization. Sometimes it withdraws into itself: but more and more it is rising up, like the early Church under the Roman Empire, to accept the challenge and become conscious of its vocation. More and more, Christians are confessing before the world that they are Christians and that they mean it.

The Church bears witness to the world in various ways —by the lives of Christians, by their impact on social life, by sermons, books, wireless, by public manifestos, by personal example. All these ways of witness are directly dependent on the individuals by whom the witness is given. But there is another way in which the Church herself speaks, more clearly, certainly and effectively than by the voices of her individual members. This is by the existence of the parish churches and the liturgy that is performed in them.

The Church liturgy is in a sense dependent on the individual members of the Church for its continuance; but its contents are mainly independent of them. The church building reflects in its ornaments and fittings the particular style of the priest and people; but it is the parish church, and its minister is responsible not only for those whose names are on the Electoral Roll, but for every soul in the parish. There are multitudes who think of their parish church almost as a place of entertainment, where services are held for the benefit of the religiously-minded. As a rule they are glad to feel that the services are there for them to attend if they feel like it; actually they rarely darken its doors except on the occasions of baptisms, weddings and funerals.

Baptisms, weddings and funerals. On these great occasions of life and death the Church still comes into their lives, and the Church liturgy has great things to say to them, if they had ears to hear, about the mystery of birth and life and death. This is significant. Other places are associated with religious experiences, as, for instance, certain large hotels for members of the Group Movement; but no one goes there for baptisms, weddings and funerals. They go to the church, because the church is the House of God and the home of the people, even though these multitudes have almost forgotten what the Church means. Home is still home, even when the children have strayed away.

By the influence of the Church service the regular Church people are moulded; for the things which they do in church make a deeper impression than the teaching which reaches their minds. Often they have thought that they came to church chiefly to hear the sermon. This, however, they mostly forgot; but there were responses and prayers, commandments, creeds and scriptures, which impressed themselves on their mind by constant repetition. All these things, the church building and the ritual and the ceremonies which take place in it, speak of the reality of God after a manner different in kind from the exhortations and instructions of the preacher.

There is the ritual of baptism. It is one thing to discuss the theory of baptismal regeneration, or to take sides in the controversy which raged on this subject in the middle of the last century: it is quite another to see the baptismal rite performed, and perceive how the act itself, with the words which accompany and explain it, shows the saving work of God in action. The child is brought to the church: the parents and sponsors know in part for what purpose they are bringing it, and also know that the meaning of the act is greater than they know. The act is one of initiation, washing, signing with the Cross. The words of the rite refer constantly to the Divine Goodwill, shown in the act of Jesus in blessing the children who were brought to Him, and shown in the rite of baptism which is the sign of His will to receive this child. The child is named by its Christian name, and baptized in the name of God. The whole action is as mysterious, as pregnant, as the planting of a seed in the ground. It speaks of a real relation of this young life to the unseen God, and of a purpose of God reaching from now on, through the span of three score years and ten, and forward into eternity.

The same applies to the Eucharistic Sacrament about which controversies have raged for centuries. But the act itself is of a different order from all sacramental doctrines or beliefs. Something is done, which is expressed in the four Biblical verbs: He took bread, blessed, brake, gave it to them. The simple action is infinite in meaning. The people come to perform a sacrificial rite, and eat and drink together before God, according to the institution of Jesus Christ.

The same principle runs through all the sacramental actions of the Church. F. D. Maurice expresses it with reference to the consecration of a bishop:

'If you appeal to books of argument in favour of Episcopacy, you will find proofs drawn out in an exact and logical form to show that such an ordinance must belong to the Church, and that all who have not that ordinance are not members of it. *Here* you will find no statements regarding Episcopacy, but the actual sending forth of a Bishop to be the Shepherd of a flock, the Father of a family which God has committed to him, over which he is to watch, for which he is to give account. Is there not the width of a whole heaven between the one of these modes of presenting the subject and the other? In the first all is dry, cold, exclusive, negative. What is this necessary ordinance? How is it connected with Christian life and doctrine? The question is asked, and the mere arguer is silent. He brings forth his title-deeds: the worth of the estates which they assure to us is not his concern. But the worth of the estate is all that our practical countrymen care for, and if we enter into the spirit of our service, we shall be rejoiced that it is so. We shall tell them that these Fathers-in-God are witnesses to us, one and all, that God is our Father, the witnesses of this truth to the outcasts in our country and our towns, the witnesses of it to our brethren who have left us to found distant colonies and be the beginners of new worlds. We shall tell them that these Fathers-in-God testify of an universal brotherhood, which has no limits of language or of race, that they do not testify of the exclusion or excision of any portion of the Church, but rather that all are one in Christ Jesus, that all who are baptized in the one uniting Name constitute a portion of God's great family, and are intended to bring the whole earth within the circle of that family.' [1]

The church building and the liturgical acts performed there express something about Christianity which the preacher's words can never give. We hear him preach, and we say he is a holy man, or a clever man, or maybe the reverse. If the Church service consisted of preachings, we should conclude that the Church was a religious movement. But you cannot sum up as merely the home of a religious movement the building where baptisms, weddings and funerals are celebrated—not to speak of the rest. It is the home of the people, the House of God. It speaks of a real and permanent relation of God with men. It witnesses to a truth deeper and greater than the truth of human beliefs and ideas—the truth of that which underlies man's own existence, the Source and Ground of all Being.

Returning now to the question with which we started, we see that we have the beginnings of an answer: and we see that the assumption of the modern world that

[1] F. D. Maurice, *The Church a Family—Twelve Sermons on the Occasional Offices of the Prayer Book*, Parker, London, 1850.

Christianity exists to provide religion for those who want it, and that religious belief is purely the concern of the individual, is a wrong assumption. Christianity is not in the first place a religion, but a faith.

In seeking to answer our question, we shall devote five chapters to a study of Christianity, adopting (as we hope) a truly realistic point of view, and trying to show not so much what Christianity ought to be, as what it has actually revealed itself to be in the life of the Church. When we envisage the problem thus, it becomes impossible to identify the Christian faith with some theological system, or to treat Christian religion as if it were simply a way of personal holiness; we have in both respects to reckon with the fact of the Church. In the second part of the book, we shall try to view the fact of Christianity and the Church in relation to the problem of the modern world.

PART I
CHRISTIANITY

CHAPTER II

CHRIST THE FULFILLER

*

I. THE PROBLEM OF THE WORLD-RELIGIONS

We have refused to allow Christianity to be summed up as religious experience: but we ourselves have come near to summing it up as a ritual. We have deliberately pointed to the church building and the rites and ceremonies performed in it as testifying by their objectivity to a real relation of man with God.

Such an argument may well seem to be a double-edged weapon. It is commonly assumed among the up-to-date adversaries of Christianity that it is just one of the great world-religions. It is evident, for instance, that the Christian rite of baptism shows marked affinities with the ceremonial lustrations which are found in all the religions and that the Christian Eucharist can be paralleled from sacrificial meals and mystery rituals. Christian Churches stand in many cases on the sites of heathen sanctuaries; the Christian congregation that meets for worship there is doing some of the same things as the pagan crowd centuries ago. No doubt the Christian worship is purer and more moral. But all the rituals stand together as rituals. And it is not difficult for the critic to assume that all are equally products of fantasy, projections of man's own fears, hopes and ideals, creations of man who now as always makes his gods in his own image.

The anthropological facts have been conveniently stated

45

in Professor James's recent book,[1] the great value of which
consists in the fact that he sets the pagan and Christian
rituals side by side. He summarizes a mass of material
which has been collected since the trail was blazed by
Frazer's *Golden Bough*, and shows how Christianity has
adopted the same 'ritual pattern' which is seen in the
rites of many nations, Egypt, Babylonia, Canaan, the
Graeco-Roman world. The ritual pattern is formed from
certain inter-related *motifs* which constantly recur: the
divine-human king: the dying god, rising again to life:
the death of the winter and the resurrection of the spring:
fertility rites connected both with the crops and with the
birth of human offspring: conflict with evil spirits and
the threatening powers of darkness and of death: the
triumph of the divine champion: the hope of immortality.
Out of these ideas is woven the coronation ritual of the
Egyptian and the Babylonian king; and the same features
appear in a transformed shape not only in Christian
coronation rites, but also in the fundamentally similar
consecration of a bishop, and in the rituals of baptism
and eucharist, marriage and the profession of nuns, and
the last rites performed over the dead.

Thus, for instance, the ancient ritual pattern is seen in
the ancient Baptismal services, of which the main outlines
survive in the Anglican Prayer Book. The baptismal rite
—constructed originally for adult candidates—is a service
of consecration in which the candidate receives a share
in a divine, heavenly life: he is made a child of God, a
member of Christ, an inheritor of the Kingdom of Heaven.
The rite expresses 'a death unto sin and a new birth unto
righteousness': it involves a conflict with evil, both in the
ascetic requirement of the fast preceding it,[2] and in the

---

[1] E. O. James, *Christian Myth and Ritual* (Murray, 1933).

[2] See the first rubric of the Prayer Book form for the 'Ministration
of baptism to such as are of riper years'.

solemn renunciation of the devil and all his works, and it rests on the victory over evil won by a divine champion. The water which is the 'matter' of the sacrament is the ancient symbol of life-giving fertility. Baptism is completed by Confirmation, which in the West is a puberty rite conferred at or before the time of adolescence, and leads up to Holy Communion, which 'completes the union of the initiate with the divine order and makes him a recipient of life immortal'.[1]

There is a problem here which Christians must not evade. To say flatly that the Christian rites and beliefs are contrasted with those of paganism as light with darkness, is an attitude which brings its own nemesis. It involves one in difficulties when one is confronted with degenerate types of Christian practice—in Latin America, for instance, if it is not desired to look for examples nearer home. But many of the early Fathers, and the best Christian theologians generally, have been ready to allow a measure of truth in the pagan religions. More than this, we have before our eyes the Prologue of St. John's Gospel, which was almost certainly written at Ephesus, in the midst of the splendour of Greek civilization, and speaks of the Divine Word as the source of all that was good and true in the pagan world.

It is also true that much in the pagan rituals was denounced by the Christians as idolatrous and as immoral. This protest has been continued by Protestantism, which in general has sought to return to the 'pure gospel', and to eliminate as far as possible the elements which Catholicism derived from the pagan rituals. We shall have to take up an attitude with regard to this question.

Let us begin by quoting a statement of the actual difference between the Christian sacraments in the early Church

[1] James, p. 122.

and the pagan mysteries. It will give us at once the central point of all.

'The fundamental difference, which no forced comparisons or accidental resemblances must be allowed to obscure, is the difference between myth and history. In both cases the worshipper finds help from the contemplation of the past as present to faith in the ritual act of worship. But while in the one case the "past" is a cult-legend of Attis, Isis, or Mithra, in which not even the best will in the world could find a grain of historical truth, in the other it is the story of a human life whose essential historicity no sane critic can for a moment doubt.' [1]

The Apostles' Creed corresponds to the pagan myths of the saviour-gods. It repeats the age-long theme of the dying god. But the startling words in it are the words 'suffered under Pontius Pilate'. This salvation myth was enacted in the full light of history. This saviour-God really died and rose again.

II. THE FULFILMENT OF JUDAISM

We must now go on to ask what is the relation between the two. We shall find help in the exceedingly suggestive argument which forms the main contention of the Epistle to the Hebrews. It deals with the relation of Christianity to the Jewish sacrificial system, but it is capable of being applied with little alteration to its relation to the religions of the world. We shall endeavour to give the pith of the argument, in language as little technical as possible.

The difficulty of the Epistle is that we no longer have the covering letter which would have explained the actual situation; we have therefore to reconstruct it from internal

---

[1] Brilioth, *Eucharistic Faith and Practice* (S.P.C.K., 1930), p. 53; cf. p. 34. Cf. Sassé in *Mysterium Christi* (ed. Bell and Deissmann, 1930), pp. 99–102.

II. CHRIST THE LORD

evidence. The historical situation which the argument requires seems to be correctly given by the older commentators.[1] A group of Hebrew Christians, on the eve of the outbreak of the Jewish War which ended in the destruction of Jerusalem by Titus in A.D. 70, are being strongly tempted by their Jewish fellow-countrymen to throw in their lot with the national cause, and to reconcile this attitude with their Christian faith by saying, presumably, that Jesus was Jewish Messiah and moral reformer, but that the sacrificial system of the old law appeared to have been left unaltered by the coming of the Messiah. They could still go on being Jews and Christians at once. The writer of the Epistle cries, 'No! It is for you, spiritually, a matter of life and death. Either you must leave Judaism and go out into the wilderness with the Christian Church or you apostatize irrevocably from Christ' (xiii. 13).

It is evident that the Divinity of Christ is the common belief of the writer and his readers, for in Chapter I it is assumed and stated, but not proved. His whole effort is put forth to prove that the Jewish sacrificial system was never intended to be more than temporary, and has now been superseded by the coming of Christ (viii. 1–2, 6–7, 13; x.1). Jesus in being Messiah is also High Priest after the order of Melchizedek (v. 10; vii. 26–8). Evidently the readers are impressed with the glory and splendour of the Jewish sacrificial ritual, and are disposed to regard it as permanent.

The argument therefore attacks the question of the animal sacrifices of the Old Testament. We can hear them saying, 'Jesus was no Levitical priest and never offered sacrifice.' We have his reply: 'I fully admit that Jesus was not a Jewish priest' (vii. 14; viii. 4); it is the

[1] See e.g. F. J. A. Hort, *Judaistic Christianity* (Macmillan, 1904), p. 157.

foundation of my whole argument. He never offered a
Levitical sacrifice. But in being Messiah, in opening the
Kingdom of Heaven to all believers, He has fulfilled on
a higher level all that the old sacrifices meant. The old
sacrifices were wonderful and mysterious: they expressed
a profound sense that somehow, through the offering to
God of that which is precious, and through death and
blood-shedding, there must at last be a way for man to
be reconciled with God and his guilt to be taken away
(ix. 9). But it stands to reason that the blood of bulls
and goats cannot take away sins (x. 4): what God really
wanted was the self-offering of man himself (ix. 13–14).

'In the life and death and resurrection of Jesus all the
lines meet. In being Messiah He is also priest: and He
has offered, not the shadow-sacrifice of a dumb animal,
but the real sacrifice which consists in the whole giving
of human life to God: "Lo, I come to do Thy will, O
God" (x. 5–10). In Him the archetype, the Platonic
"idea" of sacrifice has descended to earth (x. 1). Thus
the old Levitical sacrifices are superseded: the word that
they were confusedly attempting to utter has been de-
cisively and finally said by Him (i. 1). The old sacrificial
order drops into its true place as the preparation for
Him. It is not discarded: it is fulfilled.'

Here is the wonder. The inadequacy and imperfection
of the old sacrifices might be called the statement of a
question, and Christ's work the answer. The answer,
when it first appeared, seemed to have nothing to do
with the question: Jesus appeared to be a prophet, a
preacher of righteousness, and to have no concern with
the sacrifices. But now that His life-work is complete,
He is seen to have given the answer to the question, not
on the level on which the question was asked, but on a
higher level altogether. He fulfils the old sacrifices by
transforming the whole conception from the merely ritual-

istic level to that of the spiritual oblation of man to God, from the level of atonement for ceremonial uncleanness to the purging of the 'conscience from dead works to serve the living God' (ix. 14).

Thus Christ is God's answer to man's need. The answer came in an unexpected way. But when it had come it was found to fit the problem and answer it by raising it to a higher level.

III. THE FULFILMENT OF THE WORLD-RELIGIONS

The precise formula which we have expressed in these last three sentences may be applied to the relation between the world-religions and Christianity. Here too we have a question: man's groping after God and his efforts to get into touch with the unseen powers. Here too the answer appears in an unexpected place, within the one nation which was isolated by its claim to exclusiveness from the general current of the religions of the world: but when Christianity comes out into the wide world, it is found to possess the answer to the question.

All over the world man is seen groping after God; trying to manipulate the course of nature and secure fruitful harvests; facing the mystery of life and death, and celebrating rituals which promise immortality. No doubt we may call it the projection of man's need for supernatural help and protection: certainly man devises these forms to express his soul's need. He reaches out into the unknown and cries in the dark for light. The pagan religions are conscious that the rituals represent a question rather than the answer: for no one knows whether religious beliefs are true, and it is always allowable for the devotee to undergo several different initiations. The religions are tolerant of one another just because none of them can make any certain claim to truth.

But there is one nation in the ancient world which is intolerant because it believes that it has the truth, and therefore jealously guards its religious tradition from pollution. Exclusiveness is of the very essence of Judaism: 'I am the Lord thy God: thou shalt have no other gods but Me.' It is true that throughout the Old Testament the thought recurs from time to time that ultimately this faith in the living God must be for all nations. 'In thee (Abraham) and in thy seed shall all the nations of the earth be blessed' (Gen. xii. 3; xxii. 18). 'I have set thee for a light of the Gentiles, that thou mayest be my salvation unto the ends of the earth' (Isaiah xlix. 6). But these hopes remain unfulfilled: Israel cannot help but remain obstinately nationalist; those of other nations who desire to have Israel's faith must either become naturalized in the Jewish nation, or else remain sitting on the doorstep as 'proselytes of the gate'.

In this exclusive religious tradition Jesus is born and grows up. His ministry is confined to Israel: though according to our earliest sources a Syrian-Phoenician woman and a Roman centurion make requests for Him to perform works of healing, and not in vain, and though He seems to go out of His way to speak well of Samaritans, yet He makes no gesture admitting non-Israelites to the privilege of the Covenant.

But He always deals with the Jew on the broad human ground. Following John the Baptist, who had said 'Think not to say within yourselves, We have Abraham to our father', and had compelled ritually-clean Jews to accept a baptismal lustration because the real uncleanness was that of sin, Jesus refuses to accept the programme of a nationalistic messianic kingdom, and proclaims that in the order of the Kingdom of God the Levitical law of clean and unclean is done away, and that it is the evil thoughts proceeding from the heart that defile man.

Since to the Jew the Gentile was ritually unclean, the barriers are here in principle thrown down.

But more than this: in dealing with the Jew as a man, He pierces to the depths of the human soul, appealing to the man in men, and relentlessly exposing the self-complacency and falsehood which is the special temptation of religious men. He called them 'hypocrites', that is, according to the Aramaic meaning of the word, 'ungodly' or 'impious'.[1] Nor must we think that those Pharisees were worse than other men, or that He struck a specially bad patch. According to conventional human standards, they did not for the most part deserve so severe a judgement; but this was the judgement of God. There was in them the same root of pride and self-justification which is in you, reader, and in me.

The same relentless severity is seen in His dealings with the disciples, who have left all to follow Him. It seems as if all that is bad in them is compelled to come to the surface. They are found helpless and bewildered when He prophesies His passion; they are found seeking chief places in the kingdom; they say almost in despair 'Then who can be saved?' Jesus in founding His kingdom must penetrate to rock-bottom: nothing but the best will do for God.

Finally the Passion of Jesus seems to call out all that is ugliest and worst in human nature. One disciple betrays Him, another denies Him. The godly and respectable members of the Sanhedrin, about to keep the holiest festival of the Jewish year, snarl round Him like a pack of hyaenas when He confesses Himself to be Messiah. In the crucifixion itself, it must surely be right to think of a whole flood of evil let loose upon the soul of Jesus: He who has come to bring to men the Kingdom of God, the real reconciliation of man with God, is now faced with

---

[1] These are the synonyms of 'hypocrite' in the Septuagint. The data are given in Hastings' *Dictionary of the Bible*, s. v. 'Hypocrite'.

apparently conclusive proof that these men are not worth saving, that they have proved that they are not fit for the Kingdom of God and do not want it. He must face the evil in man at its worst, the evil as in reality it is. There is a fitness therefore in the fact that when on Easter morning the Church hails Christ as Victor in the conflict, the words of the introit should be taken from Psalm cxxxix, 'O Lord, thou hast searched me out and known me.' The paschal conqueror has searched the depths of human denial and despair: He has been made sin for us: He has borne the curse and turned it into a blessing.

The mission of Jesus was to Israel according to the out-wardness of things; but when we regard the inwardness of the story, it was the man and not merely the Jew that He had come to save. That which He had done for the Jew was in principle universal. There was therefore a fitness, of which St. Mark is fully aware, in the testimony which he puts in the mouth of the centurion at the Cross, after the death of Jesus, 'Truly this man was the Son of God', even if the centurion only meant 'a son of the gods'. There is also a peculiar dramatic fitness in two other incidents of the Passion. After the prisoner has been condemned, the Roman soldiers in mocking Him crown Him, as it seems, as King of the Saturnalia, and array Him in the garments of the god of the spring. And after Jesus on the Cross had cried 'Eloi, Eloi', a bystander is reported to have said 'Behold, He called Elijah'. But it is scarcely credible that a Jew should have mistaken the name of God, and therefore it is possible that the Old Latin MS. k preserves the true reading: 'Behold, He calleth on Helios, the sun-god.' [1] It was a pagan. Thus, as it seems, the mystery-religions are not unrepresented in the Passion story; there are presages of the future.

[1] See C. H. Turner in the *New Commentary* (S.P.C.K., 1932) on Mark xv. 35, p. 118.

Within a few years, a devout Roman centurion, being no less a man than were the Jews to whom Jesus had ministered, was baptized by Peter; Paul and Barnabas, speaking in the drawing-room of the Governor of Cyprus, found that in that assembly representative of the Roman world there was no spiritual power that could stand up to them [1]; at Antioch in Pisidia pagans who had had no previous contact with the Synagogue believed the Gospel and were admitted into the Church. St. Paul's Epistles are full of echoes of the pagan mystery-religions, and it became plain that the Christian Gospel was concerned with precisely those questions which the mystery-religions asked, about God and the soul, salvation and immortality.

It was therefore natural and inevitable that the answer should be stated, more and more as time went on, in the terms in which the question was being asked, and that Christianity should appear before the world as one of the mystery-religions, and the ritual of its sacraments should follow the lines of the mystery-rites. Christianity had indeed possessed from the beginning its two primary sacraments, the origin of which can be so fully explained in the light of Jewish antecedents that the attempt to derive them from imitation of the pagan rites has now been given up by serious students. It is in the outward ceremonial dress which the sacraments acquire that the influence of the pagan rites is seen. It was as a mystery-religion that Christianity appealed to the ancient world, and it prevailed over the others as inevitably as the disciplined Roman legions conquered the barbarian armies. So Professor James writes:

'Thus in very truth, along this line of reasoning Christ came not to destroy but to fulfil; to give a higher significance to those age-long rites and beliefs by which the

[1] H. F. B. Mackay, *The Adventure of Paul of Tarsus* (Philip Allan, 1930), p. 83 f.

world was being prepared for the final revelation when the fullness of the time was come. On this hypothesis, it might be argued that God left not Himself without witness through the ages, the Holy Spirit working through the ancient pagan systems in order to prepare the world for greater things than these. Regarded from this standpoint, Christ becomes the Heir of the ages, and the ritual pattern the Divine Scheme for the redemption and reconciliation of the human race to God. In the present volume, however, it has not been our aim to establish a theological thesis. . . . Happily it is possible to be strictly scientific without having disregard to a sense of the fitness of things.' [1]

And Archbishop Söderblom, a life-long student of comparative religion:

'A wonderful continuity, this. We are accustomed to read the Old Testament with the New: the Epistle to the Hebrews applies to Christ the sacrificial conception of Israel, in all its fullness and depth of meaning. But a day is coming when the science of religions will have learnt to interpret the much wider continuity of our Saviour's death and resurrection with the ancient pagan rituals. There also it will see a prophecy and a fulfilment: it will see types created by the longing of the human soul and its dim perception of reality, till the time came for them to become flesh and blood. Then it will be seen how strangely Christ fulfils even the idolatrous rites of weeping for Tammuz, which the women in the eighth chapter of Ezekiel are seen carrying on in the Temple of Jerusalem; and how the Roman soldiers had a dim sense of an inner meaning, when they arrayed Pilate's prisoner as a king of May revels, with purple robe and crown.

'For very many years I have had to busy myself

[1] *Christian Myth and Ritual*, p. 325.

with these subjects in thought and study; and still my wonder never loses its freshness. I can never cease marvelling, how since primeval times our race has connected suffering with its deepest idea of the Divine—till in the end an instrument of execution became the greatest of all religious symbols: the Cross.' [1]

Here, above all, Christ is the Fulfiller. Death, after all, is the one thing common to all mankind, amid all diversities of character, temperament, race, and education; even the pitiful sub-human beings in the *Brave New World* have got to die. Therefore the Christ, the Son of Man, must go down to death, tasting it in all its horror. There was no halo of glory about the actual crucifixion. It meant to every Jew that this Jesus was branded before the eyes of the nation as an accused impostor, who had laid blasphemous hands on the highest of all vocations, claiming to be Messiah: but God had broken out on him, and condemned him by the voice of the High-priest to the death on which His curse rested, for 'cursed is every one that hangeth on a tree'. The Crucifixion seemed to mean the utter and complete failure of all that Jesus had given His life to accomplish. He must accept it all, and fulfil to the very end His own words about the losing of life and the denial of the self. He must lose literally everything except God.

The fulfilment lies in the Resurrection. God raised Him from the dead. The Divine Act of the Resurrection means that the Divine, eternal, real meaning of the Crucifixion is triumph beyond all defeat, because Love has endured all that hate could do, and has still remained love. [2]

[1] *The Mystery of the Cross* (S.C.M., London, 1933), p. 23.

[2] 'Its effectiveness is, potentially at least, unlimited and all-inclusive, just because its method is one which turns very loss into gain and very defeat into victory.' O. C. Quick, *The Christian Sacraments* (Nisbet, 1927), p. 92. The whole chapter, pp. 78–100, deserves to rank among the classics.

It is the fulfilment, because here it is declared that God has a meaning for all the sufferings of suffering humanity, for the million million deaths of men. It is the fulfilment of Jewish and pagan sacrificial rituals, of the myths of the 'dying gods', of the Song of the Suffering Servant in the Book of Isaiah. These were symbols, pointing forward to that which was to come. The Easter message is the fulfilment.

IV. THE FULFILMENT IN CHRISTIAN RELIGION

To say that in Christ the pagan rituals are fulfilled means that they are transformed: and that which was capable of being thus transformed cannot have been wholly evil. To say that Christ is the Divine answer to man's question implies that God had not been absent in the process of stating the question. As the Epistle to the Hebrews is emphatic in asserting that God had ordained the imperfect and ineffectual sacrifices of Israel, so the Prologue of St. John's Gospel, as we have seen, asserts that the Word of God was the Light that was present, contending with darkness, throughout the pagan world. In our day theology is emphasizing with great vigour the transcendence of God and His real action; in doing so it is too apt to forget that man is made in God's image and that creation as well as redemption is God's work. The pagan religions were right in believing that God makes the corn grow. The early Greek science investigating the order of the natural world, and Greek philosophy investigating the moral order of human life, were seeking to learn His laws.

It seems therefore that Catholicism has in general taken up a sounder attitude than Protestantism with regard to our question. Protestantism has always tried to go back to the 'pure Gospel', the authentic essence of Christianity, and has repudiated as far as possible the forms derived from pagan sources, as being tainted with idolatry and immorality: Catholicism, on the other hand, has sought to redeem them and purify them, as being fundamentally good. In this it has incurred the risk of failing to purge out the paganism in them, and of dragging down Christian practice to a sub-Christian level: and here Protestantism supplies a necessary corrective. Some of the things said by Protestantism have also been said by the Savonarolas of the Catholic Church. But if God had been present not only in the giving of the answer but also in the stating of the question, it is plain that Catholicism is on the right lines.

We might illustrate this from the ancient ideas of fertility and birth to new life. The Roman form for the Blessing of the Font in the Easter Eve service, which was originally the service for the night before Easter Day, when solemn baptisms were administered, contains phrases which recall strongly the language of primitive rituals.[1] The Font is described as a womb:

'Pour forth the Spirit of adoption to recreate the new peoples, with whom the font of baptism is in travail . . .'

'Grant that he (the Holy Spirit) may make fruitful this water prepared for the regeneration of men by the hidden admixture of his divinity, that sanctification being conceived from the spotless womb of the divine font, a heavenly offspring may be brought forth, reborn into a new creature; and that those who temporally are diverse in sex and age, may by grace their mother be brought forth into one infancy.'

This language has behind it not only the pagan ritual tradition, but also that of the New Testament and the teaching of Jesus. For though, as we have said, the Palestinian tradition in general stood apart from the religions of the world, yet the apocalyptic symbolism in

[1] See James, pp. 115 ff.

59

which the teaching of Jesus finds its outward form contains the idea of a messianic re-birth in such phrases as 'regeneration' ($\pi\alpha\lambda\iota\gamma\gamma\varepsilon\nu\varepsilon\sigma\acute{\iota}\alpha$, Matt. xix. 28) and 'eternal life'. The same thought of a new life come down from on high is implied in the Parable of the Sower (Mark iv. 3), in which the figure of the Sower is unmistakably that of Jesus Himself, and the (divine) seed which He sows unites with the (human) soil to produce the crop of wheat. But—and here is the important point—the spiritual fact represented by the growth of the wheat is a radical $\mu\varepsilon\tau\acute{\alpha}\nu\omega\iota\alpha$, a whole re-orientation of the moral and spiritual life in renouncing the self-centredness of the natural man and making over the whole personality in surrender to God's holy will. Very significant in this connexion is His teaching about the meaning of authority (Mark x. 42–5): 'Those who are supposed to rule over the Gentiles' (note the sarcasm; we all know that it is really the staff who carry on the work) 'lord it over them': the position of rule is taken as a means to the inflation of the ego of the ruler. 'But it will not be so among you: but he that is chief among you will be your servant', the general bearer of the burdens of all and of responsibility for the common welfare: 'even as the Son of Man came not to be ministered unto but to minister, and to give himself a ransom for many'.

Our Lord Himself takes the accepted symbolism, and fills it with a new meaning: a meaning which depends on the recognition of the reality of God and of God's claim on men. The Liberal Protestantism of the last century sought to see in His moral and spiritual teaching alone the essence of Jesus' message, and to discard as completely as possible the eschatological forms in which it is clothed. The modern study of the Gospels recognizes that this is impossible, and that it is necessary to give its full value to the eschatological symbolism. But if so, our Lord was only doing with the inherited symbolism of Jewish apocalyptic what the Church did later with the partly similar symbolism of the pagan rituals: accepting the forms, and filling them with a new moral and spiritual content. The same re-orientation is expressed by St. Paul, in the same conjunction with the idea of new birth, and the Holy Spirit, who regenerates to new life:

'The mind of the flesh is enmity against God: for it is not subject to the law of God, neither indeed can it be, and they that are "in the flesh" [self-centred, carnally minded] cannot please God. But ye are not in the flesh but in the Spirit, if so be that the Spirit of God dwelleth in you' (Romans viii. 7–9. Cf. Ephes. ii. 2–5).

Similarly in St. John:

'As many as received Him, to them gave He power to become sons of God, who were born again not by right of carnal descent, nor by the will of human nature, nor by the will of a man, but born of God' (i. 13).

'Verily, verily I say unto thee, Except a man be born of water and of the Spirit, he cannot enter into the Kingdom of God' (iii. 5).

The new birth to eternal life is here also correlated with a re-orientation of the whole life after the pattern of Christ who says, 'I seek not mine own glory', and 'My meat is to do the will of Him that sent me'. In the second passage (iii. 5) the reference to baptism is plain, and we are almost within reach of the phrases of the Roman Blessing of the Font.

In fact, a book is waiting to be written on the great symbols round which the Johannine theology revolves—Life, birth to eternal life, the Bread of Life, life through death, the Resurrection and the Life; and Light, spirit, eternal truth—illustrating these symbols both from the old pagan rituals and from the text and the ceremonies of the Christian liturgies. Such a book would show how these symbols have been transformed in Christianity by the historical fact of the coming of Christ to express the re-orientation of human life involved in faith in the reality of God. The transformation is effected in the person of Christ the Fulfiller.

But the most difficult and controversial instance is the cult of the Virgin Mary. The facts are clear enough. The worship of a female deity was common to many nations of antiquity, under many names, the Mother of the Gods, Athene, Venus, Proserpine, Dictynna, Demeter; but, says Apuleius, 'her true name is Isis'. 'In her celestial capacity she was "queen of the sky" and "mother of the stars", and as the female counterpart of the syncretistic solar deity she was also identified with the moon. She is "parent of nature, mistress of all elements, first-born of all the ages, highest of all divine beings (*numina*), queen of the dwellers below, manifestation in one shape of all gods and goddesses", and finally the mediatrix, "saviour of the human race", or "saviour-goddess".' 'That Mary in her capacity of the Theotokos of Christian tradition gathered round her in due course many of the attributes of the Magna Mater, is now scarcely a matter of dispute among scholars.' [1]

Protestantism is unanimous in repudiating the cult; and indeed it might well seem that there could be no clearer instance of a paganizing of Christianity, by the introduction into it of the cult of a goddess. A writer who has Huguenot blood in his veins cannot help feeling in himself a strong impulse to join in denouncing it. To many, Lourdes looks like the shrine of a pagan goddess.

But this is not the whole of the matter. The danger of a paganizing of Christian religion at this point is most

[1] James, pp. 224, 226. Quotations from Apuleius, *Metamorphoses*, Bk. XI.

serious when the pagan origin of the cult is either not known or not admitted. When it is admitted—and it must be—the admission itself is bound to put Catholics on their guard against the danger, and also to open their minds to the idea of 'fulfilment'. The human race, making its gods in its own image, created the Magna Mater, a symbol not only of divinity but also of humanity; and in the fullness of time the Son of God was made very man of the substance of the Virgin Mary His mother. As the mother of the Incarnate, Mary of Nazareth stands as the representative of humanity. But perhaps the possibilities of this 'fulfilment' are better shown by the pictures facing pp. 113, 128, than by any words of ours.[1] Here she is surrounded with pagan symbols; yet she is no goddess, but the handmaid of the Lord, willing that it may be unto her according to His word.

Fulfilment means transformation. In the next chapter we shall see something of the transformation of the mysteries in the sacramental worship of the early Church. As with Judaism, so with the world-religions, Christ came not to destroy but to fulfil, to redeem, to transform.

[1] Illustrations VIII and IX.

CHAPTER III
LITURGY

*

If Christ is the Head of the Ages, the Fulfiller, the Divine Answer, how is this Answer mediated to us? How far by means of a ritual, and in a liturgy? How far as a revelation of truth addressed to the mind? How far in the religious experience of the soul? We shall deal with these three questions in successive chapters. It has become common for Christianity to be regarded as a system of belief, or else as a way of holiness for the individual; thus the formal liturgy of the Church comes to be disparaged as an external act, less 'spiritual' than the private prayer in which the individual soul holds communion with God. But in the patristic period there can be no question that the common prayer of the Church holds the primary place, and provides the setting in which dogma is seen in its true perspective, and in which the individual drops into his place as a member of the worshipping Body.

In his little book, *Kirche und Seele*, a study of the religion of the early Church in contrast with that of the Middle Ages,[1] Dr. Herwegen, Abbot of Maria Laach, starts by comparing it with the mystery-cults:

'Mystery in its general sacral meaning is the re-presentation (*Gegenwärtigsetzung*) of the salvation-myth on which is based the existence of the cult-community which meets for

[1] *Kirche und Seele*, by Ildefons Herwegen (Aschendorff, Münster-in-Westfalen, 3rd and 4th edition, 1928), pp. 15 ff.

III. BASILICA OF ST. CLEMENT, ROME

the celebration of the mysteries. Similarly, the Christian Mystery is the re-presentation of the saving work of Christ, on which the existence of His Church is based.'

He goes on to explain that the word 'mystery' is here used not in the sense of an intellectual mystery, an inscrutable revealed truth, but in the sense in which the Roman Missal speaks constantly of 'these holy mysteries'; the Latin for μυστήριον is *sacramentum*. So understood, it has two characteristics. First, the commemoration of Christ's saving work is not a subjective and personal act of remembering, but an objective remembrance by means of a ritual: it is therefore not in the first place a psychological fact, but an ontological fact. This does not mean that the sacrifice of Christ is in any way regarded as repeated in the Mass in the order of time and space, but that it is re-presented after a sacramental manner: as St. Gregory the Great says (P.L., vol. 76, col. 1279), 'as often as we offer the sacrifice of His passion, we show forth again His passion for our pardon'.

His second point is that the celebration of the Christian Mysteries is a social act, by which the worshippers are brought out of their isolation into fellowship with one another in the Church, which is Christ's mystical Body. Thereby not only their religious life but all their individual and social life is re-orientated towards God as its centre, and is transformed, sanctified, and glorified.

It will be convenient for us to follow this order.

I. THE CHRISTIAN MYSTERY

In the initiatory rite of Baptism the convert takes upon himself the Christian faith. The Apostles' Creed is in its origin the western form of the summary of the baptismal instructions which he learnt and repeated before his Baptism. The so-called Nicene Creed is the corresponding formula used at Jerusalem, as amplified by the

Councils of Nicaea and Constantinople to exclude the Arian heresy.

The character of Baptism as a celebration of the Christian Mystery is well illustrated by the series of lessons read during the all-night vigil of Easter Eve, to which we have already alluded. The candidates for Baptism have spent the season of Lent in intensive preparation: the twelve lessons immediately precede the Blessing of the Font, and thus form the final act of the candidates' preparation for Baptism, and also the entrance of the Church on the central festival of the Christian year.[1] The interest

---

[1] The subjects of the Lessons are as follows:

(1) The Story of the Creation (from Gen. i–ii) is the necessary starting-point, since God is Creator as well as Redeemer. This, like all the lessons, is followed by an invitation to prayer and a collect.

(2) Noah's Ark (from Gen. v–viii), a type of the Church, the Ark of Salvation.

(3) The Sacrifice of Isaac (from Gen. xxii), typical of the sacrifice of God's only begotten Son.

(4) The Crossing of the Red Sea (from Exod. xiv), typical of God's deliverance of His people from the dominion of all the powers of evil by the passion and resurrection of Christ. This ends in a chant, the triumph-song of Moses (from Exod. xv).

(5) (6) (7) (8) are prophetic passages, from Isaiah liv–lv (Ho, every one that thirsteth, come ye to the waters)—Baruch iii—Ezekiel xxxvii (the Valley of the Dry Bones)—Isaiah iv, followed by a chant from Isaiah v.

(9) The Institution of the Passover (from Exod. xii)—Christ our Passover is sacrificed for us.

(10) Jonah's preaching to Nineveh (Jonah iii). The whole story of Jonah, including his deliverance from the belly of the whale, was a favourite type of the Resurrection (cf. Matt. xii. 40).

(11) Moses viewing the Promised Land (Deut. xxxi), followed by another chant, the Song of Moses (Deut. xxxii).

(12) The Three Children in the Burning Fiery Furnace (Dan. iii), another type of the Resurrection.—From the *Roman Missal*, the service for Holy Saturday. The baptismal rite is described in Duchesne, *Christian Worship* (E.T., S.P.C.K., 1904), pp. 308 ff. See also, for an admirable description of these Symbols, G. M. Bevan, *Early Christians of Rome* (S.P.C.K., 1927), pp. 34 ff., 54 ff.; and cf. p. 243 *infra* and illustration No. IV.

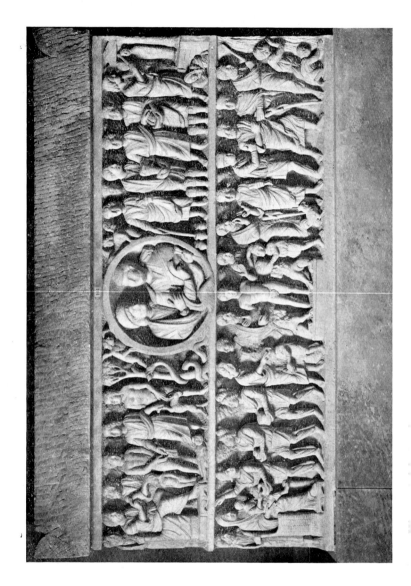

of these lessons is not merely that the Church in which they took shape evidently found the nourishment of its devotion in the strong meat of the Holy Scriptures, but also in the choice of subjects. Each lesson speaks in some way of God's relation to man as Creator and Redeemer, and tells the baptismal candidates something about the mystery of salvation through Christ. They also are passing through the Red Sea, and receiving the benefits of a mighty deliverance. They too, like the Ninevites, are called to repent; they too are being brought near to God and are going through the burning fiery furnace, in being buried with Christ in His death and rising again with Him in His Resurrection.

The eucharistic liturgy presents the saving work of Christ in a variety of ways.[1] The historical commemoration is set forth in the liturgical year, with its two series which centre respectively on Christmas and on Passiontide and Easter. This ends at Pentecost: and every Christian Sunday is in truth a 'Sunday after Pentecost'. It is set forth again in the Scripture lessons. At every eucharist the Holy Gospel is read, containing nearly always some words recorded as spoken by our Lord while on earth. The Beatitudes which we hear on All Saints' Day, read to a crowd of people in the church, are spoken to them now as His words who once spoke them to another crowd on a hill-side in Galilee.

But the historical commemoration in the Liturgy centres in the eucharistic act itself. In the eucharistic prayer of the Greek liturgies of the Syrian-Byzantine type,[2] the account of the Last Supper is framed in a long act of

[1] See Brilioth, *Eucharistic Faith and Practice*, pp. 34-41, 280-2.
[2] The chief of these are : Syrian—the so-called *Clementine Liturgy*, in Book viii of the 'Apostolic Constitutions' (Fourth century) and the *Liturgy of St. James*, the Jerusalem rite : Byzantine—the *Liturgies of St. Basil* and *St. Chrysostom*, of which the latter has remained the standard rite of the Orthodox Churches.

thanksgiving, which covers in one mighty perspective the history of the world, with its centre in the Cross and the Resurrection of Christ: it recapitulates the Creation and the Fall, the Law and the Prophets, the Incarnation in the fullness of time, the redemptive work of Christ, and His Second Advent as Judge, and then invokes the Holy Spirit to 'make present' the mystery of salvation in the consecration of the bread and wine. This may be illustrated from the *Homilies of Narsai* (Syrian: fifth century); the idea which the author seeks to convey to his readers is thus summed up by Dr. Frere:[1]

'They are to see in the Great Entrance the funeral procession of the Lord, represented by the Bread and Wine carried in by the Deacons and accompanied by the procession of priests. The altar is the tomb: the veil is the stone which seals it . . . the sanctuary is the garden of Joseph. The commemoration of the Incarnation of the Lord and of the acts of His earthly life, recited as it were over His tomb, leads up to the Invocation of the Spirit who "comes in the power of His Godhead to dwell in the bread and the wine and completes the mystery of the Lord's resurrection from the dead".'

In the Roman liturgical type, the meaning of the association of the Consecration with our Lord's words of institution is that He is the true celebrant of every Mass; this may be illustrated by a well-known prayer from the Mozarabic rite, which links the liturgy up with the Last Supper:

'Be present, be present, O Jesus, thou good priest, in our midst, as thou wast in the midst of thy disciples: sanctify this oblation, that we may receive the hallowed gifts by thy holy angel's hand, O Holy Lord, eternal redeemer.'

[1] Frere, *The Principles of Religious Ceremonial* (Revised edition, 1928), p. 52.

We cannot here enter on the discussion which of these types is the more primitive. We are concerned with what is common to both: namely, that in the liturgy the past is apprehended as present, and Bethlehem, Calvary, the Mount of Olives are brought into the *here* and the *now.* Or, better, the liturgy is really enacted as in the heavenly places, and past, present, and future alike are seen *sub specie aeternitatis.* On Christmas Day Christians go even now to Bethlehem with the shepherds to greet the new-born Saviour in the manger. If the Gospel of the day tells of a miracle of healing, the same Christ is still present to bestow healing and health of soul and body. On Good Friday He still calls as from the Cross, 'O my people, what have I done unto thee, and wherein have I wearied thee? testify against me', and the Church takes upon herself the guilt of humanity which crucified Him. On a Saint's festival, the life of the Saint is viewed in its whole meaning, and the Church contemplates lovingly his conflicts and even his failures and sins, in the light of the perfected work of grace and the final victory over sin. In the service for the dead, the Church seems to stand now with the dying man in his last agony ('from the gates of hell deliver their souls, O Lord'), now with his soul in its blessed entry into paradise ('eternal rest grant unto them, O Lord, and let light perpetual shine upon them'). All is seen as from the eternal point of view: as St. Paul says, 'our citizenship is in heaven', and it is as citizens of heaven that we take our part in the liturgy with angels and archangels, even when at another part of the service we have cried *Kyrie eleison*, and prayed for help amid present conflict. For the Resurrection of Christ, the central point of the Christian Mystery, is that which gives its meaning to the conflict and turns the conflict into triumph.

When therefore in the eucharistic act the Church 'proclaims the Lord's death till He come', this is much more than a mere commemoration of a past event. It is commemorated as an event in history; it is also re-presented as the central point of all history, as that which gives the meaning of all history. Christ is the Fulfiller and the Head of the Ages.

Therefore it is necessary also that all history should be seen in the light of that which gives its meaning; and this is what is done in the Eucharist. The lives of the worshippers at each Mass are part of history, and they themselves are conscious that the whole content of their lives is here brought into relation to God's redeeming purpose, and conscious also that the same is true of all the other lives which make up God's universal Church. Every Mass is therefore a Mass of the whole Church; and if it were possible for us to comprehend its full meaning, we should see there, focussed in one point, God's whole redeeming work for all mankind, past, present, and future.

Thus in the eucharistic prayer that bears the name of St. Gregory (of Nazianzus),[1] the celebrant speaks to God in the name of the whole human race:

'As the lover of man thou didst create me as a man: thou hadst no need of my service, though I had need of thy lordship: of thy compassion thou didst bring me into existence, thou didst stablish the heavens above me as a roof, thou didst make the earth firm for me to walk upon: for my sake thou didst confine the sea: for my sake thou didst give life to animals in their kinds: thou didst put all things under my feet, nor didst thou permit me to lack any of thy glorious works. It is thou who didst fashion me and lay thy hand upon me—thou didst endue me with the gift of speech—thou didst open to me the paradise of delight—thou didst bestow on me the instruc-

---

[1] Renaudot, *Liturgiarum Orientalium Collectio* (Frankfurt, 1847), vol. I, p. 94. Translation from J. M. Rodwell, Occasional Paper of the Eastern Church Association, No. xii (Rivington, 1870).

tion of the knowledge of thyself—thou didst reveal to me the Tree of Life—didst make known to me the thorn of death: from one tree didst thou debar me that I might not eat of it: I ate it of mine own will: I rejected thy law: I neglected thy commandments of my own mind: I brought on myself the sentence of death.

'Thou, O Lord, didst convert my punishment into salvation: like a good shepherd didst hasten to seek that which had gone astray: like a good father didst labour with me who had fallen: didst bind me up with all remedies which conduce to life. It is thou who didst minister salvation to me, though I had transgressed thy law: didst arise, as the true light, upon me who had erred and was in ignorance.

'Thou who didst ever exist, camest for us on earth, didst enter the Virgin's womb, albeit God that cannot be contained: thou didst not think it robbery to be equal with God, but didst empty thyself and take on thee the form of a servant, didst bless my nature in thyself, didst fulfil thy law for me, didst make known to me how to rise from my fall, didst give remission to those who were detained in Hades, didst take away the curse of the Law, didst destroy sin in the flesh, madest known to me the power of thy dominion, gavest sight to the blind, raisedst the dead by a word, didst reveal to me the dispensation of thy clemency, enduredst the injuries of the wicked, yieldedst thy back to the stripes, didst give thy cheek to blows, for my sake, O my Lord, thou didst not turn away thy face from the shame of the spitting.

'Thou didst go forth like a sheep to the Cross, didst manifest thy solicitude for me, didst slay my sin in thy sepulchre, didst take my firstfruits up into heaven, didst reveal to me thy second advent wherein thou shalt come to judge the quick and the dead and to give to every one according to his deeds.

'I offer to thee, Lord, the symbols of my service: my actions are a copy of thy word. It is thou who hast given unto me this ministration which is full of mystery: thou hast given to me the participation of thy flesh in the bread and wine: for in the night in which thou wast betrayed, by thy sole will and power, thou didst take bread into thy holy and spotless and immaculate and life-giving hands. . . .'

The idea which is here expressed in a liturgical form is pictorially represented in the mosaic from St. Mark's, Venice, which we reproduce opposite p. 78. This is not an illustration of what might be supposed to have been visible to an observer at the Empty Tomb, but a representation of the Christian Mystery. Christ in His Resurrection tramples the devil under foot, shaking out of his hands the keys of death, and rescues Adam and Eve. These are not two historical individuals; Adam is Man, you, I, the person who lives next door, the same common Man whom we have just heard speaking to God in the Gregorian eucharistic prayer. And it is this same common humanity that is understood to be speaking to God in the traditional use of the Psalms.

The Psalter, being the work of many psalmists, represents a much wider range of experience than that of any individual. It is therefore fitly used in liturgical worship as the utterance of Christ and of the Church His mystical Body: the members of the Church, while reciting it, feel their solidarity with the whole of the humanity which Christ redeemed.[1] This thought is magnificently expressed in many places by St. Augustine, as for instance in the following passage from the *Enarration on Psalm* lxi. (lx) 2, on the text 'From the ends of the earth will I call upon thee, when my heart is in heaviness':

'Who is this one man who calls from the ends of the

[1] We shall return to this point in Part II, p. 215 ff.

earth? Only that heritage of which it was said to the Son, "Desire of me, and I will give the heathen for thine inheritance, and the uttermost parts of the earth for thy possession." This is Christ's inheritance, this is Christ's possession, this Body of Christ, this one Church of Christ, this unity which we are, calling from the ends of the earth. . . .

'He shows us Himself, through all nations, in the whole world, in great glory but in great temptation. . . . He is in heaviness and He calls to God from the ends of the earth, but He is not forsaken. For us, His Body, He willed to prefigure in that body in which He died and rose again and ascended into heaven that whither the Head has gone before, thither the members might trust that they shall follow.

'Therefore He transfigured us into Himself, when He willed to be tempted by Satan. . . . In Christ thou art tempted, because He took to Himself flesh of thee; from Himself to thee He gives salvation: from thee to Himself death, to thee from Himself life: from thee to Himself insults, from Himself to thee honour: from thee to Him temptations, from Him to thee victory . . . See thyself in Him tempted, and Him in thee victorious.'

The recitation of the Psalms, with the reading of the Scriptures, forms the staple of the Breviary, which was monastic in origin. The common prayer of the Church, which was originally taken over from the Synagogue, is preserved in the Mass of the catechumens, the first part of the eucharistic liturgy: the Roman Missal still preserves the remains of the ancient method of alternating lessons and chants, and on certain days one or more Old Testament lessons are still appointed to be read before the Epistle.

The Graduals and Tracts which come between the Epistle and Gospel are very ancient: the chants for the

Introit, Offertory and Communion are later, not earlier than the fifth century. The psalm itself was sung by cantors, while the antiphon, usually taken from the psalm, was sung by the people between the verses.[1] In all but a very few cases the chants now survive only in a truncated form, consisting of the antiphon with one verse of the psalm and the Gloria. Even so, it is possible to imagine something of the splendour of the congregational psalmody of the creative liturgical period when they were put into shape.

Thus, for instance, the Introit for the Fourth Sunday after Easter (*English Hymnal*, 695) is taken from Psalm 98; in this case the antiphon is taken from the first and third verses, but instead of singing the whole psalm, we stop short at verse 2.

Ant. 'O sing unto the Lord a new song, alleluya: for the Lord hath done marvellous things, alleluya; in the sight of the nations hath he showed his righteous judgements, alleluya, alleluya.'

Psalm (xcviii. 2). 'With his own right hand, and with his holy arm: hath he gotten himself the victory.'

Repeat *Ant.* Gloria. *Ant.* again.

Another Introit, for Pentecost XVIII (E.H., 710) uses Psalm cxxii, and, by an antiphon which refers to various functions in the Church, turns it into an act of intercession for the Church:

Ant. 'Give peace, O Lord, to them that wait for thee, and let thy prophets be found faithful: regard the prayers of thy servant and of thy people Israel.'

Psalm. 'I was glad when they said unto me: We will go into the house of the Lord.'

He who would learn the meaning of the Church's com-

---

[1] Atchley, in *Ordo Romanus Primus* (de la More Press, 1905), gives a reconstruction of the Easter Day Mass at Rome in the eighth century, with the propers printed out in full.

mon prayer should write out in a copy of the Psalter these wonderful introit-antiphons. These Introits and propers were once the vehicle of a devotion nourished on the Scriptures. A day will come when the Church will no longer be content to use them in their truncated form, but will restore them to their old glory by the addition, in each case, of several more verses of the Psalm.[1]

II. THE FELLOWSHIP OF THE MYSTERY

In the great days of the liturgy the ceremonial of the rite expressed its corporate character as the common act of the Body of Christ.[2] In an age when Christian worship is commonly degraded into the familiar duet between minister and people, we may be thankful that the old ideal still remains, in a shrunken form, in the ritual of High Mass. But in the early Church the deliberate effort was made to divide up the functions of worship among as many people as possible.[3] The Bishop was when possible the celebrant, and was surrounded by his priests, who (at least at Rome) con-celebrated with him; the deacons, headed by the archdeacon, and the sub-deacons had their share in the reading of the lessons and the ceremonial of the altar: chanters and choir, acolytes and doorkeepers all had their place; the people too had their share in the action, in the offering of the gifts and the kiss of peace and the communion.[4]

We notice, first, the hierarchical character of the unity of the Church, as expressed in the Church service. From

[1] See p. 215 *infra*.

[2] For descriptions of the service in the early Church see Frere, *Principles of Religious Ceremonial* (new edition, Mowbray, 1928), pp. 38–74; Cabrol, *Liturgical Prayer, its History and Spirit* (Burns and Oates, 1922), pp. 62–79. See also Illustration No. III, p. 64.

[3] See Frere, *Principles of Religious Ceremonial*, pp. 22–37.

[4] See my article on 'Concelebration' in *Theology*, Feb. 1931, vol. xxii, p. 64.

St. Ignatius of Antioch onwards, the teaching of the Fathers about the unity of the Church has a liturgical background. The Bishop, who is the local centre of unity, as Christ is the centre of unity of the Church universal,[1] normally officiated at the Sunday Mass, and at Rome, where there were many district churches, he celebrated at each in turn: the 'station-days' at the various churches are still marked in the *Roman Missal*. The Bishop's Mass was the chief Mass of the Church on that day: but in order to mark the unity of the act of offering in all the parish churches, a portion of the consecrated Host was sent from the Bishop's Mass to all the district churches, to be placed in the chalice at the Commixture.[2]

The offertory in these early days must have been a very impressive act. The communicants brought their oblations of bread and wine (and sometimes other gifts also) and presented them at the altar: from these was taken that which was required for the Sacrament. An offertory-prayer from the Egyptian Liturgy of St. Mark shows very vividly the meaning of the act:[3]

'The sacrifices of those who offer, their oblations, their thank-offerings, do thou, O God, receive at thy holy celestial immaterial altar of incense, in the mighty heavens,

[1] Ignatius, *Ep. ad Smyrnaeos*, Ch. viii. 'Wherever the bishop appear, there let the people be, just as where Christ Jesus is, there is the Catholic (whole) Church.'

[2] The *Fermentum*. Pope Innocent I writes in his letter to Decentius (A.D. 416; P.L., vol. 20, col. 556–7): 'Concerning the *fermentum* which we send on Sundays to the titular churches, it was superfluous for you to consult us, since all our churches are within the city. Since their presbyters, on account of the congregations entrusted to them, cannot join with us (i.e. con-celebrate) on that day, therefore they receive by the hands of acolytes the *fermentum* consecrated by us, in order that, on that day above all, they may not regard themselves as separated from communion with us.' See the article on 'Concelebration' in *Theology*, xxii, p. 67.

[3] Brightman, *Liturgies Eastern and Western*, p. 129. For another illustration of the ancient Offertory-procession, see p. 244 *infra*.

by the ministry of thy archangel: the offerings of those who offer much or little, in secret or publicly, of those who would offer but have not, and of those who have made their offerings here this day: as thou didst receive the gifts of thy righteous Abel, the sacrifice of our father Abraham, the incense of Zacharias, the alms of Cornelius, the two mites of the widow: so receive their offerings, and grant unto them, in return for corruptible things, incorruptible, for earthly things, heavenly, for temporal things, eternal.'

This common act of offering has left a deep mark especially upon the Roman rite, both in the fixed prayers of the Canon, and in the variables, especially the 'Secrets' or variable offertory-collects. Thus the Secret for the 5th Sunday after Pentecost reads:

'Hearken, O Lord, to our prayers, and graciously accept these offerings of thy servants and handmaids: that what individuals have offered to the honour of thy name, may avail unto all for salvation.'

And the *Hanc igitur* and the *Quam Oblationem* of the Canon:

'This oblation therefore of our service and that of thy whole family, we pray thee, O Lord, graciously to accept: and do thou order our days in peace . . . which oblation do thou, O God, make in all ways to be blessed . . . that it may become unto us the Body and Blood of thy most beloved Son Jesus Christ our Lord.'

The offering of the gifts must always have been the speaking symbol of the people's will to offer up themselves to God; and here the self-oblation of the Church, the *Corpus Christi*, is set forth as the matter of the sacramental *Corpus Christi*. Here, as in St. Paul, the two senses of 'the Body of Christ' are allowed to run together: the offering-up of the Body of Jesus Christ in the Sacrament is one with the offering-up of His Body which is the Church.

It finds a preliminary expression in the offertory-act: it is consummated in the Communion.

This conception, which lies at the heart of the Catholic conception of the eucharistic sacrifice, is especially dear to St. Augustine, whose teaching is thus summed up by Fr. Emil Mersch:[1]

'The Mass is the sacrifice of the Saviour completed in His members, or, what comes to the same thing, it is the oblation of the Church, having its ground in the oblation of Christ, and deriving from it its fullness. The eucharist, so regarded, is not merely the sacrament of the real presence; it has also a necessary relation with the unity of the Church, of which it is the sacred symbol or, as Augustine says, the sacrament of the mystical body. These last affirmations are so familiar to our saint, that some Protestant historians of dogma have claimed that according to him the Host contains not Christ's physical body, but rather His mystical body. This is evidently an error: for it is precisely in the fact that the very substance of the Saviour is contained in the eucharist, that the life and unity of the Church are contained in it, as in their source. But the error testifies to the vigour with which Augustine in speaking of the eucharist affirms our incorporation into Christ.'

It is not necessary, perhaps, to quote the well-known phrases of St. Augustine at length, such as the great passage from the *City of God* (x. 6) in which he speaks of 'the whole redeemed City itself, the congregation and society of the saints', as 'offered up as a living sacrifice to God by the great High-priest': or again, the sacrifice of Christ 'is the sacrifice of the Church, which, since she is the Body of this Head, learns to offer up herself through Him' (*ibid.*, chap. 20): or the passage from Sermon 272

[1] *Le Corps mystique du Christ*, by E. Mersch, S.J., Louvain, 1933. Vol. II, p. 108.

V. THE RESURRECTION OF CHRIST

(P.L., vol. 38, col. 1247): 'Since you are the. Body of Christ and His members, it is the mystery of yourselves which lies upon the Lord's Table: it is the mystery of yourselves which you receive.' [1] These thoughts occur in a peculiarly interesting form, with much else that is characteristic both of St. Augustine and of the early Church in general, in a Sermon, which, as it is too long to quote here, we give in an appendix at the end of this chapter. [2]

St. Augustine is the greatest exponent of this teaching: but it would be a mistake to regard it as peculiar to him. The *Epiclesis* or Invocation of the Holy Spirit for the consecration of the elements in the non-Roman rites is a prayer not only for the sanctification of the elements, but also for the sanctification of the communicants. The regular formula is that the Holy Spirit is invited to descend 'upon us and upon these thy gifts', and the Invocation is always followed by a summary of the fruits of communion, as in the *Liturgy of St. James*:

'Send down, O Master, thy all-holy Spirit upon us and upon these gifts here set forth before thee, that coming upon them in his holy and good and glorious Advent he may hallow and make this bread to be the holy Body of Christ (Amen), and this cup the precious Blood of Christ (Amen);

'That it may be to all who partake thereof unto remission of sins and eternal life, the sanctification of souls and bodies, the bringing-forth of the fruit of good works, and the stablishing of thy holy catholic and apostolic Church, which thou hast built upon the rock of faith that the

[1] See Gore, *The Body of Christ* (1901), pp. 199–209.
[2] Sermon 227. See p. 85 *infra*. The original is printed, with much other exceedingly interesting matter, in *S. Aurelii Augustini textus eucharistici selecti* (73 pp.), by H. Lang, O.S.B., being vol. XXXV in the series *Florilegium Patristicum*, Peter Hanstein, Bonn.

gates of hell may not prevail against it, freeing it from all heresy and scandals of them that work iniquity, and preserving it unto the end of the world'.

This is followed by a comprehensive intercession for all estates of men in the Church. Clearly the Invocation of the Holy Spirit is not merely for the consecration of the elements but also for the consecration of the Church, Christ's Body.[1]

Further, in a number of places the Greek liturgies contain clear reminiscences of the great text from Romans xii. 1–2:

'I beseech you therefore, brethren . . . that ye present your bodies a living sacrifice, holy, acceptable unto God, which is your reasonable service.'

In different contexts in St. Basil, St. Chrysostom, Serapion, St. Mark, we find the unmistakable phrases 'living sacrifice' and 'reasonable service', commonly in conjunction with the phrase 'bloodless offering'. The Jewish sacrifices were associated with the slaughter of an animal, and there the victim was external to the worshipper: but in the Christian sacrifice there is no slaughter, and the worshippers themselves are offered up and become part of the sacrifice.

Here is seen the fulfilment and the transformation of sacrifice, according to the lines laid down in the Epistle to the Hebrews. It is fully clear, both there and in St. Paul, that the whole life of Christians is a sacrificial life. As the self-giving love of Christ is 'a sacrifice and offering to God', so Christians are to 'walk in love' (Ephes. v. 2). St. Paul represents himself as a sacrificing priest, the Gentiles as a sacrificial offering to God (Rom. xv. 16):

[1] See my article in *Theology*, Oct. 1933, on *The Meaning of the Epiclesis*. Also printed separately among *Theology Reprints* (S.P.C.K.), No. 14.

VI. THE HOLY FACE OF LUCCA

Rom. xii. 1–2 has been already quoted. And because the whole life of Christians is an oblation, even the gifts of the Philippians to St. Paul (Phil. iv. 18) or the songs of praise and the good works of the Hebrews (Heb. xiii. 15, 16), can be called sacrificial.

This conception is fundamental to the idea of the eucharistic sacrifice in the Fathers, and it always remains alive where the eucharist is the centre of the Church's worship, and the communion of the people is a regular part of the service. After the Memorial of Christ's sacrifice has been made, Christ in giving to the people the sacrament of His sacrifice, unites them with Himself in His self-oblation.

III. THE MIDDLE AGES

When, therefore, in the course of the early period of the Middle Ages the laity gradually dropped away from their communion, till by the twelfth century the Great Service was regularly celebrated with no communicants at all except the priest, this was a profound change which radically altered the character of Christian worship. Dr. Brilioth sees its importance, and calls it 'the great disaster' in the history of the liturgy [1]; but in general it has been strangely passed over by historians, so much so that it is difficult to find anywhere a summary of the evidence, exhibiting the stages of the decline.[2] The silence of the historians must be due in part to the fact that, since the theology of Transubstantiation was elaborated in the thirteenth century, the dogma of the Real Presence has dominated men's minds to such an extent that 'alike in the Roman, Lutheran and Anglican Churches it has

---

[1] Brilioth, *Eucharistic Faith and Practice*, p. 279, cf. p. 284.

[2] See, however, Dr. Sparrow Simpson in *Non-communicating Attendance* (Longmans, 1913), chs. VI, VII. A much fuller collection of documents is given in *De frequenti communione in ecclesia occidentali usque ad annum c. 1000*, by P. Browe, S. J.(Pontificia Universitas Gregoriana, Piazza della Pilotta, Rome, 1932, 84 pp.).

remained almost impossible to state the problem otherwise than as a Yes or No to the question whether the real presence in the elements is true.' [1] Then, also, it is commonly assumed that religion is an affair of the individual, and that the precise way in which people say their prayers is a matter of indifference: and it is forgotten that the things which people do in church leave a deeper impression than the words they hear or the doctrines which are taught.

In reality, the importance of this change cannot be exaggerated. It shifted the centre of gravity of the service to the Consecration, and produced the new ceremony of the Elevation, and in time the new practices of Exposition of the Sacrament and Benediction. It made the laity no longer in the old sense participants in the mystery, but spectators of a ritual performed in the sanctuary by the clergy and ministers. Thereby the sacramental principle itself was in large measure lost, though its external forms remained. The eucharist was no longer exhibited as the common offering of the members of the Body in union with the Head, but was perforce interpreted as the act of the priest celebrating Christ's Sacrifice. In Augustine the communion had been the consummation of the sacrifice: but in Aquinas the sacrifice is identified with the priestly action, and the communion of the people becomes an optional addition to it. Their part is no longer to share in the sacrifice, but to engage in acts of individual piety, while the priest performs his part. The worship of the early Church had been the common act of the Church of God, as of a Body with an organic structure, hierarchically graded; the congregation now become more and more an aggregation of unrelated individuals, met together for a religious service. [2]

We shall notice in the next chapter a parallel change

[1] Brilioth, p. 287. [2] Cf. pp. 205–6 *infra.*

taking place in the conception of the central dogma of
the Atonement: we must here mention, though very
briefly, the parallel development of sacred art. In the
epresentations of the Last Supper in the Catacombs,
there is no attempt at realism: usually we do not see as
many as twelve apostles, and on the table bread and fish,
symbols of the sacrament. But in Leonardo da Vinci's
great picture the whole interest is psychological—'Lord,
is it I?'—and one would not gather from the picture that
any sacrament had been instituted there at all. Again,
in early times the church was dominated by the figure
of the glorified Christ in the apse above the altar: now
the crucifix becomes common.[1] The earliest crucifixes
show Him robed and crowned, the Victor reigning from
the tree: but gradually the crucifixion descends from
heaven to earth, till finally the eyes of the Christ are
closed in death, and we see a realistic picture of human
suffering. The frescoes and mosaics in the old churches
—as still in the Orthodox East—had depicted the glory
of the heavenly Jerusalem; the church-building was the
home of a liturgy which belonged to the other world. In
the Middle Ages the wonderful new stained glass trans-
mits the light of this world, and depicts, very commonly,
historical scenes from the Scriptures or the lives of the
Saints. All this illustrates the change which had taken
place from the 'ontological' idea of the mystery and of
the sacramental fellowship of the Body, to a new emphasis
on the psychological experience of the individual.[2]

'In Christian antiquity the Mystery gave the point of
view from which the whole of life was seen and no part
of it left out of sight, not even the commonest things in
the world: through its relation to the Mystery, each indi-

[1] For this sentence and the next, see Illus. V and XV.

[2] This paragraph is mainly taken from Herwegen, *Kirche und Seele*,
pp. 22–9. See also pp. 243–5 *infra*.

83

vidual being passes out of its isolation and is incorporated into a great organic whole, without however losing its own individual light. The Middle Ages, in which men made a new discovery of this world and its beauty, separated the complex of life even more clearly into two spheres, the natural and the supernatural. The cleavage shows itself in individual men: a great joy in this world stands side by side with a vastly increased mortification, a warmer and gladder openness to this world with a tense personal and spiritual piety. The early Christian found Christ in the Mysteries, above all in the eucharistic offering and the fellowship of the mystical Body the Church, in which the Christian became an *alter Christus*. The medieval man seeks Christ in the historical life of the Saviour according to the Gospels and in His ethical teaching: to him Christ becomes a moral example.' [1]

So Dr. Herwegen. His aim is purely descriptive; but at the end of the essay he expresses his judgement that, as the end of the Middle Ages marked the end of an artistic period, and Gothic art died of exhaustion, so we are now at the end of an age. 'If today we observe in religious life a weariness and in places a dying-out of supernatural power, these phenomena can be understood as the signs of the self-exhaustion of the subjective religious tendency.' [2] If this be so, there is little hope in attempts to galvanize into new life a personal and individualistic piety; but there is great hope in a return to the unexhausted source, the Mystery of the redemption once accomplished and its fulfilment in the Body of Christ.

[1] Herwegen, *Kirche und Seele*, pp. 29, 30.   [2] *Ibid.*, p. 32.

An Abbreviated Translation of St. Augustine, Sermon 227

I had promised to you who have been baptized a sermon about the Sacrament of the Lord's Table which you have received. The bread which you see on the altar, when it has been sanctified by the Word of God, is the Body of Christ, and the chalice the cup of His Blood. By these means Christ has willed to convey to us His Body and His Blood which He shed for us for the remission of sins. If now you have received aright, you are what you have received: and so the Apostle expounds the Sacrament of the Lord's Table: *We who are many are one bread one body.*

This bread signifies to you how you ought to love unity. It was made out of many grains of wheat, which were originally separate, but were united by application of water, by a kind of rubbing together (*contritio*) and baked with fire. So have you been ground together by the fast and the exorcism, wetted in Baptism, and baked by the fire of Christ and the mystery of the Holy Spirit. Notice this in the lections which begin at this season from the Acts of the Apostles: for when you come to church you must put away vain fables and be intent on the Holy Scriptures. Notice how at Pentecost the Holy Spirit comes: He comes in fiery tongues, to inspire the love whereby we are to burn towards God and despise the world, and our chaff be burnt away, and our heart refined like gold. So the Holy Spirit comes—after the water the fire—and you are made bread, which is the Body of Christ: and here is the symbol of unity.

Immediately after the prayer you are exhorted to *lift up your hearts*: for this befits members of Christ. The members have a Head: where is the Head? You repeated in the Creed, *On the third day He rose again, He ascended into heaven, and sitteth on the right hand of the Father.* Therefore our Head is in heaven: and you reply *We lift them up unto the Lord*. And lest you should attribute this lifting up of your hearts to your own strength, your own merits, your labours, because to lift up your hearts is the gift of God, the bishop (or the priest who celebrates) continues, *Let us give thanks unto our Lord God*: let us give thanks, because, if He were not to grant this, our hearts would still remain on earth. And you bear witness, saying *It is meet and right* that we should give thanks to Him who has made us lift up our hearts to our Head.

Then after the consecration of God's sacrifice, because He willed that we ourselves should be a sacrifice unto Him, we say the Lord's Prayer, which you have learnt and repeated. Then is said *Peace be with you*, and the Christians kiss one another with a holy kiss. It is a sign of peace: as the lips express, so let it be in the heart. As your lips approach the lips of your brother, let not your heart draw away from him.

The Apostle says, *He who eats the Body of Christ, or drinks the cup of the Lord unworthily shall be guilty of the Body and Blood of the Lord*. What is it to receive unworthily? It is to receive mockingly or contemptuously. Let it not appear common to you because you see it. That which you see passes away: the invisible thing which is signified thereby passes not away, but abides. It is received, eaten, consumed. But is the Body of Christ consumed? Is the Church of Christ consumed? Are the members of Christ consumed? No. Here they are purified: there they are crowned. The thing signified abides eternally, though to sight it passes away. Receive therefore thoughtfully, having unity in your heart, having your heart ever lifted up. Let your hope be not on earth but in heaven. Let your faith be firm in God, let it be acceptable to God. For that which you here see not, but believe, there you shall see, and rejoice for evermore.

CHAPTER IV

DOGMA

*

I. THE NATURE OF DOGMA

The Creed was in its origin the baptismal confession of faith. It did not originally belong to the eucharistic liturgy; it was not added to the rite till the fifth century in the East, and the tenth century at Rome. But it was natural and fitting that it should be added, because the same dogma which the liturgy expresses in the form of a mystery-rite, is expressed by the Creed in the form of a statement of belief. This connexion between liturgy and creed is of fundamental importance for the right understanding of Christian dogma.

What is dogma? 'Dogma' we are told 'consists of a set of opinions about religious matters imposed by ecclesiastical authority, and thereby depriving the individual who accepts that authority of the freedom which he would otherwise have to hold other opinions: these opinions are dignified with the name of 'revelation', and churchpeople are taught that they must hold these opinions, not on reasonable grounds, but because they are guaranteed by Church authority. These opinions include the doctrine of the Trinity, and Christians rather glibly take upon themselves metaphysical assertions about the nature of the Supreme Being, which they only dimly understand and are not even able to state accurately.'

It must be admitted that Christian theology has often given only too much justification for reproaches such as

87

these. Yet all Christians know that the faith by which they live is radically different from their personal opinions, even if they cannot explain precisely what the difference is. From the earliest times to the present day, there have been martyrs who have laid down their lives rather than surrender or compromise their Christian faith: and men do not give their lives for the sake of mere opinions. The faith of the ordinary Christian, halting and imperfect though it be, is nevertheless an apprehension of something divine, something not of man nor from man, something which is to him a well-spring of life. This faith finds expression in the form of beliefs and even of opinions: yet it is felt to be more profound than either. We can argue about beliefs and about opinions: but there is something in faith which is of a different order from the mere assent of the intellect to propositions.

The point has been well expressed thus:

'Suppose I launch a question at you, my good friend (never mind who you and I are), "Does God mean anything to you?" Suppose you should answer, "Yes, a great deal," and I reply slowly, "I wonder. But please, do not answer me. Ask it of yourself." How would you answer then?

'If I dig right down to the bottom of my own mind— it is a very average dry soil—I must say, "Most times God means nothing consciously. I am just busy. Sometimes He means everything. But again, busy or not, conscious or not, I am quite conscious that He is just all the meaning there is."

'Let us turn the question on to some one else; and suppose he replies, "What do you mean by God?" I answer, "Maker of heaven and earth, the beginning and end of all things: ruler and judge of your life and mine: of whom, in whom, through whom, all things consist." Meaning— as above—God is just all the meaning there is for anything.

'Then suppose he answers, "Oh yes, I quite agree with that." Some people do answer that way, and I never know what to say next: though I know what my inner mind says: "Agree! Agree to what?" I was pointing to something. The man who can only see opinions to agree with has plainly no least idea of what I was talking about.' [1]

About opinions we can argue: the basis of the argument is an assumed mastery or comprehension of the subject. But faith is an effort to apprehend something which exceeds the grasp of the apprehending mind. It therefore fitly expresses itself in the word of prophecy, which always has something imperative about it, and is a demand on the understanding. 'Thus saith the Lord', or its equivalent, is a formula proper to the pulpit: the preacher stands there that he may speak in God's name: and it is painfully incongruous when a message which is really a word of God is introduced by some such formula as 'May we then not reasonably conclude that . . .' It is equally incongruous, on the other hand, when the note of authority proper to a word of prophecy is used to impress on the audience something which is matter of opinion, and needs to be supported by reasonable argument: a speaker who thus dogmatizes about politics or disputed questions of Biblical history is felt to be guilty of presumption. Some of the things which the clergy have to say are best said from the pulpit, and the hearers need to be left to meditate about them; for others the proper place is a study-circle, where there is room for discussion.

There is then this deep difference between the word of prophecy and rational argument, between faith and opinion; and dogma evidently belongs to the former class rather than the latter. Or rather, its subject-matter belongs to the region of faith and of prophecy, while its

[1] Father Kelly in the *S.S.M. Quarterly*, Michaelmas, 1933, p. 72.

form is that of a reasoned statement. The mind with which the preacher analyses and makes clear a prophetic message is the same mind with which he forms his opinions about political or theological questions of dispute. While listening to his prophetic message and profiting by it, we can at the same time be analysing and criticizing his presentation of it. We can distinguish between the essential content of dogma and the form in which it is expressed.

It is always possible, therefore, in the case of any given doctrine, that the truth which is seeking to find expression may not have found for itself an adequate vehicle. It is clear, for instance, that the early Fathers, such as Ignatius, Justin, Origen, are not yet fully at home in the forms in which the Christian faith is to be expressed. The work of Origen especially is experimental: he is avowedly seeking to find his way among the forms of Greek thought, going down first one road and then another in order to explore it. His work is immature in comparison with that of later theologians like Basil and the two Cappadocian Gregories, and some of it came in for formal condemnation. So today in the mission field Christianity has to create for itself a new terminology in the native languages. The word 'worship' in its Christian sense expresses the reverence and the service which is due to God alone. The heathen Basuto naturally had no word to express this: the word that was adopted meant simply 'to kneel before' some one, and has been criticized as being quite inadequate to express the idea. It is however in process of learning its new meaning, and the Christians never use it except in relation to God. The imperfection of Christian terminology in such languages provides an interesting parallel to the difficulty which dogma regularly has in finding for itself adequate forms of expression.

Then, too, since the content of dogma is a truth of God,

it can prove difficult and unacceptable to human reason in proportion as it is true. St. Thomas Aquinas says of the Incomprehensibility of God (*Summa Theologica*, I. xii. 1):

'That which is in itself supremely knowable, may not be knowable to a particular intellect on account of the extent to which the greatness of the thing known exceeds the knowing mind, just as the sun, which is supremely visible, cannot be looked at by the bat on account of the excess of light.'

Here is a principle, which is more clearly and directly expressed in the words of the Gospel, 'Thou hast hidden these things from the wise and prudent, and hast revealed them unto babes' (Matt. xi. 25). That which is in itself supremely simple is hidden from men because of their own lack of simplicity. It is not that our Lord commends uncritical credulity or stupidity: on the contrary, He is continually saying, 'He that hath ears let him hear,' and βλέπετε τί ἀκούετε, 'look what you are hearing,' 'look at it'. When He commends the childlike spirit, He means that the condition of learning anything is the readiness to listen. Or again, St. Paul says in a famous passage (1 Cor. i. 18 ff.) that the word of the Cross is 'to the Jews a stumbling-block, to the Greeks foolishness': to the former it seems rank blasphemy that one who suffered the death that was accursed above all deaths should be proclaimed as Messiah: to the latter it seems utter fatuity, stark staring madness, that a Divine Being should be believed to suffer such disgrace. It seems utterly contrary to reason.[1] It seems so to these men because they themselves are wrong, because to them it is self-evident that the ego is the centre of the universe. They will come to

[1] See A. Nygren, *Agape and Eros* (S.P.C.K., 1932), pp. 158–64, on the 'reversal of the values of antiquity'. To Celsus and to pagan thought generally the Christian gospel seemed utterly absurd.

learn the meaning of the Cross only when they themselves have undergone the Copernican revolution, which will bring them to see that God is the centre of His own world. Just because the Cross is God's truth, it cannot be judged at the bar of human reason. Men cannot indeed help judging it; but while they judge it, it judges them.

It is not that the message of the Cross is irrational: on the contrary, later theology will have to express in a systematic form the doctrine of the Atonement, a work for which St. Paul himself lays the foundations. The mystery of the Cross lies open to human reason to analyse and understand; and there can be no apprehending it without in some degree understanding it. It is not mysterious in the sense of an unverifiable formula which the mind must accept blindfold. Man must labour to understand it, but the one chief hindrance to his understanding of it will lie in his own lack of simplicity.

There is then a divine and a human element in dogma. It is 'a treasure in earthen vessels'. The divine element, as always in Christianity, is mediated in and through the human, and creates for itself a body out of human materials.

II. THE DOGMA OF THE INCARNATION

We will now apply what we have said about dogma to the central point of all, the dogma of the Incarnation, which is the proclamation that the Divine Goodness has been manifested in Christ *in carne*, in the flesh.

It is possible to show that the claim of Jesus to a Divine origin and mission is found in many texts of the Synoptic Gospels, texts which are found in the earliest sources from which our present Gospels have been constructed. These texts can rightly be held to show that Jesus believed Himself to have come from God bringing in God's name the Kingdom of God to men. But it cannot be sufficient to justify the doctrine of the Incarnation merely by an appeal to isolated texts, any one of which may be disputed. If it is true, the essential principle of it will be found to be present everywhere in the Gospels, and is woven into their very texture.

The principle is the manifestation of God's goodness *in the flesh*, that is, in and through human nature. Here we may see the deepest reason why Jesus rejects the popular idea of the Kingdom of God as given in the *Psalms of Solomon*, according to which the coming 'Son of David' would with Divine help establish an ideal political kingdom: men would live under ideal conditions, with just laws and good government, and would have every encouragement to live good lives. But such a programme would leave no place for any radical dealing with the evil in man, or the manifestation of God's own goodness in the flesh. All that could be hoped for would be an increase of human virtue. Again, He modifies profoundly the 'eschatological' view of the Kingdom of God as set forth in the *Similitudes of Enoch*, according to which this world, as it is, is unredeemable, and God can do nothing with it; God will therefore make a complete break, and will send the 'Son of Man' from heaven to inaugurate the Divine Kingdom on a transformed earth under wholly new conditions. The term 'Son of Man' is derived from a famous passage of Daniel (vii. 13), where it is a symbolical human figure representing the 'Kingdom of the saints of the Most High' (vss. 18, 22, 25–7); but Enoch uses it to describe an angelic being, usually called the 'Elect One', who shall appear on the clouds of heaven as Judge and Deliverer.

Our Lord adopts this term, 'Son of Man', and uses it often in the same apocalyptic sense. But He also uses it regularly, according to Mark, in His prophecies of the

Passion, and elsewhere, to denote the earthly humiliation of Him who 'had not where to lay His head'. Thus it sums up in itself the idea of the Incarnation; the literary allusion to Daniel and Enoch involves the meaning of the Saviour come from heaven, and the fact that He who thus speaks of Himself is a man on earth links with this the natural meaning of the word, as Man and Brother of men.

In His teaching, He does not chiefly exhort men to prepare for the coming Judgement, but rather to live the life of children of God here and now, here in this world: 'that ye may be sons of your Father which is in heaven' (Matt. v. 45). Here in this world the Divine Goodness is manifested: here and now the seed sown by the Divine Sower grows up transforming the lives of men, as the leaven transforms the dough: here and now the power of the Kingdom of God is seen in the mighty works, for 'if I by the finger of God cast out devils, then verily the Kingdom of God has arrived in your midst' (Luke xi. 20). To the scribes who say in their hearts 'Who can remit sins but God alone'—God being far away in heaven, at a safe distance—He claims by word and deed that God is near, that the 'Son of Man' has power on earth to heal both the body and the soul. The whole Gospel is permeated with this principle that God's power and goodness is present in the flesh, first in Christ Himself, then in His disciples, or, in Pauline language, first in the Head of the Body and then in the members.

It is just this that makes the Gospel of Jesus so terrifying. Men crucify Him because they dare not allow God to come so close. It is so much simpler to have a law and make the observance of its rules into a substitute for the real service of God. Pharisees and Sadducees alike dare not face the real thing.[1]

Here is the central principle of Christianity: the mani-

[1] See Söderblom, *The Mystery of the Cross* (S.C.M., 1933), pp. 42 ff.

festation of the Divine Goodness in the flesh, in Jesus as the Son of God first, and then through the Holy Spirit in the members of His mystical Body. And the essential meaning of heresy is, that every heresy in some way or other shirks, evades, weakens down this simple principle. The principle is utterly simple; but it is difficult to men because of their lack of simplicity.

The Gnostic heresy, the conflict with which is discernible already in the later books of the New Testament, from *Colossians* onwards, expressed the attitude of the Greek world which believed in a salvation through *Gnosis*, by lofty contemplation and wonderful mystical experience and soaring speculations about the unseen world, but could not believe that marriage was holy or that there was any possibility of glorifying God in the common actions of daily life. For them salvation meant an escape from the body, not the redemption of the body.

The Arians, like the pagan philosophers, thought of God as utterly remote from the world and unknowable by men: Jesus was the Logos, an intermediate being between man and the unknown God. Man might aspire to the virtues of Christ, but God was not really the Father, and the goodness of God had not been manifested in the flesh.

The Apollinarians said that Jesus was a sort of theophany, a Divine mind and spirit in a human body: He was therefore not true man, and human nature had not been redeemed.

The Nestorians thought of Jesus as a wonderful man, so good and so sinless that He had been found worthy to be taken up into the Godhead. Again, God had not been manifested in the flesh; God had not redeemed human nature.

The Monophysites regarded the manhood of Jesus as merged in the Divine, like a drop of honey in the ocean;

the divine took the place of the human, instead of redeeming it and transforming it. And all these heresies reappear under different forms in modern England; for we too are equally tempted to evade the simplicity of the Gospel of God's coming to us in the flesh.

Finally Pelagius, the typical heretic of the West, and a native of Britain, denied the doctrine of grace, claiming that if man is to be saved at all, it can only be by his own moral efforts. This is a very popular belief today; but it is the direct denial of the doctrine of grace, that is, of the presence of the Holy Spirit in the flesh, as the regenerative and transforming power of God in the hearts and lives of men.

Thus the definitions of the great Councils, and the controversies waged by the orthodox theologians against these various teachings, are so many efforts to guard the simplicity of the Gospel of God. It is not that the heretic has seen and understood the orthodox opinion, and conscientiously believes another opinion to be preferable: it is that in each case he has never seen what the Christian faith really is: 'Except a man be born anew, he cannot *see* the Kingdom of God' (John iii. 3). He misses it, owing to his own lack of simplicity.

The Liberal theologians of the nineteenth century were missing the point when they took the orthodoxy of Nicaea and Chalcedon to be a construction of speculative theology, a Hellenization of the original Christianity, 'the work of the Greek spirit on the soil of the Gospel'. The ground-conception of Harnack, underlying his great *History of Dogma*, was all wrong, and much of his work will have to be done all over again. The fact is rather that the orthodox Trinitarian doctrine represents the self-defence of Christianity against the Greek spirit, the guarding of the Divine truth against the endeavour of human reason to drag it down to its own level.

VII. THE WORD WAS MADE FLESH

III. SYSTEM-MAKING

It would be true to say, as a broad generalization, that it is not till the Middle Ages that we get a truly speculative theology.

Dr. Aulén, now Bishop of Strängnäs, Sweden, has drawn out for us the contrast between the typical view of the Atonement in the early Church and in the Middle Ages.[1] The Fathers regularly present the Atonement under a series of images and symbols, in which they describe the work of God in delivering man from the power of sin, death and the devil, under such figures as the redemption of prisoners by the payment of a ransom-price, or the conquest of the bandit-chief who holds man captive by the King who is man's rightful Lord, or the artifice of the Deception of the Devil. It has been usual to regard these expositions as tentative approaches towards the rational theory which was worked out by St. Anselm in the twelfth century; but this is a misconception. The Fathers have before their minds the Christian Mystery, and they use symbols not altogether unlike the parables of the Gospel, to describe God's redemptive work. In this they stand in contrast with St. Anselm, whose constant refrain is *nihil rationabilius*, and who provides a systematic theory why there must be an Atonement, since there must be a satisfaction offered to the Divine Justice. In general this rationalism is characteristic of the medieval and post-Reformation theologians: but the final conclusion of the rationalizing method does not appear to be drawn till a Protestant writer of the early nineteenth century, Philippi, makes the very astonishing assertion (which nevertheless on his premises is logically justifiable) that, since God has through Christ's satisfaction received full

[1] G. Aulén, *Christus Victor* (S.P.C.K., 1931). See esp. Chaps. II, III, V.

compensation for our fault, 'we could even demand everlasting life from God's justice' as a right (Aulén, p. 147).

It is a significant fact that the change of attitude towards dogma coincides in time with the change in the habits of worship which came over Western Christendom in the early Middle Ages, and in particular with the loss of the communion of the people from the great Sunday Service, to which we called attention in the last chapter. The change with regard to dogma is closely parallel with the liturgical change. In the earlier age Christian dogma is the expression of the mystery of Divine grace by which all human life is redeemed and sanctified: in the later it becomes a mystery in the intellectual sense, a sacred doctrine taught by the clergy and accepted by the laity with *fides implicita*, whereby they accept on trust propositions which they do not understand.

It was plausible enough. The Christian dogma was 'true', the demonstrable conclusions of philosophy were 'true': why should not both be combined in a rational system which, if its reasoning were coherent, would be true in all its parts? The existence of God could be proved by reason, if not by St. Anselm's ontological argument, at least by St. Thomas's cosmological argument, which argues from the non-self-explanatory character of this changing world to its necessary ground in a Being who is His own *raison d'être*. It was possible to go on and demonstrate the Divine attributes, the absoluteness, perfection, infinity, changelessness, eternality and unity of God, His creative knowledge, His omnipotence. So far Reason could go. Revelation made known to man truths which were beyond the reach of reason: thus the doctrine of the Trinity could rest on Revelation alone, and similarly the doctrines of the Incarnation, Atonement and the Sacraments. But Revelation was essentially a revelation of doctrines, and faith an intellectual belief in these doctrines.

At the very beginning of the *Summa Theologica* St. Thomas speaks of Revelation as making conveniently accessible to the ordinary man truths which could equally be arrived at by reason (S.T., I. i. 1):

'Even with regard to those truths about God which can be investigated by natural reason, it was necessary that man should be instructed by Divine revelation; because the truth about God investigated by reason would only reach man through a few, and after a long time, and with the admixture of many errors: yet on the knowledge of this truth depends the whole salvation of man, which is in God. Therefore, that salvation might reach men more conveniently and certainly, it was necessary that they should be instructed about Divine things by Divine revelation.'

Here the distinction between dogma and human belief has been lost. The way is open for a comprehensive theological system to be constructed, providing an intellectual map of the universe, competent to answer all questions that can be asked. The Bible, as the Book of Divine Revelation, must necessarily be taken as free from error in all its parts. This view of the Bible is as necessary to the scholastic scheme as to the modern Fundamentalism which, rejecting the greater part of its theological system, accepts one corner of it. Underlying both is a common assumption about the nature of truth. For St. Thomas, greatest of Christian philosophers, the scheme rests on the authority of Church tradition and the Bible and upon sound reasoning. But in view of the criticisms which subsequent thinkers made upon the Thomist construction, it was inevitable that the system should require infallible ecclesiastical authority for its guarantee.

It must indeed be allowed that the Roman Catholic

Church has preserved to the common Christian a genuine faith in the supernatural, more effectively on the whole than the Protestant Churches have succeeded in doing. But on the intellectual side we may well ask whether the scholastic system is not to be chiefly blamed for the confusion of the modern world in matters of faith. The first stage was the blurring of the fundamental distinction between dogma and human opinion, so that many things which belong to human opinion were exalted among the *credenda* of Christian faith: the last is the modern state of confusion, in which all religious belief is commonly regarded as a matter of opinion, and the common faith of the European nations has almost been lost, and a man's opinions about the relation of God and man are regarded as his private concern.

The centre of the whole business is the conception of truth: and here there are two criticisms to be made from a philosophical point of view.

First, what is the relation of human knowledge to Truth, real Truth, Truth as it is in the mind of God? When the question is so stated, it is evident that human knowledge and human truth are partial, limited, relative. 'As the heavens are higher than the earth, so are My ways higher than your ways, and My thoughts than your thoughts.' Man does not stand at the centre of the universe, able to survey the whole order as from its centre. He is himself involved in the movement of the universe; he is one of the products of the universal scheme. It is our common assumption that the view of truth which a man takes is limited and conditioned by his state of development, his character, his environment, his prejudices, his nervous condition. When I open a book of philosophy or history, I do not approach it as containing absolute truth: I am concerned to know what manner of man the author is. In fact, in pronouncing our judgement on philosophy or history, we men are in the first place pronouncing judgement on ourselves, registering our own reaction to those things which we are describing.

At the same time, this is not the whole of the matter. In the act of affirming that every human view of truth is relative and limited by the limitations of the percipient, we are affirming that it is *true* that every human view of truth is relative. In other words, every human judgement does claim to be really true. Round this antinomy all philosophy revolves. What does it mean? It means that man, tiny animal though he be, living for a few years on a little planet, big to him, but relatively to the stellar universe infinitesimally small, can yet speculate about what the meaning and purpose of the whole scheme may be: creature though he be, yet in his self-determining personality with its artistic faculties he has yet a little spark of his Maker's creative power. He is made in the image of God.

But though he can reason, and is bound by the law of his nature to trust his reason, he is manifestly not in a position to reconstruct the scheme of the whole universal order. He cannot construct a comprehensive theological system and claim that he has made a map of the universe. If he does, he is forgetting his limitations, and is guilty of a Titanism which brings its own nemesis.[1]

'Natural Theology' is rather the statement of a question than the finding of the answer. It starts from the question: 'Here am I in the midst of a changing universe,

[1] 'I must abide for ever in a state of mental docility, with my lesson never fully learned. In such a world the sceptic and the Platonist and the Christian are equally at ease, but the rationalist is an outcast; and against such a state of pupilage the intellect rebels with the pride of a Satan.' So writes Dr. P. E. More, in his important new book, *The Sceptical Approach to Religion* (Princeton, 1934, p. 99), in which he follows up and sums up his earlier series on *The Greek Tradition*.

myself also subject to change: what is the meaning of it all?' The conclusion of the cosmological argument, that that which is caused implies a first cause, is in reality no more than a more exact statement of the question. 'The meaning of this changeable universe cannot be found within itself: it must be found in something outside itself, in a super-nature.' The conclusion is still a question: we have learnt only where the answer is to be looked for. The answer remains still as unknown as ever; as Aquinas says, God has to be described by negative terms, such as infinite. The answer, the only answer, comes in Revelation. God's answer *is* Christ, who is proclaimed to be the Word or self-expression of God, embodied in the flesh. The answer comes in the form of a Person, not in that of a formula. We are not told *why* God allows all the woe and suffering of the world; we are shown Christ suffering and triumphing through suffering. The answer is greater than we are able to grasp. 'What I do thou knowest not now, but thou shalt know hereafter.' 'So foolish was I and ignorant, even as it were a beast before thee. Nevertheless I am alway by Thee: for Thou hast holden me by my right hand.'

This brings us to our second point, which is the fundamental distinction between the thing-in-itself and our concept of it, between reality and our idea of reality. The thing itself is always infinitely complex, in its own structure and in its relations to other things: Tennyson shows us that if we fully understood the 'flower in the crannied wall' we should understand the universe. I see the thing, I observe its behaviour, I analyse its characteristics; but even if I spend years on the study of the beetle, there will always be far, far more to be learnt. And always the reality of the beetle itself remains different in kind from my pictures, diagrams, hypotheses and conclusions.

There can be no doubt of the fact that according to

the New Testament the Revelation of God, the Word of God, is Christ Himself, not a doctrine about Christ. And if our analysis can never exhaustively describe the reality of even the commonest thing, much more must this be the case when the object of the analysis is of a higher order than our minds. God's Revelation in Jesus Christ must always be more than our minds can take in (cf. John xvi. 14, 15). It is true that our apprehension of it must always find expression in an intellectual formulation. So the New Testament describes Jesus as the Son of Man, the only Son of God, the Messiah, the Lord, the Divine Wisdom, the Logos; but each and all of these formulations is what we have seen described as 'a pointer', not an exhaustive definition. So it is with the Atonement. The Atonement is the fundamental reality of the Christian faith: it underlies every sacrament and every liturgical form and all Christian prayer; it is expounded, well or ill, by every theologian and every preacher. Certain forms of expressing the idea of the Atonement are commended to us by the Bible and by the Church. But there is no official theory of the Atonement, authoritatively sanctioned and guaranteed. The Church believes in and lives by the fact of the Atonement, as a reality which can never be exhaustively defined. So it is with the Christian sacraments. There is no official doctrine of the eucharistic sacrifice: the reality apprehended needs always to be expressed and re-expressed, but can never receive a final and complete formulation. Hence the best books on the eucharist are not those which seek to expound 'the Catholic doctrine of the Holy Eucharist' or 'the Evangelical doctrine of Holy Communion', but those which, like Dr. Brilioth's book, seek to set forth various aspects under which it has been apprehended in Christian experience.[1] And always the objectivity of the sacrament itself, as *this*

---

[1] See Brilioth, *Eucharistic Faith and Practice*, esp. pp. 276, 288.

ritual action, *this* bread and wine, remains different in kind from all human apprehensions of it and all human reactions to it.

The Revelation of God is thus proclaimed as in the first place a fact rather than a doctrine. This, as we saw in the second chapter, was the fundamental difference between the Christian and the pagan mysteries. Christianity is the Announcement that God has been incarnated in the flesh, and suffered under Pontius Pilate. Christianity therefore appeals to history: and every effort to evade the appeal to history is an evasion of the Gospel of the Incarnation. In selecting the books of the New Testament, the Church was citing the Apostles as witnesses to the historical facts; for the basis on which the books were accepted was not their religious value, but the fact that they were known or believed to be the work of Apostles, or at least, as in the case of St. Mark's Gospel, to contain Apostolic testimony.

Two interesting points may be cited as evidence of the sensitiveness of the New Testament to the sovereign importance of historical fact. While Thucydides is regarded with justice as the father of scientific history, even he does not name his witnesses as does St. Paul in 1 Cor. xv. 3–8: 'I delivered unto you first of all that which I also received, how that Christ died . . . was buried . . . was raised . . . was seen by Cephas, then by the Twelve, then by 500 brethren at once of whom the greater number are still alive . . . then by James, then by all the Apostles; last of all by me also.' St. Luke in the Acts does not name his sources of information, but the subtle transition from 'they' to 'we' and back again, between chap. xx. 5 and the end of the book, marks the points at which the writer was in St. Paul's company. It is a highly interesting instance of historical conscientiousness and regard for fact.

If the Church appeals to history, she must stand by the

appeal. Clearly, then, it is the principle of the Incarnation itself that forces us to accept the methods of historical investigation and Biblical criticism. It is proclaimed that the Revelation of God has been given in history: therefore the question that must be asked is, Do the accounts fall to pieces under historical analysis, and reveal themselves to be a tissue of inconsistencies? The facts, whatever they are, are God's facts, and it has been claimed that in them God has revealed Himself. If now it were to emerge as the increasingly verified result of sober and responsible investigation that Jesus Christ never existed, manifestly we could not go on being Christians. The same would be the case if the result of inquiry had been to prove that the story of the empty grave and the bodily Resurrection of Jesus dissolved away into legend upon analysis.

It is the principle of the Incarnation itself that demands that these questions should be raised and exhaustively discussed. It is not surprising that such an inquiry should give rise to much searching of heart, or that it should seem probable to many that a negative answer must be given: for, as we shall see, the issue has been seriously confused by Liberal theology. Yet even so the effort to face the facts is itself an act of Christian faith, because Christianity has appealed to the facts.

It is not surprising that Christians should be tempted to evade this appeal. This evasion of the appeal to history in panic at the seeming results of Biblical criticism, has given rise to the Fundamentalist movement. The same fear appears to underlie the answers of the Biblical Commission appointed by Pope Pius X; thus it was affirmed on 27 June 1906 that Moses must be held to be the author of the Pentateuch, at least substantially [1]; and on 19 June 1911 that Matthew the Apostle is the author of the First

[1] Denzinger, *Enchiridion Symbolorum et Definitionum* (Herder, Fribourg-in-B., 1922, Nos. 1997–2000).

Gospel,[1] that this Gospel was the first of the Synoptic Gospels to be written, and was written in Aramaic,[2] that Mark was the author of Mark xvi. 9–20,[3] that the 'two-document' theory of the Synoptic problem is in error.[4] It is a good thing that these pronouncements are probably not infallible; for they all condemn results of historical criticism which may now reasonably be regarded as certain, as far as they go. But the point is, that if historical results such as these are to be accepted or rejected on the authority of the Church, and not as the result of historical inquiry, the appeal of the Church to history has been abandoned, and with it the principle of the Incarnation, no less than if it were to be claimed that if the liturgy affirms the bodily assumption of St. Mary into heaven, her bodily assumption must therefore be believed as a fact of history, or that because the Anglican collect for St. John speaks of him as 'Apostle and Evangelist', the question of the authorship of the Fourth Gospel is closed.

But there is another side to the matter. In the syllabus *Lamentabili* of 3 July 1907 there is a list of condemned propositions attributed to the Catholic Modernists [5]: and here the modern Christian will find himself on the whole disposed to take the side of the Pope. We have, of course, no right to claim infallibility for the conclusions of modern critical study: but at least recent study tends to show that the Pope was right in condemning such propositions as that 'the faith in the resurrection of Christ was originally not so much belief in the fact itself of the resurrection, as in the immortal life of Christ with God', or that 'the teaching about the atoning death of Christ is not evangelical but only Pauline'.[6] The condemned propositions

---

[1] Denzinger, *Enchiridion Symbolorum et Definitionum* (Herder, Fribourg-in-B., 1922, No. 2148).

[2] *ibid.*, 2149, 2159.   [3] *ibid.*, 2156.   [4] *ibid.*, 2165.

[5] *ibid.*, Nos. 2001–2065.   [6] *ibid.*, 2037, 2038.

exhibit, in fact, the favourite theses of Liberal Protestant theology, as they were expressed by the Liberal theologians of Germany in the last generation. Such theses, which were believed to be the verified conclusions of historical investigation, were in reality the result of viewing the facts through the spectacles of Liberal theology—the theology of Humanism, which by its doctrine of values blurred the difference between God and man, so that it found itself regarding sin as mere imperfection, and was unable to assign to Jesus any higher role than that of Teacher and Moral Example.

In fact, the problem of Biblical criticism and the whole issue of the Christian appeal to history have been thrown by Liberal theology into a thorough confusion, from which we are only now beginning to get clear, thanks to the reaction of theological thought represented by Karl Barth in Germany and allied movements elsewhere.

All this applies above all to the central problem of the Resurrection of Jesus. Two opposed views of God and man meet at the grave of Christ. It is an *a priori* impossibility for a theology which does not believe in the redemptive action of a Transcendent God to acknowledge the miracle of the Resurrection. It is a complete mistake, therefore, to believe that the Liberal theologian is impartial and unprejudiced in such a case. In fact, if either side can possibly be unprejudiced in such a matter, it is the orthodox theologian who would have the best chance to be unprejudiced, if he were to take seriously the Christian appeal to history, and therefore accept the facts *whatever they are*, as God's facts.

IV. THE TRUTH SHALL MAKE YOU FREE

The fundamental confusion with regard to dogma is the assumption that Revelation consists in guaranteed doctrines or beliefs. This assumption is common both to the scholastic theologians and their successors, and to Liberal theology.

Scholasticism, accepting the inheritance of Aristotle, identified faith with correct beliefs. The main body of Roman Catholic theology still makes this assumption; in the Anglican Church the Tractarians took it for granted, and much Anglo-Catholic theology has continued to do so. The one great theologian of the nineteenth century who saw through the assumption was Frederick Denison Maurice,[1] that seer and prophet of the future whose importance has never yet been fully recognized. The whole centre of his teaching was his faith in the reality of God and the reality of God's saving work through Christ, and his constant endeavour to distinguish between the Divine and the human. Because he refused to identify any doctrine of man with the truth of God, and because he always rushed to the rescue of any whom he believed to be unjustly attacked, he was a storm centre of controversy. Because he criticized the current notions about hell and eternal life, he came to be labelled as a Broad Churchman: but there never was a theologian more radically opposed to the spirit of Liberal theology, or a more thorough dogmatist. It is his teaching which will form the basis of the constructive theology of the future.

On the other hand, Liberal theology consistently treats the dogma of the Church as if it were opinion. Consequently it always has misgivings about subscription to creeds: as if the profession of the Creed were a declara-

[1] See the small *Life of F. D. Maurice*, by C. F. G. Masterman (Mowbray, 1907). The large *Life*, in two volumes, by his son Brig.-Gen. F. Maurice, is now out of print. His greatest work is *Moral and Metaphysical Philosophy* in 2 vols. The only work of his which has been reprinted as yet is *The Kingdom of Christ*, 2 vols., in Dent's 'Everyman Library'. Particularly the central part of this, on the 'Signs of a Spiritual Constitution' (Baptism, Creeds, Forms of Worship, Eucharist, Ministry, Scriptures), is of first-rate importance.

tion of theological opinions, and therefore the imposition of the Creed as a condition of membership in the Church were destructive of freedom. How can a man be intellectually free, if the Church by imposing on him one set of opinions, deprives him of freedom to adopt a different set of opinions?

Now it is evident that the decisions of the Biblical Commission deprive the historical student of freedom of inquiry. But we have seen that to claim to settle such questions otherwise than by historical methods is inconsistent with the root-principle of the appeal of Christianity to history. Similarly, the misgivings of Liberals with regard to the creeds are only relevant when the creeds are misinterpreted. The form of the Creed itself reveals the error. The Creed is not a statement of doctrine, like the Westminster Confession or the XXXIX Articles. It is an act of personal allegiance[1]; a man is speaking, confessing his faith in God, in Jesus Christ the Revelation of God, in the Holy Ghost the Lord and Life-giver. Explanatory clauses must necessarily be added, to fix the content of this faith and its relation to the facts of history. But in reality, so far from being a shackle on the intellect, the profession of the Creed is the condition of its true freedom.

'If ye abide in My word, then are ye truly My disciples; and ye shall know the truth, and the truth shall make you free' (John viii. 31).

To identify 'knowing the truth' with 'holding true beliefs' would betray a complete misunderstanding of the thought of St. John's Gospel. We read there also of 'doing the truth', which is equated with 'walking in the light' and opposed to 'walking in darkness'. The one is to acknowledge in the sphere of conduct the reality of God; the other is to be lost in the blindness of self-will, and results

---

[1] Maurice, *The Kingdom of Christ*, vol. II, p. 4 (Everyman edition).

in the refusal to confess one's sins and in not loving one's brother (1 John i. 6–10; ii. 9, 11; iii. 15). Or again, the Johannine conception of 'the truth' might be illustrated from the late Professor Thomson:[1]

'There is so much to learn that ignorance in itself is no particular reproach; but the point is, to be clear when we know and when we do not, and it is one of the characteristics of the scientific mood that it will have Yes or No to this question: "Do you see it or do you not? . . . If you see it, what is it like?" '

The scientific investigator, in his sphere, knows what truth is: for he is grappling with facts. So, for St. John, 'truth' is reality: 'to know the truth' is to recognize God as real. And Christ is the truth.

Ye shall know the truth, and the truth shall make you free: free from the domination of other men's opinions, because you believe in God and not in man: but free also from the domination of your own prejudices and preconceived opinions, in proportion as you have learnt 'to know the truth'. Freedom is commonly misinterpreted by us, soaked as we are in Liberal habits of thought, to mean the emancipation of the individual from external constraint, so that he becomes 'free' to do what he likes and think what he likes. But this is a parody of freedom; for when man is not master of himself, the removal of external constraint leaves him free to become the slave of his own impulses of sensuality or pride, his own prejudices, complexes, and fixed ideas, or the opinions fashionable in his set or dictated by his favourite newspaper.

There is no freedom except in allegiance to the truth —to God, whose service is perfect freedom. This is the paradox of Christianity. There is no freedom for man except in acknowledging authority, the authority which

[1] J. A. Thomson, *Introduction to Science* (Home University Library), p. 28.

ultimately is that of God, not of man, even though it is mediated through men. In being thus under authority, man is freed from the domination of other men's opinions and of his own; he is free to obey his conscience and free also from the tyranny of his own conscience, in so far as he has learnt to obey the truth. And thus the Creed, which is man's act of allegiance to God and his acknowledgement of the authority of God's revelation in Christ is our charter of freedom.

CHAPTER V

PERSONAL RELIGION

*

I. LITURGY, DOGMA AND PERSONAL RELIGION

The three elements which we are considering in order, liturgy, dogma, and personal piety, correspond to Baron von Hügel's trio, the historical-institutional, the intellectual and the mystical elements of religion; the problem is that of the relation between them. It is clear that all three are necessary, and that the third is of decisive importance. Without piety and personal devotion, liturgy becomes external and formalistic, and dogma becomes arid and intellectualist. Further, if we are bound to regard human life on this earth as a probation and a preparation for a fuller life on the other side of death, as the eschatological teaching both of the Gospels and of traditional Christianity firmly asserts, it is clear that the relation of the individual soul to God is of primary importance. Will it then be right to regard personal religion as really the most fundamental of the three elements, and to say that liturgical worship is of value primarily in order that the individual soul may be trained up in the way of holiness, and that dogma is the intellectual formulation of religious experience, so that the *lex orandi* of the individual is his true *lex credendi*?

It is clear that the trend of religious thought for many centuries past has been largely along these lines. The piety of the Middle Ages was largely individualistic—witness Thomas à Kempis; and since the Reformation

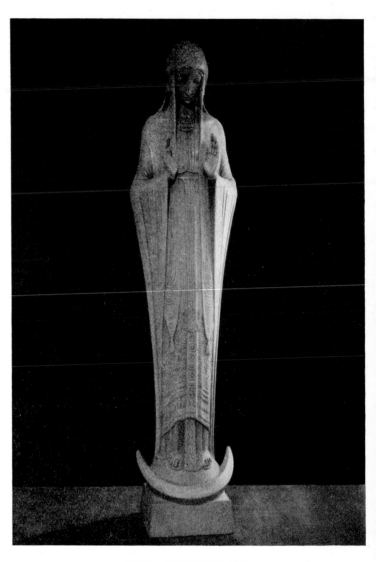

VIII. IMMACULATA

both Catholicism and Protestantism may be said to have specialized in personal religion—witness the perfecting of ascetical methods on the one side, and the Evangelical preaching of conversion on the other. Further, the modern world, while it no longer believes in heaven and hell and the traditional eschatology in general, still regards Christianity as being in the first place religion. William James' book, *The Varieties of Religious Experience*, published in 1902, marks the beginning of the modern period, in which the rationalistic agnosticism of T. H. Huxley, with its contempt for Christian dogma, gives way to a sympathetic interest in the phenomena of religious experience. Thus, it is characteristic that one of the best of the crop of books on the Tractarian Movement which have lately appeared, *Oxford Apostles*, by Geoffrey Faber (Faber & Faber, 1933), should be a psychological treatment of the chief actors in the story, by one who 'does not approach the Movement from any definite religious or theological or ecclesiastical angle', yet has found the study of it 'absorbingly interesting' (pp. ix, xii).

On the other hand, the whole line of approach which we have adopted in this book runs clean contrary to this modern view of Christianity as being primarily religion, clothed in institutional and dogmatic forms. Christianity, we have said, is in the first place not a religion but a faith (p. 42). In the second chapter we discussed the meaning of the fact that a certain 'ritual pattern' is common to Christianity and the world-religions. We found that while the ritual similarities must be admitted and emphasized, Christianity never claims to be merely the purest and most moral of the religions of the world: it claims to be sharply different from all the others in that its salvation-myth is historically true: its Saviour-God was crucified under Pontius Pilate. The Christian dogma expresses in a reasoned form what the Christian mystery expresses in a liturgical form, the gospel of the Divine Action which took place in history. But the pagan religions have no dogma in the Christian sense. They are normally tolerant of one another because none of them makes a definite claim to be true; they are intolerant of Christianity because it does.

There is an illuminating passage at the end of the sixth book of Virgil's *Aeneid* (vi. 893–8). Aeneas and the Sibyl have seen the underworld: on their way back, they come to the two Gates of Sleep; there is a gate of horn by which true dreams come, and a gate of ivory, for false dreams. Anchises sends them out by the ivory gate. What does this mean? Professor Sidgwick, puzzled, says, 'An imaginative close to a most imaginative book.' What Virgil really means is, 'Children, I have told you this pretty tale about the world beyond death, but whether it is true I have not the least idea.' To apply the name of 'dogma' to the conceptions and ideas—or we should rather say, the symbols and images—of paganism, is to read into the pagan religions something that does not belong to them.

Religious experience, like ritual, is common to all the religions of the world; its nobler forms are found in all the higher religions. Mysticism is pagan in origin; it is highly developed in Buddhism, and Plotinus the neo-Platonist attained to the experience of ecstatic union with God. Religion is a way of man to God. But Christianity is the proclamation that God has made a way to man, in the Incarnation: 'Herein is love, not that we loved God, but that he loved us.'

Clearly then it must be false to the nature of Christianity to assign to religious experience the primacy among the three elements: to do so will be to miss the essential nature of the Gospel of the Incarnation. If so, it may be that one of the chief causes of the religious confusion of the modern world lies in the fact that it treats Christianity primarily as a religion.

II. THE MIDDLE AGES

There can be no doubt that for many centuries past there has been a drift within Christianity towards an emphasis on individual religion. To obtain an accurate idea of this, it would be necessary to investigate not merely the works of the great preachers and devotional writers, but also the religious life of the ordinary Christian. Much more material is now becoming available for such a study. Just as our ordinary history books no longer confine themselves to the story of kings and parliaments and wars, and just as it will at any rate soon be recognized that the history of Christian dogma cannot rightly be written without reference to the liturgy which is the constant background of dogma, so it is coming to be recognized that the history of the liturgy cannot confine itself to the liturgical forms officially prescribed, but must take into account the use which the laity made of them.

In the early Church, it seems clear that the liturgy provided the forms of the devotions of the people. The people followed the prayers that were recited: even the eucharistic prayer or Canon was in early times recited aloud: the people listened to and understood the scripture lessons, and they joined in the chanting of the psalms. They joined in the prayer of the Church. Broadly speaking, this type of devotion continues in the Orthodox Churches today: if the people do not understand the whole service, they understand some of it, and they do not occupy themselves with manuals of private devotion while the service is going on. Thus in Gogol's *Meditations on the Divine Liturgy*, originally written in Russian, it is assumed that the people know the liturgical action and the general drift of what is being said. The great exception in the early Church is found in the practice of the monks of the desert: but they stand outside the main stream of the Church's life.

It is not so easy to say how far the people followed the service in the Middle Ages in the West. To most of the people Latin was an unknown tongue, though like the Catholic laity today they knew bits of the service. The laity had lost their full participation in the ritual action, as we have seen, with the disappearance of the offering of the gifts and of the communion of the people from the great service on Sunday. It is true that the parish Mass in the Middle Ages commonly contained a vernacular interlude before or after the sermon. In England various forms of bidding prayer were used before the sermon, presenting a summary of subjects for intercession [1]; and in Germany there was the 'offene Schuld', consisting of a confession and absolution. But the main trend of popular devotion is shown in the extraordinary growth in the thirteenth century and after of the desire to see the Host[2]; Eton schoolboys would crowd into the chapel for a few minutes to see the Elevation. Already in the Middle Ages personal prayers of devotion were taught to the people:[3]

> 'Praised be thou, King,
> And blessed be thou, King,
> Of all thy gifts good,
> And thanked be thou, King.
> Jesu, all my joying,
> That for me spilt thy blood,
> And died upon the rood,
> Thou give me grace to sing,
> The song of thy praising.'

[1] Cutts, *Parish Priests and their People in the Middle Ages in England* (S.P.C.K., 1898), pp. 207–11.

[2] E. Dumoutet, *Le désir de voir l'hostie* (Beauchesne, Paris, 1926).

[3] Quoted from Brilioth, p. 80, cf. 228 f. Other instances in Cutts, pp. 243 ff.

It is clear that, in comparison with the common prayer of the early Church, such devotions are thoroughly individualistic. It is as individuals that the people adore their Saviour: they are not in the old sense praying with the Church.

It is in their doctrine of the Church that the medieval theologians are at their weakest. The earthly Church is that which sustains the vast fabric of theology and of canon law: the love of the faithful Christian for Christ's mystical Body is directed rather to the perfected Kingdom of God, the Jerusalem which is eternal in the heavens. The earthly Church was too worldly and corrupt. This may be verified from a study of medieval hymnody. The hymn writers can look back to the saints and martyrs of the past, as in the office-hymns, and they can look up to heaven, as in the *Hora novissima* of Bernard of Cluny [1]: the wonderful sequence of Adam of St. Victor, *Jerusalem et Sion filiae*, stands almost alone in finding in the visible Church the embodiment of the heavenly.[2] So in the *Summa Theologica* of St. Thomas Aquinas we look in vain for an adequate treatment of the Church. In Part III, which deals with the Incarnation, Atonement and Sacraments, the doctrine of the Church is treated only in one Quaestio, Q. viii.

III. SINCE THE REFORMATION

The Counter-Reformation did not reply to Protestantism by returning to the liturgical sacramentalism of the early Church: it set in hand a devotional reformation. It maintained the old forms of the episcopal ministry and the sacraments, and the ancient forms of the liturgy. The priest celebrating his silent Mass still repeated the remains

[1] *English Hymnal*, Nos. 371, 392, 412, 495: cf. 431, 465, 250, 251, 252, 253.

[2] *ibid*, No. 172.

of the ancient congregational chants, the Introit, Gradual, and the rest, and recited offertory-prayers implying the offering of the gifts by the people, and post-communion collects implying the communion of the people. The parish Mass was still the chief act of worship on a Sunday morning, even though attendance at Mass on Sundays and days of obligation was now treated as an individual duty, and the requirement could be satisfied by attendance at a low Mass, or at a church belonging to one of the religious orders.[1] But the parish Mass was no longer in the old sense an act of common worship. The people no longer understood the words, and while it was in progress engaged in private devotions, using the rosary or a book of private prayers, or in default of this merely honoured it by their presence. The central point of the service was the Elevation of the Host, at which all made an act of worship.

But eucharistic devotion came more and more to centre also in the cult of the reserved Sacrament. A modern Catholic writer says:[2]

'It is the white host, Jesus hidden in a piece of bread, that becomes the centre of the most popular eucharistic devotions. Those of the Middle Ages, now less in favour, such as the desire to see the Host, have been succeeded by triumphal manifestations, processions of the Blessed Sacrament, solemn expositions, "les grands saluts". For many a superficial soul, they seem to realize the highest point of Catholic worship, the supreme triumph of the "eucharistic King". Nothing on earth, it is felt, can surpass the glory of Jesus in receiving on a "throne of light" in a monstrance glittering with gold the homage of multi-

[1] See article on 'Concelebration' in *Theology*, Feb. 1931, p. 71.
[2] G. Laporta, 'Piété eucharistique' in *Les Questions liturgiques et paroissiales* (Abbaye du Mont-César, Louvain), June 1928, p. 148. Also printed separately.

tudes who acclaim Him as He passes by, or incline in silent adoration to receive the benediction.'

At other times, a few faithful watch before the Tabernacle in silent and solitary prayer, making reparation for the cold response of so many of their brethren to the Saviour there in His 'prison of love':

'In the dim cathedrals of our great cities, before the flickering light of the sanctuary lamp, a few faithful souls keep watch, alone, while outside there is the rush of the indifferent and ungrateful multitude to its pleasures and its business.'

He continues:

'However excellent may be these pious practices, one regrets that these devout souls, stirred by emotions which are often somewhat unreal in their concrete form, have not always a satisfactory grasp of the meaning of communion and of the holy sacrifice. The first, too often, is thought of as a simple visit to the Sacrament, while the Mass is regarded by them simply as the exercise of a miraculous priestly power, whose end is the consecration of the Holy Sacrament purely for the sake of the holy table and the exposition.'

Such conceptions are, as he says, so evidently defective that no priest or teacher could be satisfied with them. And it would be easy to make out a long list of abuses, like the Jesuit instructions, quoted by Pascal, for saving time in hearing Mass by getting within range of four simultaneous masses, one of which is at the beginning, another at the Gospel, another at the Consecration and another at the Communion.[1] But it is manifestly an unfair method of treatment to collect abuses. In judging the Counter-Reformation, or any other period of history, we must look out for what is genuinely typical.

[1] Pascal, *Provincial Letters*, No. ix (Ancient and Modern Library), p. 150.

In this case there can be no doubt that the individualism which we are considering is no exception, but is typical of the best as much as of the worst. The organic unity of the early Church liturgy in which various functions of the mystical Body were represented by various persons and actions, has almost completely gone. The whole *raison d'être* of extra-liturgical devotions to the Blessed Sacrament is that those present may perform individual acts of adoration. It is altogether typical that during this period Holy Communion comes to be given, not as the climax of the common act of offering, but from the Tabernacle before or after Mass. It is regarded almost exclusively as the communication of Divine grace to the individual soul.

The same individualism appears in the other 'new devotions', such as the cult of the Sacred Heart, or the Stations of the Cross, or the Rosary. It appears in the new type of ascetic practice; new methods are worked out for the training of the soul in ways of prayer and the practice of the spiritual life; retreats are instituted to plough up the soil of the soul and induce a thorough conversion. In this work the Jesuits are the pioneers, and St. Ignatius's *Spiritual Exercises* the great classic. St. Francis de Sales, followed by a long line of great spiritual writers, especially in France, labours to raise the standard of the priestly life, and to work out the practice of the devout life no longer merely for those living in monasteries, but for those living in the world and engaged in its affairs.

We shall come shortly to the parallel movement of Pietism in the Lutheran Churches, and Evangelicalism in our own land. Both the Catholic and the Protestant Pietism are characterized by an intense devotion, and they really stand very close to one another, in spite of all diversities of external form, in their love of Our Lord. Perhaps the most important difference is that while

Protestantism has laid the greatest stress on conversion, and has on the whole shrunk from codifying the practice of the spiritual life, the Catholic teachers have applied themselves with great diligence to studying the methods by which the soul may make progress in the life of grace. The result may have been that Catholic piety to a certain extent assumes stereotyped forms and shows a lack of spontaneity; nevertheless it must be admitted that the risk has been worth taking. Post-Reformation Catholicism has here made a contribution of priceless value to the treasures of the Church universal in its development of meditation and mental prayer and spiritual direction. A proof of this is to be seen in the Anglo-Catholic movement, on which the Counter-Reformation has exercised a powerful influence, amounting at times to a fascination. There was, in fact, and there is still, very much to be learnt from this quarter, which neither the old-fashioned Anglican Church observance, nor even the influence of the Evangelical School, could give. In the modern Anglo-Catholic movement, the use of mental prayer, and of retreats, and of devotions before the Reserved Sacrament, has been to countless souls a means of spiritual deepening. This tendency may be illustrated by a recent book, *The Art of Mental Prayer*, by Fr. Bede Frost. This book shows an altogether exaggerated estimate of the importance of the Counter-Reformation in the history of the Church Universal, and a complete failure to grasp the meaning of the Church's common prayer, which we studied in the third chapter; but its positive contribution is that it gives a most valuable compendium of the ways of mental prayer, as taught by the great Catholic masters of the spiritual life. Or again, at a recent conference of Anglican and Free Church theological students, the Free Church students were found sitting at the feet of a young Anglo-Catholic priest, asking him, 'Can you help us to say our prayers better?' and receiving instruction in these same methods of mental prayer.

To sum up, it can scarcely be wrong to accuse the Counter-Reformation of a defective sense of the Church. It is true that the Church occupies a great place in men's minds, as a hierarchical quasi-political institution of immense power, as the infallible authority guaranteeing the system of belief and practice, as the one Christian denomination which is altogether in the right, all others being in heresy or in schism or both. But there has not been, at least till quite recently, a strong sense of the meaning of the Church as Christ's mystical Body, God's universal Family, God's building composed of living stones, or a strong realization in worship of this common life.

Clearly, then, it would be quite untrue to accuse the Reformers of having robbed Protestant Christendom of the doctrine of the mystical Body of Christ and led it into religious individualism. To a large extent, the thing had happened already. It would be truer to say that Luther's message was primarily 'theological', if we may use the word in its true sense: he called men back from the dry intellectualism of the Scholastics to faith in God's real action. The personal, sovereign act of God in the Incarnation and the Atonement, and God's free justification of man through faith, was the living centre of his message.

St. Paul had been able to combine this Gospel of justification by faith with a strong doctrine of the fellowship of Christians with one another as members of the Body. If Luther failed to do this, he was typical of his age. In an age which was thinking mainly along individualistic lines, the very strength of Luther's appeal to the conscience of man tended to isolate the individual and set him alone in the presence of God. It is natural therefore that a tender personal piety mixed with an anxious self-scrutiny should come to be a characteristic of Lutheranism, should appear in the Pietism which was its offshoot, and appear again in the preaching of John Wesley and the Evangelical religion of which he set the type in this country.

Yet even so the coming of Protestantism did bring back something of the old sense of fellowship in Christian worship.[1] Dr. Brilioth shows how in the Lutheran Churches the communion of the people was triumphantly restored, and how the normal type of Sunday service continued for nearly two hundred years to be the Eucharist with sermon and communion.[2]

In the eighteenth century in Germany and in the nineteenth century in Sweden the celebration of the Eucharist became less and less frequent, and the service became predominantly a preaching-service, as it has been in the Reformed Churches from the beginning; for in those churches the tradition of the quarterly Lord's Supper remained unbroken from the time of Zwingli.

In this type of service, Reformed and later Lutheran, the congregational element was chiefly supplied by the singing of hymns: and here, on both sides, there was a wonderful blossoming of hymnody.

'A French refugee in a letter to Bishop Briçonnet, written in 1525, gives an enraptured picture of the service in Strassburg, that blessed city, and specially mentions the effect of the blending of the men's and women's voices in the singing of the psalms.'[3] We can still imagine the joy and gladness of the young Calvinistic congregations when we sing such a tune as that which is set to *English Hymnal*, No. 277: and the Lutheran chorales are among the musical treasures of Christendom.

[1] The sense of the fellowship of the mystical Body is by no means absent from Luther. See Brilioth, *Eucharistic Faith and Practice*, pp. 96 f.

[2] *ibid.*, Chap. IV, esp. pp. 125 ff, 133 ff.

[3] Brilioth, p. 174.

Dr. Edwyn Bevan says in a striking passage [1] that it is in such hymns as those of Paul Gerhardt and Gerhardt Tersteegen, and in the English Methodist hymns, that the heart of the old-fashioned Protestant devotion is best revealed; and that this devotion approaches closely, at its central burning-point, to the most representative Roman Catholic devotion. In both cases:

'. . . it is devotion directed to the vividly apprehended Person of Jesus, apprehended not as a mere human figure which might be the object of a sentimental affection, but as one who is God come down in the infinite condescension of love, and love for whom is fixed with the awe and worship belonging to God.'

Quoting St. Bernard of Clairvaux, G. Tersteegen, and Charles Wesley, he continues:

'Some of these Protestants may have thought it wrong to use a material crucifix in order to set before their eyes the supreme self-sacrifice. But they would use all the resources of language to create in the mind a visional image exactly corresponding. . . . And if the reaction to such an image in the worshipper was a new resolution to devote his whole person to the great Lover and to the utmost service of the men for whom he died—a service in which self-righteousness would be kept off by the thought of the tremendous debt which could never be paid—was there much to distinguish that from the state of mind with which a Roman Catholic rose from his knees before the crucifix or before the Blessed Sacrament on an occasion when his offering of prayer had been touched by the fire from heaven?'

We must notice, however, not merely that this deep and sacred devotion, shown to be common to Catholic and Protestant, is intensely personal and individual, but also that Dr. Bevan himself manifestly regards it as the

[1] *Christianity* (Home University Library), pp. 201–3.

normal type of Christian devotion, and misses completely the deep difference between it and the corporate self-oblation of the Church as Christ's mystical Body which was characteristic of the early Church. Dr. Brilioth, however, has seen the point. He writes of Thomas à Kempis:[1]

'The disciple answers (*De Imit. Christi*, iv, ch. 9), "Thine, O Lord, are all things that are in heaven and that are in earth. I desire to offer myself up unto thee as a free-will oblation, and to continue thine for ever. . . . Receive thou me with this holy oblation of the precious Body, which I offer unto thee this day in the presence of angels invisibly attending: and may this further the salvation of myself and of all thy people." Here then we meet again the Augustinian view of the eucharistic sacrifice, but with a characteristic narrowing. The self-oblation of the Church to share in Christ's sacrifice has now become the individual's oblation of his own soul. The medieval mystic has wholly missed the thought of communion-fellowship; communion regularly means for à Kempis just the meeting of the individual Christian with his heavenly Lord and Friend.'

He adds immediately the necessary corrective:

'The element of communion-fellowship is altogether indispensable to a balanced evangelical view of the eucharist. But the fellowship of the Christian Church never excludes the union of the individual soul with her Lord: and this side of Christian experience has scarcely ever found deeper expression than in some parts of the fourth book of the *De Imitatione*.'

IV. THE LITURGICAL MOVEMENT

In our day there has arisen all over Christendom a movement of return, going back on the notion of a purely individual piety, and seeking to learn again more fully

---

[1] *Eucharistic Faith and Practice*, p. 90.

the meaning of the Church. Nowhere is this Movement more vigorous or more fruitful than within the Roman Catholic Church itself. The so-called Liturgical Movement is concerned with things vastly more important than mere ritualism, the shape of chasubles and the correct ordering of the ceremonial of the liturgy; its deepest interest is in that which underlies all the rites and ceremonies, in the Christian Mystery itself, in the inmost life of the mystical Body of Christ.

It is necessary for an Anglican, writing about that which is happening in the Roman Catholic Church, to disclaim the right to pose as an authorized interpreter of it, and also to utter a word of warning against certain possible misconceptions. Thus, the fact that in many respects it breathes a very modern spirit does not mean that it has any affinity with the Catholic Modernism of the last generation; it is tenaciously orthodox. Again, it would be a mistake to interpret it as a party-movement, in the sense familiar to us in England. The Movement always traces its origin to the *Motu proprio* of Pope Pius X (22 Nov. 1903): 'Active participation' says the Pope 'in the public and solemn prayer of the Church is the primary and indispensable source of a true Christian spirit.' The *Semaines liturgiques* held annually in Belgium, to which we shall refer later, receive the cordial support of the Episcopate. Nor is it specially a Benedictine movement; it is being taken up very widely, and it is clear that such a writer as Fr. Mersch, S.J., the author of *Le Corps mystique du Christ*, is moving in the same direction.

At the same time the Benedictine order has played and continues to play a leading part in the Movement. The Benedictines live by the liturgy, the *opus Dei*; and the main effort of the Liturgical Movement is to recall the faithful to the treasures which they possess in the liturgy, and to realize anew the ancient ideal of Christian worship as the common prayer of the Church, the act of the whole Body, in which all the members have a part.

The origins of the Movement are commonly traced to the work of Abbot Guéranger,[1] the re-founder of Solesmes Abbey and the restorer of the Benedictine order in France in the middle of the nineteenth century. He was an ardent infallibilist, and was responsible for a wild slaughter of the still not inconsiderable relics in France of the ancient traditions of ceremonial, to make room for a uniform observance of the Roman ritual and calendar. This destructive work was criticized by the Roman Catholic liturgist Edmund Bishop in no measured terms.

Nevertheless, these excesses, which are closely parallel to the similar mistakes of Anglican zealots in remodelling usages and in restoring churches, testified like them to a reviving interest in liturgical forms and practice. His books include *Considérations sur la liturgie*, 1830, *Institutions liturgiques*, 1840, and the famous *Année liturgique*, begun in 1841.

A period of more serious scholarship followed. Liturgical science began its work of minute investigation, seeking to unravel the complicated history of liturgical development, and learning increasingly in the process to recapture the spirit of the old liturgies. For some years now the Roman Catholic scholars have been the leaders of Christendom in this work of research; it is only necessary to mention the names of Duchesne, Batiffol, Cabrol, Connolly, Wilmart, de Puniet, and the monumental work now being issued in French, *Dictionnaire d'archéologie et de liturgie chrétienne*.

Further stages in the growth of the Movement are marked by the pronouncement of Pope Pius X, the foundation of Beuron Abbey in Germany, and the work

---

[1] The *Catholic Encyclopaedia* gives a rather inadequate biography, which, however, contains the main facts of his life.

of Dom Lambert Beauduin in the period before the War. His important little book, *La piété de l'Eglise*, published in 1914,[1] was soon in every one's hands. After the War, the Abbot of Maria Laach began the issue of an important series, *Ecclesia Orans*, the first of which, by Romano Guardini, has been translated into English under the title *The Spirit of the Liturgy*.[2]

The Movement is active in many countries, Germany, Austria, Belgium, France, Italy, Portugal; it seems to be most backward among English Roman Catholics. However, a writer in the *Universe* (8 Sept. 1933), on 'The People and the Liturgy', after noting this fact, expresses his belief that it is making real progress; in particular the laity are learning more and more to follow the service. He goes on to discuss possible methods, such as a 'liturgical week' after the Belgian pattern, and the making of the responses by the people at Mass—what is called abroad the *messe dialoguée*; he quotes also an article by Dr. E. J. Mahoney in the *Clergy Review*, with an admirable summary of the principle:

'The faithful share in offering the Mass, *meum ac vestrum sacrificium*, because they are united to Christ as members to their Head, and because the priest at the altar acts in the name of the whole Church. The part of the faithful is not merely passive, sharing in the fruits of the Mass,

[1] Abbaye du Mont-César, Louvain. An English translation, under the title *Liturgy the Life of the Church*, is published by The Liturgical Press, Collegeville, Minnesota, U.S.A. The same house also publishes *The Spirit of the Liturgy*, by Abbot Emmanuele Caronti, translated by Dom Virgil Michel, O.S.B., and a number of other works; also a four-weekly periodical, *Orate Fratres* ($2·50 per annum).

[2] Published by Sheed and Ward. A French translation, *L'Esprit de la liturgie* (Plon, Paris), contains a valuable introduction. In 1924 the monks of Maria Laach issued their big book, *Die betende Kirche* (St. Augustinus Verlag, Berlin); this book covers much the same ground as Abbot Cabrol's *Liturgical Prayer, its History and Spirit* (E.T., Burns and Oates, 1922), but with much greater fullness.

IX. OUR LADY OF THE LILY

but active; and the spirit behind the Liturgical Movement, which has had such striking results in recent years, is to make the faithful conscious of this fact, by encouraging them to follow the Liturgy and understand its solemn beauty.'

On the Continent very much is being done. To begin with the ritual and ceremonial, it has been found possible in some few places to revive the ancient Roman practice of so arranging the altar that the priest can stand on the far side of it facing the people,[1] with the express object of bringing the people more in touch with the liturgical action. This is, of course, the only possible position for the celebrant at the high altar of the old Roman basilicas. Perhaps more widely the old offertory procession is revived: at the offertory a server comes forward bearing the box of altar-breads, and those who are going to communicate take each a bread and offer it at the altar. The underlying symbolism is that at the Holy Sacrifice the lives of Christians themselves are offered up to God to be a living sacrifice in union with the Head. Most important of all, the people are encouraged to make their communion during the Mass, not from the Tabernacle, because the communion of the people is the culmination of the eucharistic sacrifice.

Various attempts are made to overcome the admitted difficulty arising from the fact that the Mass must be celebrated in Latin. As in England, books are procurable containing the service in Latin and in the vernacular in parallel columns; leaflets are distributed containing the whole service thus printed out for each Sunday.[2] It is admitted that these expedients do not fully meet the case

[1] cf., *Les Questions liturgiques et paroissiales*, Aug. 1931, pp. 199 ff.
[2] These leaflets are distributed with *Lebe mit der Kirche* (see below). A similar leaflet, with the service in Latin and Italian in parallel columns, is issued weekly by the Opera della Regalita di N.S. Gesù Christo, Piazza S. Ambrogio 9, Milan.

for the uneducated worshipper, who can never share quite fully in a service celebrated in an unknown tongue. At the same time it is recognized that a vernacular liturgy would not by itself solve the problem; the participation of the people in the liturgy is not a mere matter of saying words in common, but of a spirit of common worship. And much can be done. In some places the people sing parts of the service, such as *Gloria in excelsis*, in the vernacular, while the priest says the Latin words at the altar; or the Latin words including the responses are said or sung by all, in the *messe dialoguée*. And everywhere, by one means or another, the people are helped to use the words of the rite as the medium of their devotion; and since the 'propers' of the Mass are nearly all taken from Scriptures, this means that the Scriptures are being given back to the people, and that in the best possible way. It is not that the Bible is put into their hands for each man to make of it what sense he can, but that it is given to them in direct relation to the mystery of salvation which the liturgy sets forth, that it may become a vehicle of their prayers. This is well illustrated in the village sermon, preached to an Austrian congregation, which we print at the end of this chapter.

This sermon is taken from the issue of *Lebe mit der Kirche* for 21 August 1932. This is a penny magazine issued weekly from Klosterneuburg; this number contains also notes on the liturgical commemorations of the week, with brief lives of two saints; a second sermon on the Gospel for the day, which throws a pathetic light on the economic distress in Austria; a study of Ecclesiasticus, part of an Old Testament series; a study of Mark i. 39–45, part of a course on the Gospels; a children's page; a popular Latin lesson; and a setting to a simple chant of a German translation of the 'propers' for the Sunday.

'Liturgical missions' are held in parishes, and continuous courses of instruction on the Liturgy, culminating sometimes in festival services at which congregations of many thousands from the surrounding parishes meet to sing Mass in the Cathedral. Then there is in Belgium the annual *Semaine liturgique*, which in 1932 was held at Namur, and attended by six bishops and several hundred clergy and crowds of laity. We will now give some extracts from an article on this congress in the *Liturgische Zeitschrift* for Nov. 1932.[1]

'The great functions at the Cathedral, daily Pontifical Mass, and solemn Vespers and Compline, show that eucharistic worship really does make its appeal to the modern man, and that it gains its highest point in the acts of the pure and simple traditional worship. During the whole week, apart from the brief service of Benediction on the Sunday, there were no other extra-liturgical devotions to the Sacrament.'

The writer goes on to speak of the plainsong singing, but emphasizes that in reality the most important aspect of the Liturgical Movement is its theological side, which he sets forth thus:

'It is a matter of the conception of the living Church, and of unity in a catholic and common life of worship, dominated by the Christian mystery, which is the translation into liturgy of the Divine work of redemption, and the means whereby that redemption continues as a living power in us and for us. From a practical point of view this doctrinal aspect is the most important of all. There was a general sense that all the rest—the plainsong movement, the honour paid to the eucharist, the liturgical instructions in the Cathedral—were really subordinate to

[1] The *Liturgische Zeitschrift* (Friedr. Pustet Verlag, Regensburg) is the chief review of the Movement in German, as *Questions liturgiques et paroissiales* (Abbaye du Mont-César, Louvain) is in French.

Semaines liturgiques have also been begun in other countries: Portugal, Holland, Italy.

the exposition of doctrine, as given in the sessions of the Conference. . . .

'From this point of view the full and informative press-reports fall into a unity. Taken together, they contain a compendium, on whose leading points it is good to dwell: it is the theology of the life of the Church as a supernatural organism, of which we form a part, of the life of the Church in which the mystery of redemption finds its continuation and accomplishment. Then there is the fellowship established between Christians through their unity in Christ, a fellowship whose effects extend to their moral conduct, but which reaches its highest level and its completest expression in the worship that is carried out in union with Christ and in His name. Then the corollary of sacramentalism, the inalienably corporate character of worship, by which it is attached to a system of rites and symbols, whose reality, independent of the worthiness of the ministers, makes on the faithful an imperious and urgent demand for conscious participation, by which it attains in them its full glory—the selflessness of voluntary self-surrender which forms its basis, in virtue of the object which it seeks and the motives which control it. "The Church fulfils in worship a threefold aim: she unites, she sanctifies, and she adores. But she unites only in order to sanctify, and she sanctifies only in order better to adore." '

'Christianity is, in fact, not merely a religion or a confession in the modern sense of these words, that is, a system composed of a number of dogmatic truths, which one accepts and believes—a *Weltanschauung* (!)—or a sum of moral precepts, which one must endeavour to observe with as good a will as possible. No, Christianity is above all a Mystery; that is, a Divine Action through which God wills to save mankind and every individual, and exalt us to a participation in His Divine life.'

132

It is clear, however, that it was the Liturgy itself which formed the great feature of the *Semaine liturgique* held at Liége from 3 to 7 June 1934. The reports glow with enthusiasm over an experience of common worship which surpassed all expectation. As far as Liége was concerned, the occasion seems to have been made into a diocesan festival, under the leadership of the Bishop. On the opening day the solemn Mass was celebrated in the Cathedral; on the other days the ancient stational procession was revived, and at 6.30 each morning a procession set out from the Cathedral for a parish church.[1] 'Sceptics had said that attendance at Mass for four days at half-past six was too much to hope from the Liégeois. But on the first day the procession which started from the Cathedral was 750 strong; on the fourth it certainly exceeded 1,200; and in the church there were 2,000 and more each day.'

'From the attack of the Introit *Cibavit eos*, which was sung with the psalm through the whole of the celebrant's preparation, and was thus repeated four or five times, one was thrilled with the enthusiasm which penetrated the whole congregation, as they took up the chant sung by the choir. . . . The congregational singing, "like the sound of many waters", like successive waves of sound bearing to the altar the faith and adoration of all this people of God, was an amazement to all. No director of music had expected it. That congregational singing is possible, that it has a rare and incomparable beauty of its own, was proved to us four times over.'

The Gradual and Alleluia were sung by the choir; but the congregation, provided with copies of the words and music, insisted on singing the sequence *Lauda Sion Sal-*

[1] The account which follows is a résumé of the report in *Les Questions liturgiques et paroissiales* for June–August 1934 (a double number), pp. 171–3; cf. also Abbot Capelle's article, pp. 158–66, and *The Universe* for 29 June.

vatorem right through, and of course the Creed. From the offertory anthem and onwards it is noted how the dialogue maintained the unity between the people and the altar. After the choir had sung the offertory anthem, there was a deep silence (*un haut silence*) while the priest —their priest—prepared the elements. Then the dialogue, the Preface, the *Sanctus*, and the Canon, during which there was 'the same religious silence which demands of each that he lets the priest speak in his name, and maintains his will in intimate union with that of Christ who speaks and acts through the priest at the altar'; at the close of the Canon a resonant and unanimous *Amen*. Then the Communion, the procession towards the Holy Table, the participation in the Banquet, the coming of Christ among His people. Meanwhile the choir sings the communion anthem *Quotiescumque manducabitis*,[1] while six or eight priests distribute the sacrament to the two thousand people. 'The chant of the *Quotiescumque*, repeated several times, is taken up by all these voices; seized with an irresistible enthusiasm, they unite themselves with the choir and sing the anthem as they approach the common Table of the Banquet. St. Augustine says sometimes, *Dictum est decies*, *dictum est vigesies*, it was repeated ten, twenty times, in describing the great ceremonies in his Cathedral at Hippo, or in thanking his people for their zeal at the great liturgical solemnities. He could not have failed to mark the same enthusiasm at Liége.'

There had, of course, been much preparation and organization beforehand; directions for the congregation, provision of the words of the service with translation,

---

[1] 'As often as ye eat this bread and drink this cup, ye do show the Lord's death till he come: wherefore whosoever shall eat of this bread and drink of this cup of the Lord unworthily, shall be guilty of the body and blood of the Lord, alleluia.' I learn from a correspondent that the psalm sung with this Antiphon was Ps. 33 (34): 'I will give thanks unto the Lord: his praise shall ever be in my mouth.'

and the music of the people's part; there had been forty
journées paroissiales at Liége. But at the festival, 'it was
the Mass itself which aroused the response of the multitude; the Mass by itself, without any secondary attraction, without any compromise or diminution. Simply
the liturgy of the Sacrifice, integrally restored in all its
dynamism, and becoming the living expression of an
enlightened faith, and of a rediscovered solidarity of
one with another in Christ: the drama with all its ceremonial, but also with all its doctrinal richness and supernatural vitality, expressed in an active and continued
co-operation, and thus becoming on the one hand by its
expressive symbolism the culminating point of the subjective life of each member, and on the other by its
sacramental efficacy the objective source of the authentic
Christian spirit and of Catholic renewal.'

We will now go and sit under the preacher at Klosterneuburg. The sermon was preached on the 14th Sunday
after Pentecost, and it succeeds in bringing in nearly all
the scriptures and propers of the Roman Mass for the
day. (The arrangement is slightly different from that of
our Prayer Book. The collect and the gospel are the same
that we have on Trinity XIV, and the epistle and the
other propers, according to the *English Hymnal*, on Trinity
XV.) The author adds a note to explain that at Klosterneuburg they have revived the primitive custom of the
offering of the gifts by the people at the offertory. It may
be added that the text of the sermon seems to imply that
the altar faces the people, so that they have to go round
behind it in order to bring their gifts to the priest.

'If we would sum up the main idea of today's Mass in
a picture, we might do it in the words of the offertory
anthem: "The angel of the Lord standeth round about
them that fear Him, and delivereth them: O taste and
see how gracious the Lord is."

'First we sketch out the picture. It is the offertory procession; the congregation is engaged in offering the holy sacrifice. The people mean to unite themselves with the sacrifice of Christ; therefore they go up behind the altar, and deposit their offertory gifts. Behind this visible picture there is another which is not visible to bodily sight. The altar is Christ, the King of the divine kingdom; there He sits enthroned, and round the King are gathered His soldiers, the Christian hosts; round these again is a wall of angels, warding off the assaults of the evil one; and the King gives to His people their nourishment. Or alternatively, at the altar Christ is enthroned, as the Head of God's family; His children are gathered round Him; guardian angels defend this family against the assaults of the enemy, and the children receive from their Father the family bread. This is the picture.

'Next, let us draw out the main points.

(a) 'The Place. Here in God's house is the meeting-place of God's children. God is the Father, Christ is our King and the Good Shepherd; the Church is our mother, God's house is our Father's house, a little bit of home on earth. O that we might grasp ever more closely what this means—the Church is our home. We have it in the beautiful words of Psalm 83 (84): "O how amiable are thy dwellings, thou Lord of hosts; my soul hath a desire and longing to enter into the courts of the Lord. . . . Yea, the sparrow hath found her an house, and the swallow a nest where she may lay her young; my home is Thy altar, O Lord of hosts." We sing this for the Introit. After the toil of the week, how should we not long on Sunday to hasten to our Father's house, to the presence of our Lord! Here should our heart, hungry for happiness, seek and find rest; as St. Augustine said, after the wanderings of his life, "Our heart is restless till it finds its rest in Thee."

(b) 'The Father. Note throughout how full of trust is the tone of this Sunday's Mass. The relation of the Christian to God is set forth throughout as that of a child to his father. The thoughts of the gospel fit in very beautifully with this. Our Saviour encourages us to trust in God's fatherly providence. He speaks of the birds and of the lilies, which sow not, and are not anxious about raiment, yet the heavenly Father feeds them and clothes them. We should be like birds, gladly and happily flying round the tree of the Church. We should be like lilies, arrayed in the white beauty of sonship to God.

'Free from care, free from anxiety, we should feel ourselves safe in God's hand, knowing well that we have a Father who loves us and cares for us. He gives us even now in the Mass the proof of His love, because there He freely gives His Son for us. So let us grasp the idea of our picture: the family, the soldiers, gathered round the Lord.

(c) 'Defended. This family, this army, is surrounded by enemies; these are the powers of evil. So the Church sets before us once again the familiar antithesis of the two kingdoms. So long as we are on earth the conflict continues in us. Is the lower nature or the higher manhood to prevail? In today's epistle St. Paul shines a light into our hearts; he describes the works of the flesh and the fruits of the Spirit. Christ too speaks in the gospel of the two masters, whom we cannot serve both at once. The collect recognizes our human frailty, and prays that God will keep us ever by His help from all things hurtful, and lead us to all things profitable to our salvation. Our picture shows us that in the conflict we are not left to our own resources; there are guardian angels who watch over us.

(d) 'The Bread. But it is not only angels who aid us in our spiritual warfare. One greater than they takes the field with us, Jesus Christ our King, who has triumphed over the enemy of mankind: "I have overcome the world." In His triumph ours is included. So our picture directs our attention to the heavenly bread: "O taste and see how gracious the Lord is." This is the Holy Eucharist.

'Here is the key to the understanding of this Sunday's Mass. Why does the Church show us the two kingdoms? Not to invite us to choose between them, but to show us that in the conflict we have the one great means of succour, the one weapon of victory—the sacrifice of the Mass and the heavenly bread. In Him we are victorious over the enemy. How beautifully St. Paul speaks in the epistle: "They that are Christ's have crucified the flesh with the affections and lusts." This happens in the Mass, for in it we do not merely represent the death on the cross, but we ourselves hang with Christ on the cross, we unite ourselves with His sacrifice.

'The thoughts of today's Mass may be summed up in the words of the communion anthem, "Seek ye first the kingdom of God, and all these things shall be added unto you." Christians, let us stand faithful to Christ, let the kingdom of God be our first care. Then we are strong, then we are victorious over the world; and the heavenly Father will not forsake us in our bodily and spiritual need.'

CHAPTER VI

PERSONAL RELIGION AND THE CHURCH

*

I. MYSTICISM

The last chapter has been occupied with a historical survey. We must now go back over the same ground and examine the relation of individual religion to God's own saving action and to the corporate life of the Church.

We have described a great change in the habits of Christian devotion, which in all essentials was complete by the thirteenth century. To give anything like an adequate account of its causes would require a deep analysis of the history of many centuries. We have noted some of its outward signs: the decline of communion, the change in the religious practice of the people, the changed attitude to dogma, the change in the character of Christian art. Dr. Herwegen is inclined to attribute the change to the break-up of Graeco-Roman civilization and the influx of the Germanic peoples, with their individualistic and psychological approach to religion, their interest in morals and their need of moral discipline.[1] But there is another factor which has at least powerfully contributed to the result, a factor which arises out of the inmost life of Graeco-Roman civilization itself—the rise of Mysticism. We are not called upon to discuss the many difficult problems which Mysticism raises; but it is essential for us to see what light it throws on the problem of individual religion.

[1] *Kirche und Seele*, pp. 21 ff.

Mysticism was adopted into Christianity from paganism. It is found in a fully-developed form in the neo-Platonists, who have already formulated the three stages of the mystic way: the purgative, which is the purification of the soul from the defilements of sense (κάθαρσις), the illuminative, which is the progress of the soul in heavenly enlightenment (ἔλλαμψις), and the unitive, which is the ecstatic union of the soul with the Deity (ἕνωσις). Mysticism passed into Christianity to a large extent through St. Augustine, who before his conversion was for a time a neo-Platonist, but still more through the influence of pseudo-Dionysius the Areopagite (late fifth century), who 'carried the thought of Plotinus and Proclus to its logical conclusion in the *via negativa*, and at the same time gave it a thin veneer of Christian respectability'.[1]

At least from the twelfth century the work of pseudo-Dionysius exercised a powerful influence in shaping the type of Western mysticism seen in Richard of St. Victor, the author of *The Cloud of Unknowing*, Walter Hilton, Tauler, Eckhardt, Ruysbroeck, Father Augustine Baker, St. John of the Cross.

We have seen in our discussion of the pagan religions that the Christian religion is compelled by the law of its nature to assimilate pagan elements: Christ is the Fulfiller. But it is all the more necessary for the theologian to distinguish clearly the pagan elements from the Judaeo-Christian. In this case, Dr. Nygren of Lund has presented the contrast with all possible sharpness in his book, *Agape and Eros*.[2] The 'heavenly Eros' of Plato, which is quite distinct from the sensual and earth-bound Eros of carnal

---

[1] Paul Elmer More, *The Catholic Faith* (Princeton, 1931), p. 242. The last chapter of this book has been re-printed by S.P.C.K. under the title of *Christian Mysticism*.

[2] A. Nygren, *Agape and Eros, A Study of the Christian Idea of Love*, Part I (S.P.C.K., 1932).

desire, is the upward movement of the soul towards the Divine, her endeavour to escape from the entanglements of the flesh and attain to knowledge of the real and the eternal, to her heavenly home and her true rest. Thus Eros is called into being by the attractiveness of its object. But the Agape of the New Testament is God's own spontaneous self-giving: 'God commendeth His own agape toward us, in that, while we were yet sinners, Christ died for us' (Rom. v. 8). Agape is the very nature of God Himself, for 'God is agape', and 'God so loved the world' (John iii. 16; 1 John iv. 8); it is manifested in Christ, and it is seen in men as the presence of the Holy Spirit, which is God's own agape shed abroad in our hearts (Rom. v. 5).

The criticisms which have been made on Dr. Nygren's book centre round the problem of the relation of Agape to Eros, a problem which in this volume he makes no personal attempt to solve. He confines himself to presenting the contrast. He compares them to two streams which have their sources very far apart, in two widely different traditions, which approach one another and for a time flow side by side, till at last they meet. But this is insufficient; his exposition of the contrast cries out for a theological statement of the relation between the two. However much it may be true that the conceptions of Agape and Eros represent respectively the Judaeo-Christian and the Greek modes of thought, yet the fact remains that Eros describes a human activity; and since in the Incarnation Agape has become embodied in the flesh, manifestly there must be an ultimate synthesis between it and man's seeking after God. If the two are contrary and there is a tension between them, this will be the same tension which is necessarily involved in the clash of God's will and man's will, of God's saving work and man's response, God's grace and man's faith and works. If God saves man by His own free grace, man cannot be saved unless he loves God with all his heart and mind and soul and strength.

We have then a tension between two opposites, a tension which is not merely theoretical but practical, and demands a synthesis in the life-story of every Christian soul. We may set out the contrast as follows:

The Way of Agape starts from God's coming to man in the Incarnation. As God took on Himself true human flesh and blood, so man's body as well as his soul is redeemed; hence Christianity is thoroughly and essentially sacramental. And as He took our common human nature, so Christianity is not for an *élite*, but for mankind; and the sacraments exhibit men as reconciled to one another in being reconciled with Him.

Mysticism, the typical expression of the Way of Eros, is manifestly for an *élite*, for the religiously gifted, for the few choice souls. It is a solitary path; the mystic pursues his way alone, and is not thereby united with his fellows. It does not involve any redemption of the body, since it proceeds by the exercise of the faculties of the mind and spirit, and in its pagan forms it desires above all to escape from the body. And in so far as it proposes to attain to the end of union with God by mystical experience, it stands in no particular need of the Incarnation or of the sacraments.

This statement of the opposition of the two elements must not be misunderstood. In Christian Mysticism, as in all Christian religious experience, some sort of a synthesis of the two is attained. St. Paul states the problem: 'Work out your own salvation with fear and trembling, for it is God that worketh in you' (Phil. ii. 12–13). But there is always the danger, as in every such tension of opposed elements, that the true balance will be lost. Either Christians may assume that since the Divine gift is so unspeakably great in comparison with any faith or works of theirs, no spiritual discipline on their part is called for; in this case we find either a formalistic trust in outward observances, or a false 'assurance' of salvation, or a quietism, resulting in a neglect of spiritual endeavour. Or the tension may be resolved by placing the whole practical emphasis on the upward movement of man to God, and losing hold of the principle of the Incarnation.

Our study of the tendency of Catholic devotion in the Middle Ages, and since the Reformation, has shown clearly how strongly the current has been setting in this latter direction, towards individual piety and the attainment of holiness; and this is precisely the Way of Eros. We have emphasized the positive value of the working-out of the methods of the ascetic life. But we must not allow the recognition of this value, or the appreciation of the heroic sanctity of the great mystics, to obscure the other side of the picture. When the emphasis is laid on this side, there is always the danger that religion will come to be regarded as the affair of the devout, and that the common man, whose nature Christ took, will be left out in the cold; and that it will come to appear that Christianity is concerned with only a part of man's nature, namely his religious faculties, and not with the redemption of his whole life to God.

It is the same danger that appears in Monophysitism. The Monophysitism of the fifth century was the doctrine that the human nature of Christ was absorbed into the Divine and lost; instead of the human nature being the exhibition of manhood transformed by Divine power, its place is taken by the Divine. The Transubstantiation of the thirteenth century asserts that the substance of bread in the sacrament is instantaneously converted into the substance of the Body of Christ. Similarly, modern religion, instead of claiming for God and transforming the whole of social life, including the schoolboy's football and the shopkeeper's profits, leaves these on one side and limits itself to the life of piety lived by the devout. The principle of the Incarnation is lost; we are moving no longer in the faith of the redemption of all life to God, but in that of moral and spiritual uplift.[1]

Religion can thus come to be regarded as a department of life, in which the inner circle of the devout are the specialists. If the modern world regards Christianity as the special concern of the religiously-minded, and therefore leaves it on one side, it is because Christians themselves have set the example. We Christians have interpreted our Christianity to a large extent in terms of Eros, and have lost our grip on the full meaning of Agape. The element of Agape involves the redemption of the body and of common life by the Incarnation, and the fellowship of the common man with the religious specialist in the Church which God has provided for all.

II. EVANGELICAL RELIGION

It is clear, however, that this criticism applies only in a limited degree to Evangelicalism. Evangelical religion has always desired to rest wholly on faith in the Cross of Christ and God's own saving agape. It has exercised a mighty influence in our land. In the eighteenth century the preaching of Wesley transformed the life of England. Since his day Evangelicalism has produced a long line of saintly souls: nothing could be purer or more holy than the converted life as exhibited in Handley Moule or Frances Ridley Havergal. It gave rise to the noble Clapham sect at the beginning of the nineteenth century, and achieved a splendid record of social work in such men

[1] See an article by Fr. Kelly, 'Monophysitism and Transubstantiation', in *Theology*, June 1927, pp. 344–52.

as Wilberforce and Lord Shaftesbury. It has sustained a wonderful missionary work.

The appeal of the Gospel of Christ to the individual soul has been the strength of the Evangelical school in the Church of England: it has been an appeal to experience, which has constantly been justified in experience.[1] But has not this been also its weakness?

The actual spiritual issue is this. If justification is by faith, and salvation is mediated through experience, it is clear that the doubtful factor is not God's faithfulness but mine. So long, therefore, as I am faithful, my life will be rightly lived. Hence justification by faith is in constant danger of becoming a trust not in God's faithfulness but in my own perseverance: faith, that is, in my own faithfulness. All good Evangelical preaching continually recalls the soul to trust God and not itself. But the constant reminder of the need of a right response does, in fact, produce a paralysing self-scrutiny—'Am I saved?' It is just here that the objectivity of the sacrament is the great defence and refuge. But Evangelical churchmen, largely through fear of Anglo-Catholicism, have rarely been sufficiently courageous here, and have been misled by the receptionist doctrine of the sacrament, which lays the stress on the faith of the recipient.

The weakness of the appeal to experience has been seen over and over again, in those who have been taught to expect an experience of conversion. Many have been driven, in default of an overpowering experience of 'irresistible grace', to a partly uneasy trust in their good intentions and their desire to be converted. Many more, believing that the mark of a genuine Christian is conversion, and knowing that this conversion can only come

---

[1] See, for instance, the account of the ministry of E. H. Bickersteth at Christ Church, Hampstead, in Carpenter, *Church and People, 1789–1889* (S.P.C.K., 1933), pp. 400–3.

by a gift from above, and not by a manipulation of the proper psychological strings, have gone on from year to year, hoping for the wonderful experience to come to them: meanwhile they have perforce organized their lives without it, till at last the hope has faded away, and they have gradually drifted away from the outward observance of a religion which has never obtained a real hold on their life. It is a fact to which many who have been brought up in Evangelical circles can testify, that the children of Evangelical families often drift away from religion in later life: a minority follow in the steps of their devout parents, while the majority become lax or indifferent. It would seem that Anglo-Catholic families compare favourably with Evangelical families in this respect; the children on the whole remain faithful to their religion. The reason is fairly clear. The Evangelical has been taught to rest everything on personal experience: but the Catholic finds in the objectivity of sacramental worship something independent of his experience and prior to it. He has learnt to forget himself and believe in a truth.

The sum of the matter is this: The letter killeth, but the spirit giveth life. Evangelicalism has been afraid of the letter, and has desired to live by the spirit. But the spirit does not work *in vacuo*: it takes the letter, and gives life to the letter. The spirit needs forms in which to work: apart from those forms, it finds nothing on which to get a grip. Therefore Evangelicals also find that what is precious to them is after all enshrined in the forms whose use is so easily perverted into formalism: forms of prayer, sacraments, the visible Church. Ecclesiastical and liturgical forms are the safeguards of the authentic Christian experience which Evangelicalism treasures.

III. THE IDEA OF THE CHURCH

Let us now see, by way of contrast, an expression of Christian piety from the great Russian theologian Khomiakoff, who lived in the middle of the nineteenth century:[1]

'We know that when any one of us falls, he falls alone: but no one is saved alone. He who is saved is saved in the Church, as a member of her, and in unity with all her other members. If any one believes, he is in the communion of faith; if he loves, he is in the communion of love; if he prays, he is in the communion of prayer. Wherefore no one can rest his hope on his own prayers, and every one who prays asks the whole Church for intercession, not as if he had doubts of the intercession of Christ the Advocate, but in the assurance that the whole Church ever prays for all her members. All the angels pray for us, the apostles, martyrs, and patriarchs and, above them all, the Mother of our Lord, and this holy unity is the true life of the Church.'

'Just as each of us requires prayers from all, so each person owes his prayers on behalf of all, the living and the dead, and even those who are yet unborn: for in praying as we do with all the Church, that the world may come to the knowledge of God, we pray not only for the present generation, but for those whom God will hereafter call into life. We pray for the living that the grace of God may be upon them, and for the dead that they may become worthy of the vision of God's face.'

'Let no one say: "What prayer shall I apportion to the living or the departed, when my prayers are insufficient even for myself?" For if he is not able to pray, of what use would it be to pray even for himself? But in truth the spirit of love prays in him. Likewise let him not say:

[1] From Birkbeck, *Russia and the English Church* (London, 1895), pp. 216 ff.

"What is the good of my prayer for another, when he prays for himself, and Christ Himself intercedes for him?" When a man prays, it is the spirit of love which prays within him. Let him not say: "It is even now impossible to change the judgement of God," for his prayer itself is included in the ways of God, and God foresaw it. If he be a member of the Church his prayer is necessary for all her members. If the hand should say that it did not require blood from the rest of the body, and that it would not give its own blood to it, the hand would wither. So a man is also necessary to the Church, so long as he is in her: and if he withdraws himself from communion with the Church, he perishes himself and will cease to be any longer a member of the Church. The Church prays for all, and we pray together for all; but our prayer must be true, and a true expression of love, and not a mere form of words. Not being able to love all men, we pray for those whom we love, and our prayer is not hypocritical: but we pray God that we may be able to love all, and pray for all without hypocrisy. Mutual prayer is the blood of the Church, and the glorification of God her breath. We pray in a spirit of love, not of interest, in the spirit of filial freedom, not of the law of the hireling demanding his pay. Every man who asks: "What use is there in prayer?" acknowledges himself to be in bondage. True prayer is true love.'

The idea which underlies Khomiakoff's words is that Christianity means unity—that is, not merely that charity is a Christian virtue, but that God has created and established a unity for mankind, through Christ, to draw men out of loneliness, isolation, and enmity with one another, into the fellowship of His universal Family, a fellowship which the Church exists to express. It is the explicit denial of the common assumption that Christianity means the free access of individuals to God, each for himself: it is the assertion that the only way to God is to come to Him ἐν Χριστῷ, that is, as a member of Christ's mystical Body.

The idea of the mystical Body of Christ can truly be regarded as the culminating point of the whole Bible. The purpose of Christ's coming is to 'open the Kingdom of heaven to all believers'. The message of Jesus is not in the first place a calling of individuals to a moral and spiritual reformation of life, but a call to enter into an order of salvation which God has prepared. The Kingdom of God is regarded as existing prior to the individuals who are called to enter into it: it is a Wedding-feast to which they are bidden to come, a Home to which the Prodigal Son returns, a Sheepfold to which the Lost Sheep is brought back. Again, the work of Jesus is compared to the sowing of seed in a field by which the souls of men are born again to new life. He comes among men as the Heavenly Messiah incarnate in the flesh, bringing to men the Kingdom of God.

The Old Testament, as seen from the Christian point of view, is the preparation for the Kingdom of Christ. The New Testament is built on the foundation of the Old. To Abraham and his seed were the promises made: Abraham, the father of a family. In the time of Moses God made His Covenant with Israel, and constituted Israel as His people; the story of the Old Testament is the story of a nation in covenant with God. The Law is always interpreted in the New Testament as Divine but incomplete: as God's word, but not God's final word. The Prophets look forward from the imperfect present to a future salvation: they announce God's judgements, they seek to discern the purpose which God is working out. And always this purpose is concerned not primarily with the salvation of individual souls, but with individuals as members of a nation; and even when the nation as a whole is declared to be apostate, and Isaiah sees the hope of the future in a righteous Remnant, it is still a corporate and social salvation that is in view.

The announcement of the New Testament is that all has been fulfilled. The Church of Jesus Christ is the New Israel, the true heir of the Old Testament: into it first Jews and then Gentiles are called to enter. The phrase of St. Cyprian, *extra ecclesiam nulla salus*, is exactly true of the New Testament teaching, because the Church is the sphere of the salvation accomplished through Christ. The Church is described as a Family or Household; or (in terms of an eschatological image derived from the Gospels) as the Bride of the Messiah; or as the Body of Christ, composed of many members; or as a Temple, built of living stones, taking the place of the material temple at Jerusalem; or as the City of God, the Heavenly Jerusalem. All these images are rich in associations, and are applied in great detail throughout the New Testament in various ways.

The maturest summary of all is that of the Epistle to the Ephesians, in which St. Paul, or one writing under Pauline influence, presents a philosophy of history as the working out of the eternal purpose of God, culminating in the saving work of Christ and in the Church as Christ's Body—in the establishment of the Unity which God has made for men, breaking down the middle-wall of partition, and reconciling the enmities between man and man, nation and nation, class and class. As in Galatians iii. 28, 'there can be neither Jew nor Greek, there can be neither bond nor free, there can be no male and female; for ye are all one man in Christ Jesus'. It is not that the diversities are all planed away into a cosmopolitan or sexless uniformity. The diversities remain: the Jew and Greek retain their national traditions, man or woman are still male and female, even the institution of slavery remains for the present: but the enmity is taken away, and slavery ceases to be slavery when master and slave meet as fellow-men and brothers at the Table of the Lord (cf. Philemon 16).

The diversities remain. The body is one, and has many members: the hand, the foot, the eye, are all necessary to one another: there are diversities of gifts, but the One Spirit: and if one member suffers all the members suffer with it, and if one member is honoured, all the members rejoice with it (1 Cor. xii.; Rom. xii. 1–8; Ephes. iv. 1–16). Such is Christian Unity: it is not a unity of uniformity, but of manifold diversity, brought together into a living unity by the reconciling work of God through Christ. The unity is not presented as an ideal toward, which men are to strive, but rather as an existing facts established by God, whose meaning is to be progressively realized.

'I therefore, the prisoner of the Lord, beseech you to walk worthily of the calling wherewith ye were called. . . . There is one body and one Spirit, even as ye were called in one hope of your calling: one Lord, one faith, one baptism, one God and Father of all' (Ephes. iv. 1, 4–6).

The great controversy of St. Paul's life, the battle for the admission of Gentiles into the Church on equal terms with Jews, was a battle for Christian unity. The line of least resistance would have been to allow two separate churches to grow up, so that the one would not trouble the other; but St. Paul knew that Christianity meant unity, and therefore the issue was vital.

In the Epistle to the Hebrews we get the grand image of the City, the organized πόλις with its social life and organic structure:

'Ye are come unto Mount Zion,
    The City of the Living God, the heavenly Jerusalem.

And to ten thousands of angels,
  To the festal assembly and Church of the first-born,
  Whose names are written in heaven,
And to God the Judge of all,
  And to the spirits of just men made perfect,
And to Jesus the mediator of a New Covenant,
  And a blood of sprinkling speaking better things than that
    of Abel.'

(xii. 22–4.)

In the Book of the Revelation this same New Jerusalem is presented in apocalyptic language, not merely as a picture of the eternal future, but as in the act of descending to earth and embodying itself in the Church (xxi. 2). The visible Church on earth, seen from the eternal point of view, is the projection of the eternal into the present. This is a conception which is fundamental to the New Testament and to Christianity. The Church on earth belongs both to time and to eternity: it is at once human, imperfect, militant here on earth, and divine, the heir even now of the eternal kingdom of God: 'our citizenship is in heaven'.

Lastly, St. John's Gospel, which more than any other book of the New Testament stresses the reaction of faith on the part of the individual soul (vi. 35, 47, 56, &c.), unites this emphasis on individual faith and individual judgement with the corporate aspect of the Christian hope, as in the Allegory of the True Vine (xv. 1 ff.) and the Prayer for Unity, which forms the climax of the High-priestly prayer of Christ (xvii. 20, 21):

'Neither for these only do I pray,
  But for those who believe on me through their word,
    That they may be one,
  As thou, Father, art in me, and I in thee,
  That they also may be in us,
  That the world may believe
    That thou didst send me.'

Thus throughout the New Testament the Unity of the

Church is not merely one point among many: it is rather a focal point in which all else meets. It is present in the Lord's Prayer itself: the Christian is not allowed to pray 'My Father, give me this day my daily bread': it must be 'Our Father', and he must associate with himself all those others who, by God's will and not his, have been called to be children of that Father and his own brothers in God's universal Family.[1]

So long as the Church is in the world, this unity is subjected to constant strain. It is so in the New Testament: we see, for instance, not only the threatened schism between Jew and Gentile, but also a sectarian spirit showing itself in cliques and coteries within the Church of Corinth (1 Cor. i. 12). The history of the Church has been marked by constant schisms, some of them brief and soon healed, some of them lasting for centuries and still continuing. Yet in principle no difference of kind can be drawn between schisms between churches and quarrels between individual Christians. Every such quarrel is a breach of Christian unity: and it is easy to picture a personal quarrel widening out and coming to involve first two families, then other families and groups, till it results in the setting up of two rival church organizations. But it is clear that if the unity which God has created is not destroyed by the original quarrel, it is not destroyed by the final schism. There still remains a unity which God has made, which is deeper and more fundamental than the divisions made by men.[2] In spite of the schisms which desolate Christendom, we can still declare our faith in the one Church of God.

[1] See Maurice, *The Kingdom of Christ*, Vol. II, p. 26 (Everyman edition).

[2] I have worked this point out more fully in my book *Intercommunion* (S.P.C.K., 1932, 2s.) which is a study of the sacramental order of the Church, with special reference to the problem of Reunion. See esp. pp. 88-95.

It is not only the unity of the Church which is imperfect. As the Church which is essentially one is, in fact, divided, so the Church which is holy and the witness to God's holiness on earth is also defiled with many sins; the Church, which by her very nature is catholic and universal, is tainted with a sectarian spirit; and the Church which retains the apostolic faith and order is nevertheless unfaithful to the apostolic gospel. The Divine and human elements in the Church are interwoven. It is very lamentable that the Church should be so imperfect and so unworthy of her calling. But in principle there is nothing to be surprised at in this, since the method of the Incarnation is the manifestation of God's goodness *in the flesh*, and the Christian redemption has sinful human nature for its subject-matter.

But then, how can we distinguish the Divine and human elements in the Church? It is manifestly wrong to say that it is the distinction between good and bad Christians; for the distinction which we need is between God's own saving work and the men who are thereby saved.

The distinction is seen most clearly in the sacramental order of the Church. The rite of baptism is performed on an adult or a child, a specimen of sinful humanity. The service is recited more or less reverently or irreverently. The baptismal rite is a human composition, beautiful and venerable, but evidently capable of improvement from a liturgical point of view. But the act of baptism itself, from Pentecost onwards,[1] has been the appointed sign of admission into the blessings of salvation through Christ: when the act is performed upon *this* individual *here* and *now*, it is the sign that God's universal purpose for the salvation of mankind is extended to this person in particular. If we may adapt the scholastic distinction of the Form and the Matter of the sacrament, the Divine

---

[1] See *Intercommunion*, pp. 39 ff. on the origins of Baptism.

element is the universal Form: the human element is
the particular Matter.

It is easy to apply the same distinction to the eucharistic
sacrament, and see how the human element appears in the
liturgy itself and the way in which the liturgy is performed
by this particular congregation; while the Divine element
is the Lord's own institution, which brings the sacrifice of
Christ and the Divine Gift into the *here* and *now*, so that the
sacrament is adored by *these* communicants as the Bread
of eternal life and the Cup of Salvation, and is received by
them as the sign of their reconciliation with God and with
one another in Christ.

Again, with regard to the bishop or priest who is the
minister of the sacrament, there is the same distinction of
the Form and Matter, between the office committed to
him as priest and pastor in Christ's name, and the manner
in which he fulfils it. Bishops have always been in danger
of the sin that is summed up in the word Prelacy. But
Prelacy is sinful precisely because it is the denial in life of
the office of the Bishop as priest and shepherd of the flock
of Christ in His name.

The importance of the episcopal office is constantly
misunderstood. It is regarded by many as simply a convenient method of church organization, no doubt preferable to a presbyterian system in certain respects because
it offers the advantages of the concentration of responsibility on one person. But this limited view misses completely the real meaning of the episcopal office, through
losing sight of the Divine character of the Church, and
considering it purely as a human organization.

First, because the unity of the Church is of God, that
unity is expressed in her structure. The Bishop in each
place is in virtue of his office the centre of Christian unity,
as the Father-in-God of all the Christians in that place.
At this point the divisions of Christendom, being in them-

selves utterly anomalous, throw all our thought into confusion: we shall not fully grasp what the office of Bishop
means till the schisms have been healed, and he has
actually become once again the chief Pastor not of a
denomination but of all the Christians in his diocese.
Yet even as things are, a measure of Christian unity is
actually realized in our denominational life. The Bishop
being responsible for a great variety of people, of various
classes, various interests, and even various races, can never
identify himself with any one party or cause or racial
interest without being false to the office committed to
him. By his office he represents catholicity, the unity of
all in Christ.

Secondly, as a member of the Episcopate he links this
local division of the Church with other local divisions.
From the early ages of the Church it has been the duty
of the Bishop not only to care for his own flock but to
meet in council with other Bishops and care for the welfare
of the Church as a whole.

Thirdly, by his consecration in the Apostolic Succession
he links this generation of the Church with other genera-
tions, both of the past and of the future. The Apostolic
Succession is widely denounced as a symbol of exclusiveness, because it seems to un-church those who stand outside it. But when those who are now outside it have been
brought back within it, it will be universally seen to be
what it really is, a symbol not of denominational exclusiveness but of catholicity and universality, a sacrament of
unity. The long line of the succession, reaching back to
the original message and commission bestowed by Christ
on His apostles,[1] unites the Christians of today with all

[1] See *Intercommunion*, pp. 69–74, where it is argued that the Apostolic
Succession does not depend on some disputable interpretation of the
second-century evidence, but on the nature of the Gospel, which
requires that a message and commission, derived from Christ, should
have been handed on to responsible persons in each new church.

their forefathers, as with their successors. It testifies to the existence of the Church in the world as an historical institution, beginning with Christ Himself.

The actual meaning of Apostolic Succession is nowhere more splendidly expressed than in the great prayer said by the Bishop in the Anglican form for the Ordination of a priest, immediately before the laying-on of hands:

'Almighty God and heavenly Father, who, of thine infinite love and goodness towards us, hast given to us thy only and most dearly-beloved Son Jesus Christ to be our Redeemer and the Author of everlasting life: who, after he had made perfect our redemption by his death, and was ascended into heaven, sent abroad into the world his Apostles, Prophets, Evangelists, Doctors, and Pastors; by whose labour and ministry he gathered together a great flock in all parts of the world, to set forth the eternal praises of thy holy Name: For these so great benefits of thy eternal goodness, and for that thou hast vouchsafed to call these thy servants here present to the same Office and Ministry appointed for the salvation of mankind, we render unto thee most hearty thanks, we praise and worship thee. . . .'

The Church is at once Divine and human. As a human society, she comes in for criticism and blame. But her very nature and structure testifies to her Divine character. Her ground-plan is that of the Celestial City. The Corinthians of St. Paul's day were guilty of certain very ugly sins, including incest, a presumption that did not stop short of taking part in heathen sacrificial feasts, a flagrant dishonouring of the Lord's Supper, the denial of the resurrection of the dead, as well as extreme rudeness towards their beloved Apostle. Yet St. Paul addresses them as 'the Church of God which is at Corinth'. The Church of God in our parishes is guilty of not less serious if less interesting sins. Yet even so, and however bad the sermon may be, the faithful Sunday by Sunday recite the Psalms and hear the Scriptures and partake of the Bread of Life. And in a world which treats the factory-worker as a cog in the industrial machine, the forms of the Church still proclaim him to be called to be a child of God and an heir of eternal life, and in this world a member of a fellowship that is based not on his own self-interest nor yet on other people's ideals for his welfare, but on the will of the God who made him. The Church stands as the witness, against the world, of the right of a man to be treated as a human being.

IV. THE THREE ELEMENTS

We have reviewed the three elements, liturgy, dogma and personal religion. The conclusions which emerge are somewhat as follows:

First, while personal devotion is the mainspring of all Christian life, we lose hold of the essence of Christianity if we interpret it simply as a way of holiness, having for its end the salvation and the perfection of the individual soul. Personal religion, so interpreted, becomes a way of escape from the body by meditation and contemplation. But Christianity is the redemption of the body, and of common life, by the Divine action in the Incarnation. The Christian way of salvation through Christ is salvation in the mystical Body of Christ, the Church; and the Church, while it is not *of* the world, is *in* the world.

Second: while Christianity is in its essence dogmatic, it cannot be identified with a system of dogma. The Divine Revelation is not a system of truths about God, to be apprehended by the mind: the Revelation is of God Himself, translated (as it were) into human language in the Incarnation. But such a view of Revelation makes Theology not less but more important. Theology ceases to be academic; it no longer consists of disputations conducted in the rarefied air of the schools; it comes into direct relation to life. It deals with the things which concern the common man. It is said that in the days of the Arian controversy theology was discussed in the barbers' shops: and rightly so, for the matter of the discussion was of the deepest concern for the ordinary man. If theology today has a bad name, it is because we have become used to theology of the wrong kind. We want theology, far more theology, from the pulpit: theology that will help the common man to understand the theological language of the New Testament, and see it in relation to his own daily life. We need clear thinking in simple language, as simple as the language of our Lord's parables, about God and God's impact upon the life of the actual world.

Thirdly, if Liturgy is the expression in worship of the life of the mystical Body of Christ, we need more serious study of the forms of this common worship. We need to get right away from the idea that there is something unspiritual about forms of worship, and that the only worship which is 'in spirit and in truth' is the devout meditation of the individual soul. Forms of worship can become formalistic in their use when the spirit has gone out of them: 'the letter killeth, but the spirit giveth life'. But the spirit is helpless if it has not forms upon which to work: and when the forms are there, in scriptures, creeds, prayers, sacraments, they are waiting for the spirit to come and interpret their life-giving meaning.

But above all, if Christianity is the Gospel of the manifestation of God's goodness in the Incarnation, the Gospel of the redemption of the flesh, accomplished once for all in Christ and continuing in Christ's mystical Body, it is clear that it is the function of the Church's Liturgy to interpret and express her life, and to exhibit the aim and meaning of human life in the light of the Incarnation.

To worship God in church is not a substitute for the service of God in daily life: rather, it is that which makes the service of God possible by bringing the things of daily life into the light of eternity. And as the Christian redemption is not merely individual but social, so the normal type of Christian worship is not the individual's meditation, but the common worship of the Body, when the members are met together to learn the meaning of the common life which is in Him.

PART II
CHRISTIANITY AND THE MODERN WORLD

CHAPTER VII

THE ACTUAL CHURCH

*

I. THE PRESENT SITUATION

In seeking to answer our question, What has the Church to give to the modern world? we have been compelled to discuss Christianity, and present a theological statement of the idea of the Church. But the trouble is that all this theology is failing at present to reach the mind of the modern man. It is not that it is rejected as untrue. It is set aside as irrelevant. It fails to make contact with his life. It seems to belong to another world than the world in which he lives.

Why, why, why is this? There are many who blame the Church for not being sufficiently modern. Liberal theologians and preachers seek to modernize the message of the Church, and present it in the form of attractive ideals. 'The Prayer Book is out of date, and the old prayers need to have substituted for them other prayers in a modern style. The modern man does not want sacraments: let him not therefore be troubled with them.' This style of devotion is fully represented in the B.B.C. services. It gains a certain amount of success. But it is not carrying all before it: it does not answer the real problems; it does not capture the best minds in the Church, nor does it convert the best minds in the world.

The difficulty goes deeper. It is not merely the Church, the Prayer Book and the sacraments which fail to make contact with the modern man: it is above all the Bible.

Apart from a limited range of passages which are much quoted for their direct moral appeal or their poetic beauty, such as some of the teaching and anecdotes from the Gospels, or St. Paul's hymn in praise of Charity, the Bible as a whole is set aside as irrelevant, and seems to belong to another world altogether from that in which the modern man lives. How many people read Romans, Ephesians, Hebrews or the Revelation?

If it is so with the Bible, need we be surprised if the theological teaching of the Church fails to get across to the public? A great amount of really excellent theology is being produced, on an intellectual level of which no branch of science would have cause to be ashamed. It is read by Christians, who understand the language in which it is written. It is not read by the general public.

It is not merely that faith in the unseen and the eternal, the faith that is described in Hebrews xi., is always difficult for carnal-minded and pleasure-loving man. Whatever be the faults of the Middle Ages, the Christian assumptions about God and man and the world were then accepted as the background of the life and thought of Europe. But now the world has strayed away from the Christian faith. Since the Renaissance Europe has endeavoured to build up its life more and more on the basis of Humanism, on the basis of the power of man to solve his problems and answer his questions for himself. Religion has been put into a corner. It has been assumed that Science is concerned with fact and Religion with values: Religion thus becomes a department of life, a spiritual experience which appeals to those who are temperamentally religious, and are interested in treading the way of holiness. But to the modern man these values seem less real than the world of atoms and electrons, of economic laws and material progress. These, however, cannot tell him what his life is for, and the attempt of

Humanism to answer the problems of life and to build up a stable society is ending in disillusionment and despair.

But just at this point the Church fails to give a clear witness. It is the Church's function to help the common man to apprehend the Eternal, by exhibiting in her teaching, her worship and her corporate life, the pattern of the City which hath foundations. But the state of the actual Church seems to give the lie to the exalted language of theology about the Church as the Bride of Christ and His mystical Body and the New Jerusalem really but imperfectly embodied on earth, and makes it appear hopelessly unreal. We preachers and theologians go back to our Bible and paint a glowing picture: Christianity *is* unity, God has created for mankind a Family and a Fellowship. But the actual Church is miserably divided, as we are reminded every time we walk down the High Street. Again, we speak of the Eucharist as the sacrament of the fellowship of the Body. If on every Sunday in every parish church the central act of worship were the eucharistic liturgy with the communion of the people, as in the early Church, that service would proclaim to the world what Christianity is. But as things are, Holy Communion is commonly regarded as a service of private devotion for the few, and Christian worship fails to exhibit what the Church really is. Again, we speak of the Church as Christ's witness to the world: but the actual Church is worldly and secularized, and appears to the ordinary man as a pillar of the established order, with endowments maintaining the ministers of the Gospel in ease and comfort (as he thinks), and an ecclesiastical law which makes the Church seem to be a department of the State. It seems as if the Church has failed to conquer the world, and the world has penetrated the Church with its own worldly spirit.

It is not surprising, therefore, that the modern man

should seize on the evident fact that there are still plenty of sincere and convinced Christians, and interpret their Christianity as an expression of religion, an actualization of spiritual values which is valid for them, but not universally valid or valid for him.

But then we cannot have Christianity on such terms. The Church cannot be content to be tolerated as a provision of religion for the devout, without denying its own nature. It is all or nothing: either the Christian faith is true, universally true, or it is false. Either the God whom it proclaims is the Judge of all mankind, or there can be no Christian faith. If the truth which baptism proclaims about God and man's sonship to God is not really true, baptism ought not to be tolerated: the fonts ought to be destroyed out of our Churches by an indignant people, and with them the Prayer Book and the Bible which teach the same doctrine. Mr. Middleton Murry at least sees that the Church cannot be merely tolerated. He insists that the modern world must make its choice for Communism:

'What is demanded of the conscious minority is a positive and dynamic rejection of religion. For them a purely negative lapse from religion is not merely insufficient, it is disastrous—ethically and politically. It leads to moral dilettantism and to coquetting with the empty and barren idea of Fascism. For the difference between a lapse from religion and a dynamic rejection of religion is tremendous. To reject, unconsciously, a manifestation of human life so ancient, so venerable, so evidently the vehicle of precious human values as the Christian religion is an offence against human responsibility: it proceeds from weary ignorance. Far better than such neglect is the deliberate determination to return to the Christian orthodoxy.' [1]

[1] J. Middleton Murry, *The Necessity of Communism* (London, 1932), p. 47.

Yes: either the Church's claim is true, and God is the Judge of the world, and God's salvation through Christ is valid for all men, or Christianity must be consciously and deliberately rejected as the last of the great illusions which have deceived mankind—if indeed mankind has any standard of truth left in the name of which it can still denounce it.

But we who live by the faith that Christianity is true, and that the church building which stands in each parish really is the House of God and the home of the people, however much the people may have strayed away from their home—we can never cease to bear a great sorrow in our hearts. 'Why should not my countenance be sad, when the city, the place of my fathers' sepulchres, lieth waste, and the gates thereof are consumed with fire?'[1] Sunday by Sunday the congregation assembles: not so bad perhaps as things are, but still, nothing like what it should be. We who assemble there are to think of ourselves as keeping the hearth-fires burning and the door of their home open for the multitudes who have strayed away: we are worshipping the Father of men on behalf of those who have forgotten Him: we are keeping a tradition alive in trust for those who have lost it.

Luther, four centuries ago, spoke of the Babylonish Captivity of the Sacrament and of the Church. The Church is still in a state of Babylonish Captivity: in the light of her present degradation we recite *Super flumina Babylonis* (Ps. 137), and, like the Jews in exile, look in faith for a return from captivity, and rejoice in the signs that the day is beginning to dawn.

The Church lies in bondage. She is far from being altogether helpless, altogether ineffective. If there is much in her that makes us weep—the miserable sentimentality of many of the popular hymns, the pettiness of parochial

[1] Nehemiah ii. 3.

life, the obstinacy of some of our party-rivalries, the futility of so many clergy who know, as their people know, that they have no message to give that can do any one any good—yet the Church inspires a vast amount of self-denying service, and exercises an actual influence that is greater probably than we ever guess. But the Church is very far from fulfilling her calling, and appearing before the world as that which she really is: she is very far from attaining to the measure of the stature of the fullness of Christ.

II. THE CHURCH OF ENGLAND

Where now are we to begin with our exposition of the Church's witness to the world? Clearly, we must envisage the whole Church. But Christendom is split up into fragments. Should we then go the rounds, and try to estimate the possibilities of the Roman Catholic fragment, the Eastern Orthodox fragment, the Anglican fragment, the Lutheran and Reformed fragments? The task would be beyond us: we should fail to get at the essentials, and could scarcely fail to be guilty alternately of a patronizing approbation and of partly unfair criticism.

An Anglican writer can only start from his own Church, which he knows from within, and seek to see there the lines of the universal, of God's one holy catholic Church. He will, of course, expect others to do the same, and seek to learn from the experience of their life in their own churches what are the lineaments of the whole. For in spite of all the divisions and the manifold unworthinesses of the actual churches, the Church of God is nevertheless in being, and exists as a fact in the world.

We start, then, from the Church of England, or rather, the world-wide Anglican Communion. And for this purpose, the Church of England is admittedly well placed. At the *Faith and Order* Conference at Lausanne in 1927 every one was speaking of her as the Bridge-Church. We may also quote an interesting testimony, written seventy-five years ago by the ardent papalist writer de Maistre,[1] when the influence of the Anglican revival upon our forms of worship had scarcely begun:

'If ever Christians draw closer to one another, as there is every reason that they should, it seems that the initiative (*la motion*) must come from the Church of England. Presbyterianism was a French product, and consequently an exaggeration. We are too far removed from these followers of a worship which lacks substance: there is no chance for us to be understood. But the Anglican Church, which touches us with one hand, touches with the other those whom we cannot touch; and though, from one point of view, she is a target for blows from both sides, and though she presents the somewhat ridiculous spectacle of a revolt which asks for obedience, nevertheless from other points of view she is most valuable, and may be compared to one of those chemical intermediates which are capable of bringing together elements which of their own nature are incapable of combination.'

But the Church of England is a queer concern. Even those who have given their lives in her service often shake their heads over her, half-despairingly: one can only faintly imagine what a monster she must seem to be to the tidy regimented mind of the Roman Catholic. Is she the Church of the English nation, or is she really a group of denominations held together by an accidental bond of establishment? Is she authentically Catholic or is she Protestant? Does she hold a definite belief? If so, why does she not enforce conformity of belief? Is she a tolerant, backboneless institution in which each man follows his

[1] Oeuvres du comte J. de Maistre, Tome I (*Considérations sur la France*) (Pelagaud, Lyon, 1860), p. 27. Quoted in French in *Oecumenica*, Vol. I, No. 3 (Sept. 1934), p. 199.

own private judgement? What was the real character of the English Reformation? Was it a weak compromise between Rome and Geneva, reached, not on the basis of a clear and definite belief, but merely on the basis of political expediency? It will be well to begin with the last of these questions, for it provides the key to the others.

The English Reformation did not begin with a clear assertion of principle like that of Luther; nor did it develop on the basis of a theological system, like that of Calvin. It shaped itself in the course of three reigns of terror, under Henry VIII, Edward VI's Council, and Queen Mary. The Church of England emerged under Queen Elizabeth rent by controversy between the Church party and the Puritans, yet in possession of a reformed liturgy based on the old order for the Mass and the Breviary, a Ministry continuing the ancient orders of Bishops, Priests and Deacons, the ancient creeds and the scriptures, interpreted in the light of the appeal to the early Church Fathers.

The remarkable thing in this Reformation is that it is not based on a theological system, but on something apparently much more vague. There is a Church with a definite order and structure, an episcopal ministry which has been maintained ever since, and an order of worship. The order of worship affirms the Trinitarian faith of the Church Universal, not in the manner in which it is expressed in a theological treatise like the *Summa Theologica* of St. Thomas Aquinas, but in the liturgical manner, in which God is worshipped, through the Son, in the power of the Holy Spirit: as the Athanasian Symbol expresses it, 'The Catholic faith is this, that we worship one God in Trinity.' The Church of England escaped being tied down to a theological system, as the Calvinistic Churches were tied down, and as the Roman Catholic Church was forced to tie itself down, in maintaining itself as a denomination against the other denominations into which Western Christendom had come to be divided. The nearest parallel in the West is the Church of Sweden, which has no other title than this, and did not in fact officially accept any Lutheran formula till at the Upsala-möte of 1594 it was compelled to exclude Calvinism; the Swedish Church believes itself to be the Church of God in Sweden.[1] In the East the Orthodox Churches have always maintained the same principle. They in like manner have avoided the danger of identifying themselves with a theological system, and consequently retain liberty of discussion.

If there is one man to whom we owe the position which the Church of England took up, it is Thomas Cranmer. It is easy to condemn the weakness of Cranmer's character: 'the age of the Renaissance' says Fr. Kelly 'was a paradise of bullies, and Cranmer was a commonplace citizen made to be bullied'.[2] It is less easy to understand the history of his mind, and to relate the various and inconsistent theological utterances for which he made himself responsible, with one another and with his declaration immediately before his death. Various indeed are the interpretations of him given by various writers. But surely we do wrong if we take his theological pronouncements too seriously, though he himself took them seriously enough. Father Kelly has an illuminating characterization:

'With all his commonplaceness as an individual and a controversialist, Cranmer was also a Churchman, and, above all, a supreme liturgical artist, transfigured by that strange sub-conscious intuition of the artist to do things as they had to be done in his medium, whether the

[1] For an account of the very interesting course of the Swedish Reformation, see Brilioth, *Eucharistic Faith and Practice*, chap. VII.
[2] In an article in the *S.S.M. Quarterly*, Easter 1932.

results were or were not according to the theories he
was at other times pushed or pulled to take up. At one
time he wrote a memorandum for Henry VIII suggest-
ing that bishops were only state officers for religious affairs;
but an Ordinal was an Ordinal. No one who reads either
the Preface or the forms of 1550 would guess that he ever
entertained such notions.'

A supreme liturgical artist; out of his depth in purely
theological controversy, dimly conscious, perhaps, that
he was out of his depth there, and showing by his changes
of front that he was aware of the complexity of the theological issues: such is Cranmer. But on the liturgical side
he had a vision of the possibilities of corporate worship
such as Stephen Gardiner never had. Gardiner thus tries
to persuade Cranmer that it is useless to try to make the
service intelligible to the people:

'For in times past, when men came to church more
diligently than some do now, the people in the church
took small heed what the priest and the clerks did in the
chancel, but only to stand up at the Gospel and kneel at
the Sacring, or else every man was occupied himself
severally in several prayer. And as for the priest's prayer,
they could not all have heard and understood, although
they would, and had given ear thereunto. For such an
enterprise to bring that to pass is impossible, without the
priest should turn his face to the people when he prayeth,
and occupy many prayers to them to make them hold
their peace. And therefore it was never meant that the
people should indeed *hear* the Mattins or *hear* the Mass,
but be present there and pray themselves in silence; with
common credit to the priests and clerks, that although
they hear not a distinct sound to know what they say,
yet to judge that they for their part were and be well
occupied, and in prayer; and so should they be. And
good simple folks were wont so to be, and other, more

dissolute, used to commune in the time of Mattins and Mass of other matters. And I have known that, after their little devotions said, as they called them, some used to gather by the penny or two pence such money as they had lent in gross. But as for hearing of Mass in deed, some, well occupied, heard not, and some, evil occupied, heard not neither. And thus it hath been practised; so as that can be taken for none argument of hearing. And I gather no opinion by divination, but by plain comprobation of the fact, and after that sort I speak. . . .'[1]

Christopherson, 'one of the most learned and most respectable of the Romish party', writes in his *Exhortation against Rebellion*, in the reign of Queen Mary, A.D. 1554:

'And lette them not so greatly passe for understandynge what the priestes saye, but travayl themselfe in fervent praying, and so shall they hyghly please God. Yea, and experience hath playnlye taught us, that it is much better for them not to understande the common service of the Churche, than to understand it . . .'[2]

Clearly then, the people had not been in the habit of following and understanding the service; and both at the time when the Prayer Book was first being prepared, and after, there was no lack of advice to the effect that it was impossible and undesirable to try to bring them to understand it. The Western insurgents of 1549 were emphatic on the point.

But Cranmer held to the higher vision, and in his Prayer Books he gave the Church of England liturgical forms on the lines of the ancient offices and missal, in

---

[1] Written in July 1547. From No. 125 in *The Letters of Stephen Gardiner*, ed. J. A. Muller (Cambridge, 1933), pp. 355 f. I have modernized the spelling.

[2] From Christopher Wordsworth, *Ecclesiastical Biography* (3rd edn., 1839), Vol. I, pp. 149 f., *note*. He refers also to the *Mirror of our Lady*, fol. 22: 'Commendation of those who attend the divine services without understanding them.'

which the people were to take their share. Here he antici-
pated in part the efforts now being made by the Liturgical
Movement in the Roman Catholic Church: and on this
side it is impossible to exaggerate the importance of his
work. The Church of England today is reproached for
her lack of liturgical uniformity. The remarkable thing
is rather the stability and permanence which the Anglican
rite has actually shown. In spite of our predominantly
liturgical controversies, the Prayer Book still holds its
ground firmly in the Anglican Communion today, not by
an enforcement of uniformity but by its own inherent
merits.

Any estimate of the Anglican Reformation which does
not give full importance to its liturgical side is a false
estimate. On the doctrinal side, the one original feature
is that which we have noted: that we escaped the danger
of being tied to a theological system. It is further to
be noted that even today the Church of England does
not readily produce comprehensive works of dogmatic
theology. Anglican works of this character spring up
rather in the U.S.A., where the Anglican Communion is
to all appearance one denomination among many, and
to a lesser extent in the Scottish Episcopal Church: they
do not appear in England, where the Church is the Church
of England. We stand before the nation as the Church of
England: that, and not some theological system, is our title.

Hooker († 1600) has a very clear idea of the Church,
as the universal Church of God; in expounding the teaching of the Church of England, he is not in any way
defending her as one sect among many, or expounding
a particular theological system. He gives us this magnifi-
cent sentence, as the conclusion of his treatment of the
two Gospel Sacraments in the *Ecclesiastical Polity* (V. lxvii.
13):

'Thus therefore we see that however men's opinions do

otherwise vary, nevertheless touching Baptism and the Lord's Supper we may with consent of the whole Christian world conclude they are necessary, the one to initiate or begin, the other to consummate or make perfect our life in Christ.'

We note the universal appeal, and the distinction between the universal faith and men's opinions. It is this period, that of Hooker, Andrewes and Laud, that is really the classical period of Anglican theology.[1] The Church still stood on the old basis, as the Church of God in England, and the faith to which these great writers appeal is a common faith.

But after the Civil War a change sets in. It can scarcely be rash to say that it was ultimately on sectarian grounds that the Puritans beheaded King Charles I. However much the king may have infringed the constitutional rights of the Parliament, nevertheless the hereditary kingship is in itself a symbol of the unity of the nation, since the king stands above all parties. King Charles I said in the course of his trial: 'I do stand more for the liberty of my people than any here that come to be my pretended judges.'[2] But the Puritans beheaded him because, so long as the king remained on the throne, the Puritan system was not secure: they acted on the ground of a party allegiance, in the name of a sectarian belief.

When Church and King came back in 1660, the Church at least no longer stood on the old basis. The Puritans were now outside the Church, and thus the Church was compelled to take up a sectarian position in opposition to them. Englishmen now could no longer fully take the Church for granted, as the mother of whom they had

[1] See *Anglicanism*, edited by Paul Elmer More (S.P.C.K., 1935), a book of extracts from the Church writers of the sixteenth and seventeenth centuries.

[2] From the minutes of the trial as given in *England's Black Tribunal* (London, 1747).

been born: it was open to them to choose to belong to the Church or to the Independents. It was now that the denominational or sectarian principle became part and parcel of the national life, as the result of the war which had rent the nation in two. Yet the old principle of catholicity or universality still lay at the basis of the national Church. The subsequent history is the story of its conflict with the denominational principle.

We can trace it in the Tractarian Movement. Keble and Pusey were true Anglicans, and regarded themselves as continuing the Anglican tradition; it is significant that they both said that they had learnt from their mothers to believe in the Real Presence. Newman was never really an Anglican: there is in him, as in some of his successors, a sense that it is his duty to make the Church of England Catholic. Newman was always hankering after an infallible authority to give him a system of belief: this is why he was so upset in 1838 by the first mild censure on the Tracts by Bishop Bagot of Oxford, when Pusey could not understand why he took the matter so seriously.[1] It is also true, however, that all the Tractarians, partly under the influence of the dominant Aristotelianism of Oxford, assumed that Christian dogma must necessarily mean a system of theological belief. When they appeal to the Fathers, they marshal serried ranks of patristic quotations as testimonies to an absolutely true belief. A mark was thus set on the Anglo-Catholic Movement which it has retained ever since, in spite of the influence of Maurice, who represents in this respect the genuine Anglican tradition.

This attitude towards dogma has been a powerful force driving the Anglo-Catholic Movement in the direction of Rome: this on the one side, and on the other the revival of interest in liturgical worship. On this side increased

[1] Faber, *Oxford Apostles*, pp. 385 ff.

X. KELHAM CHAPEL

familiarity with the liturgical tradition of the universal
Church opened up to Anglicans the treasures of the
Roman missal and breviary, and made it impossible to
go on speaking of the Prayer Book as 'our incomparable
liturgy'; while at the same time the 'new devotions' of
the Counter-Reformation exercised, and still exercise, a
fascination upon Anglicans—and, in fact, these develop-
ments of personal piety, such as the method of retreats
and systematic training in mental prayer, contained very
much which is of permanent value. For all these reasons
the Roman Church has exercised an enormous power of
attraction upon Anglicans, even to the extent of making
them ashamed of their own Anglican inheritance. The
Roman Church seemed to be strong in all those ways in
which the Anglican Church was weak.

But we are immediately concerned with the view of
dogma as a system of doctrines. Here the Roman Church
speaks clearly and definitely, where the Anglican Church
seems to be afraid to commit herself. The marvel is, not
that so many Anglo-Catholics have joined the Roman
Church, but that very many more have not done so. The
fact that the great body of Anglo-Catholics have remained
in the Anglican Church shows that in spite of their apparent acceptance of the Roman conception of dogma,
they have had a deep faith in the Church herself and
not merely in a system of belief.

The Anglican basis has been summed up in the Lambeth
Quadrilateral of 1888—a document which came actually
from America, and should perhaps rather have been
called the Chicago Quadrilateral. It lays down as the
minimum basis for reunion the acceptance of the Scriptures, the Apostles' and Nicene Creeds, the two Gospel
sacraments, and the episcopal ministry. The fact that
this is laid down as the basis for reunion means that it
is claimed to represent the indispensable basis of the

Church Universal. It points to the Church, as existing in fact, and as having such and such a tradition, and such and such a structure. It refuses to bind the Church to the scholastic or any other theological system: it ties us, not to the theoretical construction of some theologian such as Aquinas or Calvin, but to the Creeds as confessions of the universal Christian faith, and it connects the Creeds with the Church's life of worship.

It is just this point, which we discussed in our chapter on Dogma, that Roman Catholics and 'authoritarians' of all kinds find it impossible to understand. Thus Mr. Christopher Dawson, in his book on the Oxford Movement,[1] would warn Anglicans to tread in the ways of the Tractarians, and beware of the 'modernism' of *Lux Mundi* and modern Anglican scholarship.

There is a confusion in this view. Modern historical and scientific study makes it impossible to hold certain beliefs about the Bible which form part of the older theological systems. But 'Modernism' is the name for a movement which, while using the newer methods of study, interprets them in the light of a philosophy of life which is fundamentally humanistic; having little sense of God's sovereign action, it has confidence in the power of human reason to solve all mysteries, and views Christianity as a human movement of religion. But the same methods of study are equally used by those who believe in the reality of God and in God's redemptive action expressed in history, and tied down therefore to certain historical facts. The difference lies in a radically different conception of God. It can be said quite confidently that modern Anglo-Catholics, with few exceptions, are not Modernists. They hold to the old Anglican basis, believing it to be the catholic basis of the Church Universal.

[1] Dawson, *The Spirit of the Oxford Movement* (Sheed and Ward, 1933), pp. 135–42.

But why does the Church of England openly tolerate Liberal theology, and allow those to hold office in the Church who deny the bodily resurrection of Christ—this denial being, as we have seen,[1] the symptom and the result of a belief about God fundamentally different from that of the Bible and the Church? We cannot evade this question, for it is much in the public mind both in England and abroad, more in fact than is warranted by the actual influence of Modernists in the Church. An answer to the question has been given in *Oecumenica* as follows:[2]

'With regard to the Modernist Movement the Church of England has adopted a breadth and a pliability (*souplesse*) which is to some a stumbling-block, but which testifies to her faith in the unconquerable power of Truth. The ordinary Anglican is firmly attached to the traditional Christian doctrine, but he is convinced that in periods of transition such as our own it is wiser to tolerate certain imprudences of language and even certain dangerous doctrinal rashnesses, than arbitrarily to impose silence by measures of external discipline, and so fetter the freedom of the Holy Spirit.'

The present writer took upon himself part-responsibility for this statement: but he is no longer fully happy about it. The utterances of Modernism, as represented by the *Modern Churchman*, are not those of men beset with intellectual difficulties and hazarding imprudent hypotheses: they reflect a dogmatism which is satisfied that it has comprehended all that orthodoxy has to say, and propounds an alternative teaching. To say less than this is really to be untruthful.

On the other hand, the passage from *Oecumenica* rightly expresses the Anglican method. Why do we not excommunicate heretics? It is not only because we are tied and

[1] p. 107, *supra*.
[2] *Oecumenica*, Vol. I, No. 1, article 'Notre But,' pp. 3, 4.

bound by the Establishment, for the Anglican Communion overseas ordinarily acts in the same way. It is partly because when there is a heresy-trial, the heretic has to be met, not with the voice of the Church of God herself, but with the interpretation of it that her doctors give: it is a case of 'my doctrine against yours', and the orthodox statement is not always above criticism. It was for this reason that F. D. Maurice was continually rushing to the help of heretics whose teaching he detested, because he detested the spirit and temper of their accusers almost more. It is partly also because of the danger of breaking the bruised reed: for many Modernists are on the move. They preach, and they find that Liberal theology has no Gospel for the saving of souls: their own experience teaches them the vanity of a humanistic religion. A policy of excommunication would block the road for these pilgrim souls.

The greatest danger is that which arises from the use of conciliatory phrases which cover up falsehoods. It is the urgent duty of both sides, both Orthodox and Modernists, to make the issues clear, and all the more urgent because not only the Church of England, but the whole reunion movement is concerned. In fact the present situation is so unstable that something is bound to happen. In Germany it has happened already; *proximus ardet Ucalegon*: the challenge of the Totalitarian state has driven a wedge between the opposition pastors who hold the orthodox faith, and the 'German Christians' whose faith is in the power of man—in this case the German man—to achieve his destiny. The same issue is likely to become actual in England before long in some form. When it does, the mildness of the Church of England will be justified by the fact that not a few who are called Modernists will come out on the other side.

But Anglicans are ill-advised when they claim, as they

sometimes do, that the Church of England as she stands is the best available expression of Catholicism.[1] The plea may or may not be capable of being sustained: it is the plea itself that is wrong. For those who believe in the Church of God, and are therefore bound to acknowledge the 'catholicity of the Holy Spirit' working out His purpose in all the parts of divided Christendom, such comparisons are unfitting: they assume that Christendom consists of a multitude of rival denominations or sects, among which the individual is to choose that which seems to him to be the best. The Church of England has never made such a claim. She has never claimed to be the whole of the Church of God, nor has she ever claimed to be 'the true Church', the Church of the Saints, in the Donatist and Puritan sense. What she has claimed is that, in her limited sphere as a national Church, she exhibits in her character and structure the lineaments of the Church of God.

We are looking for the principles of the Church Universal. Believing that the Church of God actually exists, and is at once Divine and human, we are bound to recognize that the treasure is in earthen vessels, and that the embodiment of the Divine element is imperfect and incomplete.

It is therefore a false assumption that the Church of God must needs be perfect, a perfectly ordered system. Both Roman Catholic and Eastern Orthodox apologists show a tendency in different ways to minimize the element of human imperfection. The obvious shortcomings of the Church of England are to some extent a safeguard against this: it is not humanly possible to deify our archdeacons and canons and diocesan machinery, and we are compelled to look deeper if we are to find the principle of the Church Universal in the visible Church.

[1] As does Prof. N. P. Williams in *Northern Catholicism*, p. 230.

Nor can we rightly give our whole allegiance to any party-programme or cause. No programme of social reform, and no party-programme such as that of the Anglo-Catholic party, as a party, can be simply identified with the cause of God or with the whole purpose of God manifested in the Church. The Anglo-Catholic party ought not really to be a party at all, since its whole aim is to seek the meaning of the Church as the Church of God.

We are looking for the interpretation and embodiment of God's meaning for our life and for the world. We men pose our problems and ask our questions. The answer is in God and in God's will, in Christ and His saving work, and, somehow, in the Body of Christ which is His Church. All that we have said hitherto points us to seek in the worship of the Church the clearest expression of what the Church really is. The Christian liturgy, we have seen, is a kind of meeting-point, in which all the elements of the Church are seen in their right perspective. Scriptures and creeds hold a central place in the liturgy; their liturgical use shows that the true meaning of dogma is seen in the setting of worship. The personal religion of the individual soul is here seen in its true setting, when the individual takes his place in the life of the Body. The fact that the Church service is the assembly of the Church of God shows the true significance of the hierarchical structure of the Church.

Our business is therefore to disentangle so far as we may the essential principles of the Church's worship and life, and to see these in relation to the actual life of men and the order of human society. We have not only to consider what we do with Christ in the Church, but what He wills to do with us in the street. The Church has indeed the key of the street. Too often she seems inclined to use it to lock herself in.

CHAPTER VIII

FAITH AND LIFE

*

I. THE REALITY OF GOD

Christian worship is in the first place and above all the worship of God, the acknowledgement by the rational creature of the sovereignty of the Creator to whom he belongs and for whose glory he exists. With worship goes confession of faith in God the Creator, the Redeemer, the Life-giver: 'Blessed be the Lord God of Israel, for He hath visited and redeemed His people.' This worship or adoration is the collective act of the Church, and is the confession of the common faith with regard to the foundation on which the universe and human society rests: it is also the personal act of each individual, the charter of his freedom as a child of God. The note of adoration runs through the liturgy: 'Thou only art holy, Thou only art the Lord': 'O come, let us worship and fall down, and kneel before the Lord our Maker.' Wherever it is lost, and the temple becomes a preaching-house and praise gives way to edification, worship has fallen to a sub-Christian level.

The adoration of God's glory is in itself a confession of the creaturely limitation of the man who adores, just as the prayer 'Come Holy Ghost, our souls inspire' is an acknowledgement of man's helplessness and need. For this reason the worship of the transcendent God does not involve an unwarranted metaphysical dogmatism. The act of praise is an acknowledgement that God's glory exceeds our power to praise Him: God is (in this, the correct sense of the word) incomprehensible; *Quia major omni laude, nec laudare sufficis*. Likewise God's purpose for our lives exceeds our understanding of it: 'What I do thou knowest not now, but thou shalt know hereafter.'

The worship of God is the deliverance of man from what the Bible calls idolatry: 'Thou shalt have no other Gods but Me. Thou shalt not make to thyself any graven image. . . . Thou shalt not bow down to them nor worship them'—whether the graven image be Power, Success, or Money and what money can buy, or Comfort, or the objects of fleshly lust: thou shalt not bow down and worship the Self, even in the more refined forms of self-worship, such as moralism and stoical self-righteousness, or again in the idolatry of the collective Ego, in a party, class, nation or clique. The individual is perpetually seeking to find in himself the end of his existence and the object of his worship, and mankind is perpetually seeking to make for human society some centre of unity other than the unity which God has made for it. This, precisely this, is Original Sin. There are only two things in the universe that man can ultimately live for: God or himself. Christ died on the Cross and rose again to save man from himself and redeem him to God.

With such a statement of the meaning of worship and faith, we have advanced far beyond the difficulties of intellectual belief which have hindered so many from worship and prayer. It has seemed to them that the act of worship involved an unjustified metaphysical dogmatism, a profession of theological opinions from which reverence would lead one to shrink: that agnosticism and suspense of judgement is a more fitting attitude than a dogmatic belief in God:

> 'There is more faith in honest doubt,
> Believe me, than in half the creeds.'

And then it has been felt that, however uncertain we might be on these transcendental matters, at least we stood on solid ground in the fact that in Christian worship we were sharing in a great upward movement of human religion. This uncertainty about God and trust in human religion was seen in the Catholic Modernists of the last generation and remains characteristic of Anglican and other Modernists today. An article appeared recently entitled 'Prayer without Theism',[1] in which the author sought to meet the difficulties of the adolescent with regard to belief in God by exhibiting the psychological side of prayer, and showing that a great deal of prayer can still go on without any definite belief in God at all.[2]

We have seen that an element of agnosticism is involved in Christian worship, which reflects the scholastic formula that God is 'incomprehensible'.[3] But the difficulty, as stated, depends on the characteristic limitations of Liberal theology with regard to belief in God. In the faith of the Bible and the Church, God is the living God; He is creative and spontaneous Agape. But to the whole liberal and humanistic tradition God is not the Seeker but the Sought, not Agape but the Object of Eros. God is the 'Totality of Values'. The highest human shades off into the Divine. The phrase 'the will of God' is regularly used to mean that which *we* are to do—since our ideals of action, in so far as they are high ideals, are Divine—and not in the

---

[1] *Theology*, May 1934, p. 254.

[2] Cf. the following, from the 'This England' column of the *New Statesman* (10 Nov. 1934): 'Would any one like to send out Coué thoughts for the success of a girl who has just finished the opening chapter of her first novel?—HER MOTHER. Advt. in *Morning Post*.' This represents the final degradation of Intercession, when it has been separated from Christian faith and the fellowship of Christian worship, and has come to be treated as a psychological method for promoting human well-being.

[3] For the meaning of this easily misunderstood word, see p. 91, *supra*.

sense of God's own sovereign action, that which He wills and does on His own account. It is not too much to say that the question of belief in God becomes almost an academic question: since the values of truth, beauty and good are the object of human striving and endeavour, it can be matter of debate whether these values must be regarded as summed up in a personal God.

Modern theology, however, exposes with relentless clearness the difference between such teaching and that of the Bible. Karl Barth proclaims God's transcendence and sovereignty: Bishop Aulén teaches the dramatic aspect of God's work of atonement, as a real conflict between the redeeming Love of God and the evil that has dominion over man. All this helps to clear the issues which Liberal theology had confused. The doubts which have tortured so many souls, whether or not they could honestly profess belief in God at all, were really due to a large extent to the fact that Liberal theology had robbed the name of God of most of its meaning, and was at variance with the teaching of the Bible.

The ultimate issue, to which every man must in the last resort answer Yes or No, is the question whether he will worship God or the Self. The question is expressed in intellectual forms: but the ultimate answer is given in life, by the will. It is the question whether each man will acknowledge a truth and a good which is not himself, or will make his own views and his own good opinion of himself the ultimate standard of reference.

It is a universal question. The pagan Socrates answered it truthfully according to his light. It was the central faith of his life that a truth existed, independently of his mind; that this truth might be known in part, but that he himself could not own or possess it. Thus it was that he justified Apollo's assertion that he was the wisest of men; he was aware of the limitations of his knowledge. To us

186

the Gospel of God has come, as the announcement that God's truth and God's righteousness has been manifested in Christ, the Word uttered by God: and each man is compelled to answer Yes or No.

Of course there are intellectual difficulties; it is bound to be so, since for us belief in God must take form in a human conception of God, and the Divine Revelation has taken place in history. It is the business of theology to disentangle the essential from the non-essential. A wrong theology may confuse the issues and make the way of faith difficult. There can be, as we have seen, a wrong doctrine of God; elsewhere there may be wrong conceptions of the meaning of revelation, which will treat the truth of Christianity as standing or falling with the literal interpretation of the account of the creation in Genesis or of the story of Jonah and the whale, or with some particular theology of the Atonement. We have to find our way through the intellectual difficulties of faith as best we may, and be thankful that there is sufficient light to walk by.

The issue which must be fought out in each soul takes form on a larger scale in human society. Just as each man must ultimately choose between the worship of God and the idolatry of the ego, so on the larger stage the issue is becoming clearer year by year, between the Kingdom of God and the Kingdom of Man. On the one side stands the Church, bearing witness by her scriptures, creeds, sacraments, and teaching to a supernatural Gospel, the sovereignty of God, and His redemptive work. On the other stands a belief in the power of man to achieve well-being by the spread of education, culture and humanitarian ideals. On this basis it is still possible to find room for religion as an embellishment of human life, and a means of providing motive power for the kingdom of man; this religion will not be the old Christianity, but a liberal-

187

ized Christianity of some sort, accommodated to the demand of the age.

In this country the issues are still much confused, though they are rapidly becoming clearer. They have become clear in Russia. Communism is apparently a revolt against the bourgeois civilization of Western Europe, which has been based on humanistic ideals: but it is in reality the logical carrying out of the ideals of Humanism. It is the supreme expression of faith in the ability of man to save himself. It calls men to abandon the selfish covetousness of Capitalism and its pursuit of individual gain, and combine to use the resources of nature and the new powers which invention has given in an organized economic life whose sole aim is the prosperity of the community.

The anti-God propaganda of Communism is therefore not an accident but part of its essence. Plato believed in the real existence of God and truth, independently of man: for him, the Idea of the Good is laid up in the heavens. Hebrew prophets proclaimed God as the Judge of men. Christianity has received the inheritance of both, and is bound to proclaim an eternal righteousness of God by which man is judged. But Communism in seeking the well-being of the State cannot permit a reference to an external standard of righteousness: in bringing men into unity as servants of the State, it cannot permit them to have ideas of their own about an external order which is superior to the State.

Similarly, the issues in Germany are becoming clear. We may well be cautious about accepting the criticisms of the Nazi régime so commonly made in this country, in the name of the Liberal ideal of individual freedom; for with all its faults, the Nazi state has actualized the unity of the German nation, as the Liberal-democratic régime which preceded it was powerless to do. When we have

said this, we may go on to say that there is here, no less
than in Communism, an intense faith in the kingdom of
man, to be realized through the working out of the des-
tinies of the German nation. The true object of worship
and inspirer of devotion, for millions of Germans, is
Germany: not the One God and Father of the Christian
faith, but the magnified corporate ego of the nation.[1]

We ought to expect that the trial of faith which has
come upon Russia and Germany, and made the Churches
in those lands into martyr-churches, will come in some
form or other upon us in England. The issue between the
Kingdom of God on the one hand and the kingdom of
man on the other will become plain.[2] When the trial
comes, it will become plain to all that Christianity stands
for something more than personal religion—if this were
all, Christianity might be derided as 'dope for the people',
but might still be tolerated as harmless. Actually Christianity stands for a view of human society as finding its
centre in God; and that is something that the kingdom
of man cannot permanently tolerate.

There is a remarkable prophecy in F. D. Maurice's
Kingdom of Christ, written nearly 100 years ago, but now
in process of being fulfilled. He has been speaking of that
part of the world which, having once been Christian,
turned Mohammedan, and goes on to speak of the rest
of Christendom:

'Another portion of it [Christendom] has declared that
they see in the Cross the symbol of love triumphing
through suffering, in the Crescent the symbol only of
power claiming dominion over weakness; that the first

[1] Since the situation in Germany is changing so rapidly, it is
necessary to add that whatever is said about Germany in this book
was written not later than October 1934.

[2] For a forecast of the lines which this development is likely to
take, see C. Dawson, 'Religion and the Totalitarian State' in *The
Criterion*, Oct. 1934.

is a bond of mutual fellowship among members of a suffering race, the other the pledge of a universal slavery. That the spirit of the Cross prevails very little in the nations which still profess to honour it, that self-sacrifice is very generally and very systematically denied to be the law of our being, most of us are ready with shame to confess. And therefore the expectation is surely very reasonable, that the experiment which was so successful in the East will be made, under other conditions, in the West. We have had many preparatory Antichrists, many sovereigns reigning by the strength of mind and will, and scorning all other right—why should we doubt that *this* image also will be yet more completely manifested?

'May God preserve those who live in the day when it is manifested, and when the world goes wondering after it! In that day when intellect and will shall be utterly crushed under the car of the idol which they have set up: in that day when the poor man shall cry, and there shall be no helper, may God teach His saints to proclaim these words to the sons of men: *He was born of the Virgin: He suffered under Pontius Pilate: He was crucified, dead and buried: He rose again on the third day: He ascended on high: He sitteth on the right hand of God: He shall come to judge the quick and the dead.* May they be enabled to say, *This* is our God: we have waited for Him.' [1]

'Thine is the kingdom, the power and the glory, for ever and ever, Amen.' A correspondent of the *Church Times* (17 Aug. 1934) writes movingly of the profound emotion of this affirmation at a German Evangelical service.

'*Die Reich*, meaning the worldly state, is a word so continually upon the lips of Germans nowadays that it was a relief and a consolation to use the same word with a different significance, to pray *Dein Reich komme*, and

[1] *The Kingdom of Christ*, Vol. II, p. 13.

affirm with this congregation in distress that it was God's and so also was the power and the glory—always.'

II. THE INCARNATION AND SOCIAL LIFE

The Incarnation of the Son of God claims the Kingdom for God over the whole of human life. It is the manifestation of God's goodness in the flesh; it involves the redemption of the body, and therefore also of the social relations of the life lived in the body, and of the whole social, economic and political structure. God has established His Kingdom, a kingdom not *of* this world, but very much *in* the world. It is wrong to assume that the concern of Christianity is only with the religious life of the individual, and the endeavour of a select circle of devout people to live a sanctified life and attain an individual perfection: it is the denial of the Incarnation. The method of the Incarnation means that the separation of 'sacred' and 'secular' is broken down. Christianity is deeply concerned with 'secular' activities of every kind: not so that the sacred becomes secularized, but so that the secular activities are redeemed to God.[1] It is impossible that he who loves not his brother whom he has seen, should love God whom he has not seen. It is impossible because of the Incarnation; the will of the God whom we worship comes to us through our relations with the common humanity which God has taken on Himself. Inasmuch as I have not served and helped one of the least of these, I did it not unto Him.

In every parish the church building stands as God's House. It is not that the church building is exclusively God's House, and that all the other buildings, factories, shops and public-houses in the parish belong to the devil, but that the earth is the Lord's: by the existence of a house

[1] See O. C. Quick, *The Ground of Faith and the Chaos of Thought* (1931), p. 38.

called God's House, these others are all claimed for Him. So the Lord's Day at the beginning of each week claims all the other days and their occupations for God's glory: and times of prayer are set apart, both for the Church service, and by individuals for private prayer, not to imply that those times only are given to God, but to claim for Him all the rest of the day.

Similarly, the clergy are set apart for the service of God in the Church, not that they alone may be holy, nor that they may be holy for themselves, but for the sake of the people whom they are sent to serve. The same principle applies to the threefold consecration of the Religious Life: its object is not a private and individual pursuit of perfection, but the good of the whole Body. The members of religious orders are called to Poverty, not as if the possession and administration of wealth were evil in itself—if so, how could Jesus have worked in a carpenter's shop?— but on the contrary, that the existence within the social order of groups of men and women, who have freely surrendered the right to possess and administer wealth, may help all the members of the Body to escape from making the pursuit of wealth into an end. They are called to celibacy, not as if any slur whatever were thereby cast on the holiness of marriage, but on the contrary to bear witness to the redemption of the sex-instinct in marriage as well as in celibacy, to be the instrument of the spirit. They are called to obedience, not as a way of escape from the responsibility of making decisions, but in order to help all men to escape from enslavement to the self-instinct and to ambition, and to live their lives in obedience to God.

The same principle is seen in a hundred other ways. In the Church service we make use of the common things of daily life: we use water in a solemn ritual washing; we use bread and wine, we eat and drink before God; we

XI. ANTONIUSKIRCHE, BASEL

read aloud, we sing in chorus, we perform ordered movements: we light candles, we make fire and a smoke—all these things are done in church in order to signify that the corresponding actions in daily life are redeemed to God. The fact that the Eucharist is the Lord's Supper makes the family dinner also a holy meal.

In actual fact, we Christians sin against the Gospel of the Incarnation by our slowness to recognize the significance of these things. We are fools and slow of heart to believe: we are even ready to acquiesce in the Church becoming a preserve for the devout instead of being a home for the people. It is indeed not so easy to lay down rules of ethics and draw up a programme of social action: but the first and the chief thing is that we should so learn to believe in the Incarnation that we learn to see more and more clearly the contrast between the actual and the ideal which is the truly real.

Here is part of the ideal : that all those who live in one place should eat and drink together before God. The Son of God has taken upon Himself our common human nature ; therefore those who are living a social life together during the week ought to meet on the Lord's Day to celebrate the Lord's Sacrifice and partake of the Lord's Supper, and so consecrate their daily life at home and work and play. If a family or an individual is absent, it ought to be felt that they are missed. Such an ideal is very far from our actual practice; we have little social life. Dwellers in villages, where every one knows every one else, are for this reason happier than dwellers in towns; the towns are for the most part aggregations of unrelated families and individuals. The task of the Church in the future will be to re-create a social life.

This common social life must include all. A pathetic story was told to me once, by an Anglo-Catholic who had been invited by some Methodist friends to help run a boys' camp. The camp, as things turned out, had a strongly spiritual side, and he learnt afterwards that they had thought of holding a communion service at the end. But they could not ask him to partake, and on the other hand they felt it to be intolerable to hold a communion service at which his place would be empty. So they went without their communion service. The story is a particularly sad illustration of the anomaly of the divisions of Christendom. But those Methodists had got hold of an aspect of the Christian sacrament in a way that puts us Anglicans to shame. We shall not recover it till we recover the ideal of the Parish Eucharist, of which we shall speak in the next chapter—till in each parish the chief Sunday service is the offering of the Eucharist with the communion of the people.

To take another important illustration: we may well ask ourselves whether the usual methods of preparation for Confirmation are not too exclusively religious. The boy assistant at the garage comes, desiring to be confirmed; he is likely to be given a good and careful preparation, consisting of a series of instructions on Christian doctrine, the Church service, and his private prayers. This is all very good, but is it certain that we are beginning at the right end? Has not the whole scheme of preparation rather the air of adding a fresh interest to the interests which the boy already has—or at least, since he has been attending Sunday School and Catechism for years, a specialization in this interest, in order that the concentration of his mind on the religious department of life may exercise a healthy influence on the rest? Ought we not perhaps to be working out a different technique of preparation for Confirmation, beginning with the boy's actual interests, his home, his football club, his work, and showing him how it is just *these* that are to be laid on God's altar and redeemed? We might show him the place of his little

194

daily job in the social structure; how the things that he uses in his daily work, petrol, oil and machinery, are God's things, used by God's children; what the Sacrament of Baptism teaches about the people who use them, that they are human beings and not wage-slaves or cogs in an economic machine, that God has a meaning for their lives: what the Sacrament of Marriage means in relation to his parents and his own future courtship and marriage, as the declaration that God has a meaning for each human family; and how in the Sacrament of the Eucharist he is to lay on God's altar all his interests and activities, and his relations to his fellows, learning thus the meaning of Intercession as the realization of the common life which he shares with them as a member of God's family, and in Holy Communion receive back from Christ all his interests and activities redeemed and transformed, as part of the interests and activities of God's universal family.

It is for the parish clergy to work out the technique of such a course of preparation: one who is not a parish priest cannot presume to say exactly how it would be done in detail, whether for instance it would require a series of individual conversations, or whether it could be done with a class. But the governing idea of the whole is clear. The preparation must be more than an intensive training in religion; it must start from actual life and show the way to the redemption of actual life.

III. SOCIAL IDEALISM

But what is going to happen to the Confirmation candidate, plunged into the moral confusion of the industrial world? The Industrial Revolution has borne its fruit in an atomistic order of society. The working-man, theoretically free to sell his labour wherever he chooses, has become a wage-slave; new methods of production, forced on industry by competition which is now international and world-wide, have replaced the craftsman by the machine; the standardization and mechanization of industry have robbed labour of most of its dignity, and have thrown on the dole the millions whose labour is not required. That the present state of things is very deeply contrary to Christian ideals is obvious. But what is the Christian approach to the problem? Ought Christians to be making plans for an improved social order, a social order which could be called Christian? Ought we, perhaps, to be Communists?

Because it is so clear that the religion of the Incarnation is concerned with the whole life, ideal schemes for the reorganization of society seem to have a great attraction for the ecclesiastical mind. We have had a noble succession of Christian Socialists: today we have a crusade of Christian Communists. Communism has set out to tackle in earnest the evils of modern society, to seek to remedy the irregular distribution of wealth, and overcome the sin of covetousness; to make the producer feel that he has a share in the social order, not as a mere tool, a wage-slave, working for the advantage of others, but as a member of a body, having a stake in the community. It is no wonder that the youth in every land feel the attraction of Communism, and go hankering after it. And would not such an order of society correspond more fully to Christian ideals than the present order? Ought not then the Church to come out boldly with a social programme, and take in hand the reordering of society, building up its own doctrine of what redeemed human society ought to be, and leading mankind in the direction of Utopia? It will be well to number our headings for the sake of clearness.

(1) It would be necessary, of course, to agree first of all about the programme, to agree as to the precise course of action to be followed. There is a great deal to be said

for experiment on communistic lines. But the Fascist experiment is violently opposed to Communism; in Nazi Germany we see a great national movement, which it is wrong and foolish to meet with mere condemnation, as it would be foolish to ignore the success already achieved. There is much to be said for Social Credit; here is a scheme which promises to solve many of our social evils and to restore economic prosperity. What is the relation of these schemes to one another? Can the Church, can the clergy, judge between them?

This at least is plain. The grace of orders does not confer on the clergy, nor does baptism confer on the ordinary Christian, a clearer insight into economic problems than is possessed by non-Christian students of economics. The question of social credit must be discussed and decided as an economic problem; there can no more be a Christian view of the matter than a Christian solution of a problem in mathematics. There exists, therefore, a well-founded dislike and suspicion of 'politics from the pulpit'. The business of the priest is to consider all these questions from the theological side: in economics and politics he deserves to be listened to, like any one else, in so far as he is well informed and has learnt to think clearly.

(2) The Church's own contribution is 'theological'— that is, she is called to view all these questions in the light of God's meaning for human life, in the light of the Incarnation and of the fulfilment of the Incarnation in the Church. The Church sees man as called to be God's child and a member of God's Universal Family. Hence the Church must always think of man as a personal being, having personal relations with God and with other men. She can never be content to think of men in the abstract or in the mass, as a bureaucracy always does, as so many cases', or as having such-and-such a potential output of labour. Thus, for instance, a street of houses is run up by

a jerry-builder, or a block of flats is built by a 'philan-thropic' organization. But the parish priest goes visiting in that street and among those flats, and he is concerned with the people who live in them, with each family as a unit having its own family life, and with the welfare of each soul.

The typical pronouncements of Christian prophets about the evils of the social order deal with the de-personalizing influence of modern conditions of life; they condemn luxury, because it cuts the wealthy off from their fellow-men, and the industrial organization because it deals with men as mere 'hands', and robs them of their dignity as human beings and of the opportunity to put something of themselves into their labour. Always the situation is envisaged not in the abstract, not in terms of statistics, but in terms of the life which men, children of God, are living.

The peril of the Christian social idealist is that he will forget this. Schemes for social reorganization deal with men in the mass, with the general conditions of life. And the Christian who occupies himself with these is in danger of overlooking just that contribution which he as a Christian ought to bring. He can envisage an ideal scheme and, because it promises increased prosperity and material well-being, call upon Christians to support it. But if he forgets that the concern of the Church is ulti-mately with persons and personal relations in a common life, and comes to think of living souls as cannon fodder, as objects for his own benevolent care, he is missing the essentially Christian view of the matter.

(3) But Christianity does not deal with men merely as individuals, merely as souls to be saved and cared for: it deals with them as members one of another, and incor-porates them into a Church whose life is based upon a common faith. This common faith need not mean that

they all learn the same catechism, and repeat the same dogmatic formulae: it is possible, for instance, for an Anglican and a Swedish Lutheran to meet, and find that amid all external differences they share the same fundamental presuppositions, the same view of God and the world. It is with this that the common faith of Christians is concerned; with the things that are said in many different ways in the Bible and in the prayers of the liturgy, and expressed in the actions of the Church's worship.

It is the absence of such a common faith that makes the awful uncertainty about the things that matter, which is evident in our novels, our newspapers, our films and drama. I read lately a detective story, one of the *Inspector Frost* series, and enjoyed it: I found afterwards that the author was a Christian. But the majority of the books which the public reads are confused and uncertain about the things that matter: the author does not know whether there is a right and a wrong, and has lost the sense of the sacredness of marriage and of birth and of death.

There can be no true common life without a common faith: and here is the real tragedy of the modern world, the root of its social disorganization, and the cause of the insolubility of economic and international problems. The root of the difficulty is not material. Given a common understanding about the things with which theology deals, there is an ample supply of raw materials in the world, and ample machinery for making them into commodities, and ample intelligence for solving the problems of distribution and consumption and the political problems of the relations of men to one another in society: but it is this common understanding which is lacking.

There is in the Old Testament an ancient myth of the Tower of Babel. Men set to work to build a great tower, and the top of it was to reach unto heaven. But it failed because of the confusion of tongues, because those who would build the tower were not able to understand one another.

The Chorus say in *The Rock*:

'You, have you built well, have you forgotten the corner-stone?
Talking of right relations of men, but not of relations of men to God.
"Our citizenship is in heaven": yes, but that is the model and type for your citizenship upon earth.'

And again:

O world! forget your glories and your quarrels,
'Forget your groups and your misplaced ambitions,
We speak to you as individual men;
As individuals alone with God.
Alone with God, you first learn brotherhood with men.' [1]

(4) Our Lord in the Temptation on the Mount rejected the conception of a political messianism, which was the accepted hope among the Pharisees in His day; the Messiah was expected to establish an ideal kingdom of righteousness and peace. He knew that such a kingdom would fail to deal with the root of evil in human nature; it would be built on the sand, not on the rock; it might be a kingdom of man, but it could not be the Kingdom of God. Therefore He attacks directly the root of evil, in man's soul, and the Kingdom of God which He proclaims is radically apocalyptic and other-worldly; as it comes to man from God, as God's gift (Luke xii. 32), so it is to reach its perfection only in the world to come. But the Gospels resolutely reject a one-sided apocalypticism; they are at once other-worldly and this-worldly. As the Messiah who is come from God and in God's name is incarnate in the flesh, so the Kingdom of God is present in this

[1] *The Rock*, by T. S. Eliot (Faber & Faber, 1934), pp. 20, 46.

world as a Divine fact, and operates by transforming the lives of men and their social relations to one another.

There is no false optimism about human nature in the Gospels or in Christianity. Throughout the story the Messiah is represented as in conflict with radical evil, and at the last He is crucified. The crucifixion of Jesus means that evil is a real fact. In the words of Archbishop Söderblom:

'The most awful thing in the death of Jesus is that it was brought about by men who were following, or believed themselves to be following, good and honourable reasons for their action. Men of various classes, the guardians of religion and public morals and of the order of society itself, united to crucify Jesus. They were men like you and me. That is why we keep Good Friday.' [1]

Therefore all schemes for an ideal social order which rest on a fundamental optimism with regard to human nature, an assumption that man is able to achieve his own salvation, and a failure to reckon with the radical evil in man, are fantasies out of relation with the real facts of life. And yet, if the Church were to withdraw herself from the world, and cease to labour for the up-building of the social order, she would be false to the principle of the Incarnation; for the Christian redemption is the redemption of the body and therefore of the social relations of men. Only, she may not identify any social or political programme with the cause of God; for the Kingdom of God cannot be built on any other foundation than that which He Himself has laid.

This being so, it is not surprising that the Church should be constantly reproached by social idealists with being content to make the best of the existing order; and it often looks as if the reproach were deserved. The self-denying labours of good people can even do harm, by making an

[1] *The Mystery of the Cross*, pp. 47–8.

evil system of employment seem tolerable; the virtues of Christians are expended upon patching up a social system which perhaps had better be allowed to fall to pieces.

But if this is so, it is because it ought to be so. The reproach is best met by being freely admitted. Whatever new social order may emerge must grow out of the old; Utopia cannot suddenly appear from nowhere. And as the Church is bound to believe that our citizenship which is in heaven is 'the model and type for our citizen-hip upon earth', so the deepest contribution which the Church can make to society must spring out of her life as the Church of God—that is, the life which finds its expression in the structure of the Church and in her liturgy. Our next chapter on the Church service ought therefore to give at least some hints of what this contribution may be.

The Church cannot identify herself with any scheme of social reformation. But in so far as she is true to herself, she is compelled to criticize the present order far more rad-ically than do those whose minds are fixed upon material well-being. Poverty, bad housing, the wrong distribution of wealth, are material evils; and, because they are evils, they must be fought against. But it is the function of the Church to keep the mind of the community alive to the spiritual side: to such evils as the lack of social life in our land, the harm which is done to the rich by the sin of luxury and the class-distinction which separates them from their fellow-men, and the evil effects of unem-ployment, not merely in material poverty but in the degradation of mind and soul.

There is a stinging text of the prophet Amos, in which he condemns those who care for their own comforts, but 'are not grieved for the affliction of Joseph' (Amos vi. 6). It is easy to reproach Christians with complacency and lack of concern about the evils of society; the reproach is easily overdone, for Christians do care about these things. Nevertheless, we have as much need as Israel of old to listen to the voice of the prophet.

Only, be it remembered, in giving his social message the prophet is not adding to the Christian Gospel something that was not there before, but simply reminding Christians of the corollaries of the Incarnation. We heard in an earlier chapter the Anaphora of St. Gregory, in which the priest speaks in the name of humanity.[1] In this spirit we are to learn more and more to use the Psalms, the *Kyrie eleison*, the General Confession, not merely applying them to ourselves, but using them in order to share the common burden of the humanity of which we form a part.[2] As Christians thus learn to exercise their priestly functions of intercession for the world, they will learn how to bring their practical contribution for the healing of its wounds. There is much to do, much to build up, much to restore: and much that the Church can do, in proportion as the Church fulfils its calling as the Church of God, and the Christian learns what it is to be a Christian.

---

[1] *Supra*, pp. 70–2.

[2] Cf. the following words of Prof. Berdyaev: 'Bolshevism appeared and conquered in Russia because I am what I am, because I lacked real spiritual strength, the strength of faith that moves mountains. Bolshevism is my sin, my fault. It is a trial which God has sent me. The suffering which it has inflicted on me is an expiation of my guilt, my sin—of our common guilt and common sin. All are responsible for all.'

'Communism should have a very special significance for Christians, for it is a reminder and denouncement of an unfulfilled duty.'

—N. Berdyaev, *The Russian Revolution* ('Essays in Order', Sheed and Ward, 1931), pp. xxii, 54. See the whole of both passages.

CHAPTER IX

THE CHURCH SERVICE

★

I. THE CHURCH

Mr. Maurice Reckitt [1] gives a remarkable illustration of the manner in which one parish congregation came to learn what the Church is:

'A parish priest found that members of his congregation were falling off from communion, precisely because the falsehoods imposed upon them as a condition of their employment made it impossible for them to approach the altar with a clear conscience. Was the priest to absolve them from responsibility as a means of recovering them for the central act of Christian worship? The danger of blunting loyalty to truth seemed far too great for such a course to be followed. What then could be done? The community of the faithful must come to the rescue with a corporate act—the rescue not merely of those of their number whose livelihood was at stake, but of the Christian witness which was imperilled in their dilemma. The employment must be thrown up, and the priest would tell the employer why; the hardship involved must be spread over the whole congregation, and a fund collected, with pre-eminent appropriateness at the Holy Sacrifice, to provide against the contingency and any similar ones that might follow it. The plan was put into operation with the full concurrence of the laity, and "a real sense of corporate responsibility developed in

---

[1] In his book, *Faith and Society*, pp. 451 ff.

204

the congregation. In fact the congregation became a church."

' "The congregation became a church." Have we not perhaps in this phrase the cue to what is arresting the capacity of religion to make its significance plain to an age helpless to move forward without the illumination and the power which the Faith is required to bestow? Has the Church become a collection of congregations whose members resort to a sacred building periodically to satisfy their religious instincts, as they resort to art galleries or concert rooms to satisfy their aesthetic instincts? To say as much would be to overstate the fact, for corporate life is assuredly not dead in our British parishes. . . . But this solidarity is turned inwards in devotion, it does not express itself outwards in a clear-cut and defined attitude to the issues and challenges of the age.'

In quoting this inspiring instance, it is necessary to guard against the suggestion that this particular procedure is held up as a model to be imitated everywhere. The point of the story is that it is an instance of the sort of thing that may be expected to happen when Christians are learning seriously what their Christianity means. When they learn what they really are—not a group of timid souls with religious ideals, but members of Christ's Body and participators in God's purpose of salvation, they can no longer stand on the defensive. They know that they have a mission to fulfil: they are in the world to bear witness that there is a God and a Saviour, and that man's true nature is not to be a de-humanized slave of the industrial machine, but to be a human being and a child of God.

The false conception from which we have to make good our escape is summed up in the two terms 'a congregation' and 'a service'. The word 'congregation', instead of bearing the sense which it has in the Bible and in the Articles, is used to mean an aggregation of persons met together for religious exercises: 'a service' is the name for the religious exercises in which they take part. It may be 'a nice service' or 'a dull service': the Holy Communion is the most sacred service, but there is no particular relation between it and other services, and no standard of judgement as between one service and another, except the degree in which the worshippers are edified and uplifted.

All this bears little relation to Christianity as St. Paul understood it:

'Paul, called to be an apostle of Jesus Christ through the will of God, and Sosthenes our brother, unto the Church of God which is at Corinth, even them that are sanctified in Christ Jesus, called to be saints, with all that call upon the name of our Lord Jesus Christ in every place, their Lord and ours: Grace to you and peace from God our Father and the Lord Jesus Christ.'

So he writes to the Corinthians (1 Cor. i. 1–3). The word *ecclesia* is not to be interpreted, as the nineteenth-century commentators were apt to do, in the light of its classical associations: we are not to think of the assembly in democratic Athens but of the Old Testament *ecclesia*, 'The congregation of the children of Israel'.[1] Christians are the heirs of the Old Testament; those who 'call upon the name of our Lord Jesus Christ in every place' constitute the New Israel, the People of God according to the New Covenant. The Church at Corinth is the local representative of the People of God; such is the Church of God at Philippi, Rome, Constantinople, London, Nottingham.

Thus the Church service is the assembly of the People of God, a Body met together in union with its Head, like

---

[1] See Hoskyns and Davey, *The Riddle of the New Testament*, pp. 26–35. Cf. also *Die betende Kirche*, pp. 188 f. Hort, *The Christian Ecclesia* (Macmillan, 1908) chap. I.

a regiment of soldiers on parade; an assembly conscious of the basis upon which it is constituted. Its existence depends on a Divine will and purpose. Therefore Christian worship is in the first place a confession of faith in God, and a commemoration of God's work of salvation; and then an expression of the application of that salvation to the whole of human life. As such, it is (in the true sense of the word) theological through and through: it depends on and expresses the relation of man to God. Then again, as the act of a community, worship is the living utterance of the life of the community. Not as a passive listener or spectator, but as a member of the Body, the worshipper joins in the prayer of the Church. In the words of a Roman Catholic writer:

'Liturgy is the Divine Service which the mystical Body of Christ, the Church as a community in union with Christ, her Head, offers to the Father in heaven. It consists in the celebration and the application of Redemption, which by means of the priesthood of the whole Body and the particular priesthood of the clergy is accomplished in the form of a mystery-rite.' [1]

II. THE PARISH EUCHARIST

The Holy Eucharist is not one service among many, but the centre of all. The Church of God assembles to celebrate the One Sacrifice upon which the whole life of salvation depends: pays to God the adoration which the whole creation owes to Him as its Lord; gives thanks to Him for all His mighty works from the foundation of the world to the second Advent, and for all spiritual and bodily blessings which each member has received; offers up to God the offering of the whole creation symbolized in the oblation of bread and wine, which includes the will of each member who shares in it to offer up his

[1] *Die betende Kirche*, p. 25.

own life to God: takes the bread and wine, and repeats with them the sacrificial rite which Christ instituted at the Last Supper, as the sacrificial Memorial of His Death and Resurrection; and in the Communion is herself offered up, through union with Him, to be a reasonable, holy and living sacrifice, and to live a sacrificial life in the world. For the individual, this act is the summing-up of all that his Christian faith means: his reconciliation with God and with his brethren, when with the other members of the family he kneels at the Table of the Lord: self-dedication: dependence on God, from whom he receives the sustenance of his life: justification by faith: forgiveness of sins; the Divine peace.

The eucharistic liturgy contains in itself all the elements of Christian worship: psalms and hymns, as the vehicle of the common praise, prayer and penitence; litanies and intercessions: the reading of the Scriptures: the preaching of the word of God: and thanksgiving, culminating in the central eucharistic act. In the other services of the Church these are developed separately, at leisure: thus, for instance, in the daily offices the Psalter is recited monthly, and the Bible is read through (for the most part) yearly. But it is from the Eucharist that these other services receive their interpretation.

'The Office circles round the fixed pole of the eucharistic showing forth and making present of the fact which stands at the centre of all Christianity: the redemptive work of Christ by His death and resurrection. . . . All the prayers of the Church and of the soul thereby become a prayer of Christ. The Spirit of Christ, the Holy Spirit, lifts up on strong wings the prayer of the congregation, and gives it a Divine value which otherwise it would not have. Thus it truly becomes prayer "in the name of Jesus"' (John xvi. 23).[1]

---

[1] *Die betende Kirche*, p. 184.

XII. THE CROSS AND THE ALTAR

As therefore the parish is the local unit of the Church of God, the Parish Eucharist is of necessity the central act of its life. It has been the glory of the Anglo-Catholic revival that it has vindicated the dignity of the Holy Eucharist, as the central act of Sunday worship. But, as things are, these efforts are confronted with a variety of difficulties.

First, it has in some measure to compete with other services, which act as rivals to it; not only Mattins, but Evensong, attendance at which can satisfy the consciences of those who feel that they should attend Church once on a Sunday, and also men's services and classes of various kinds, which are attended by many who have not been to *the* service. Consequently the clergy are overburdened with addresses; each of these events must have its address, and the clergy cannot talk well when they talk too often. Further, the laity get into the deplorable attitude of the passive listener. What are their thoughts? They do not realize perhaps, how deeply the clergy long to know what they make of the instructions which are continually being given them.

But if the laity are really members of the Body, it is not their part to be mere listeners: for a body which is living is alive all over, alive in all its parts. There are signs already of a salutary change in this direction, classes transferred from Sunday afternoon to an evening in the week, and changing their character from classes of instruction to tutorial classes, for which the members of the class prepare by reading a book and at which they learn to shape their ideas by expressing them. There is great scope here, for the hammering-out in discussion of the applications of Christianity to problems of daily life.[1] But, quite apart from this, the ground needs to be cleared for

---

[1] With the help of such books as Dr. Kirk, *Conscience and its Problems* (Longmans, second and revised edition, 1933).

the Parish Eucharist by the shortening and simplification of the rest of the Sunday programme.

Secondly, even where the Holy Eucharist is proclaimed to be the chief service, there is some ambiguity about the matter. The most common arrangement is that there is a Low Celebration, or more than one, at eight o'clock or earlier, and a Sung Eucharist at eleven. Which of these is the chief service? At eleven o'clock there is music and a sermon and dignified ceremonial, but no communion of the people. The people, or some of them, have made their communion at an earlier hour: and it is clear that the service at which any one communicates is *for him* the chief service of the day.

This arrangement does injury both to the early communion and to the Sung Eucharist. Communion can hardly escape being regarded as an individual act of religion, the approach of individuals, each for himself, to the throne of grace, to receive the divine Food for his soul's need; and the 'early service' is not the assembly of the whole Body and fails to exhibit the meaning of Communion as the fellowship of the Body. The individualism of the service is a discouragement to the young communicant, who can hardly avoid having the sense that he is setting himself up to be better than others. The late Sung Eucharist, lacking the communion of the people, is a maimed rite: however beautiful and moving the service may be, the people are spectators at the liturgy, and not in the full sense partakers in it. In fact, it becomes 'a service' in the false meaning which we have criticized above. It can never be anything else till it becomes also a communion.

The adoption of this arrangement may be pronounced without hesitation to be the great blunder of the Anglo-Catholic movement. It is not for us to criticize those who first adopted it. It was necessary sixty years ago to vindi-

cate the God-ward character of the act of worship, when
the whole emphasis in the then dominant teaching was
laid on the gift received; it was necessary to insist on the
fast before communion; it must have seemed that the
only way to secure for the Eucharist its due honour was
to celebrate it at 11 a.m.; and the example of Roman
Catholic usage probably weighed heavily with men who
had some excuse for undervaluing Anglican liturgical
tradition. But the same excuses cannot be made for its
continuance now. It can safely be said that if the Anglo-
Catholic movement after the War had been far-seeing
enough to return to the practice of the early Church and
adopt the Parish Eucharist with communion as the principal service of the Sunday, the whole situation of the
Church of England would now be different: and the
Parish Eucharist would have universally justified itself as
truly evangelical and truly catholic.[1]

What is required in many, perhaps most, parishes is
that the eighteenth-century tradition which established
11 a.m. as the holy hour for Sunday morning worship
should be abandoned, and the service held at nine or
nine-thirty. This hour, the ancient canonical hour for
the Liturgy, has many advantages. It is not too late an
hour to make the observance of the fast difficult; and
those whose work requires them to get up early during
the week value the opportunity of rising later on Sundays.
The housewife can return home in time to prepare the Sunday dinner; and families can attend the service together.
In some places it is found suitable to arrange for a Parish
Breakfast after the service; apart from its practical con-
venience, this common meal carries one stage further the
Fellwoship of the Body expressed in Holy Communion,
and shows that the fellowship which begins at the altar

[1] For the principle involved, see Brilioth, *Eucharistic Faith and
Practice*, pp. 224, 283–6; Gore, *The Body of Christ*, pp. 199–209, 269–86.

does not end when the people pass out of the church door.

It is one of the encouraging signs of the times that the Parish Eucharist with communion has become, or is on its way to become, the chief service in an increasing number of churches. No statistics are available, for there is no organization to back this movement. It is taking place spontaneously in many different places, and winning a generous response.

Quite commonly there is no choir, and the people sing the service themselves. It has too often been assumed that the only way to make religion popular is to bring it down to what is supposed to be the level of popular devotion; thus 'congregational singing', as commonly understood, means the hearty vociferation of popular and sentimental hymns. It is a different matter when the people join in the sacred music of *Kyrie, Credo, Sanctus, Agnus,* and *Gloria,* either to the old plainsong, or the sixteenth-century plainsong of Merbercke, or one of the simple modern settings which are now being produced. A new school of liturgical music is arising, under the guidance of such composers as Martin Shaw, which promises well for the future. In church after church the elaborate settings dear to the Victorian Age are being consigned to the lumber-room: most of us remember how the congregation used to listen, mute, while a trained choir performed a setting of *Gloria in excelsis* which with its intricacies and repetitions occupied quite ten minutes.

It is not for us to lay down the law in detail: we would only assert the principle that as Christian worship is the worship of the Body, its forms of music and ceremonial must be such that the people can make them their own. If in a country church they are relatively rude and bucolic, they will be none the less noble if they are for the Church of God in that place the fitting vehicle of its devotion.

That which is taking place is, in fact, a parallel development to the Liturgical Movement in the Roman Catholic
Church. Here, as there, the people are learning to 'pray
with the holy Church of God': or, in the words of Pope
Pius X, 'You are not to pray at the Mass: you are to
pray the Mass.' [1]

It is because this principle is involved that the inclu-
sion of the communion of the people at the Parish Eucharist is really a matter of importance. It is not merely that
the late Sung Eucharist does, in fact, lead many who
should be weekly communicants to substitute attendance
at Mass for communion: it is that when the service is
the general communion its atmosphere and spirit becomes
quite different. It becomes the worship of the Body: the
eucharistic sacrifice is seen in its full glory when it is not
only the Memorial of the sacrifice of Christ but also the
offering-up of the members of the Body in union with the
Head. Bishop Gore always used to say that the divorce
of eucharistic worship and sacrifice from communion
'really represents a seriously defective theology'.[2]

Finally, there can be no doubt that this is the intention
of the Prayer Book.[3] Mattins, Litany and Holy Communion form together the Anglican Liturgy for Sunday
morning; and the fourth rubric at the end of the Communion Service shows that the Prayer Book intends to
return in this respect to the custom of the early Church,
which is still the custom of the Orthodox Churches, of
allowing only one celebration of the Liturgy in each
place on the Lord's Day. It is true that the Anglican
practice of the past commonly robbed the service of its
climax and crown by bringing it to an end after the
sermon and the Prayer for the Church; it is true that
the whole liturgy of Mattins, Litany and Eucharist, with

[1] Quoted in *Die betende Kirche*, p. 26.   [2] *The Body of Christ*, p. 276.
[3] Cf. Lacey, *The Anglo-Catholic Faith* (Methuen, 1926), pp. 140–56.

music, hymns and sermon, is over-long; it is true also that, at any rate in town churches, there will always be need for at least one other celebration on a Sunday. But it is a sound principle that the parish priest should not so much endeavour to provide as many celebrations as possible in order that as many people as possible may be enabled to fulfil their individual duty of attendance at Mass, but rather so teach his people that they will desire to communicate if possible at the chief service, as the symbol of their share in the fellowship of the Body.

We must never express ourselves as though it were for us to make the Eucharist into a sacrament of the Church's unity; for it is so, always and of its own nature, and every Mass, under whatever conditions it is celebrated, is a Mass of the whole Church. But it is for us so to order the ceremonial and other arrangements as to express the true nature of the rite. The meaning of the parish priest's office is most truly seen when he stands at the altar celebrating with his people the Christian sacrifice and feast. The time will come when the bishop also, as the *sacerdos* of his diocese, will, as in the ancient 'stational Mass' spend his Sunday mornings in visiting his churches in turn, not primarily in order to preach, but to celebrate the principal Eucharist of the day for his people, as their Bishop.

III. PSALMS, SCRIPTURES, AND PREACHING

Psalms, scripture-reading and preaching all form part of the structure of the ancient eucharistic liturgy. They are there seen in their right liturgical setting, which explains their use elsewhere in the Church service.

It has been explained in an earlier chapter how great a place the Psalms held in the old Roman liturgy, and how the Introits and other propers are the abbreviated remains of the old congregational psalmody.

'Of the *Communio* which formerly as a Psalm, with the antiphon repeated between the verses, was sung during the procession of the faithful to partake of the sacrificial feast, now only the antiphon remains. But at recent Papal masses in St. Peter's the communion Psalm has again been sung in the old way, as also the verses with the anthem at the offertory.' [1]

This is an example which Anglicans ought to follow. It is of much importance that Psalms should be sung at the Eucharist: the truncated forms of the old Propers, now printed in the *English Hymnal* and used in many churches, are not satisfactory, for it is difficult to attach meaning to one verse of a Psalm in isolation from its context. We have also the precedent of the Prayer Book of 1549, which provided a whole Psalm as an Introit for each Mass. Experience shows that the use of at least one Psalm at the Sung Eucharist is welcomed by the people, and it has the further advantage of explaining the meaning of the Psalms at Mattins and Evensong.

The eucharistic liturgy is the common prayer of the Church, through Christ the Head of the Body: and this is exactly the traditional sense in which the Psalms are recited in church. The 'I' of the Psalms is not the individual worshipper, but Christ speaking in His own person, or speaking in the members of His Body:[2] for the Psalms are recited corporately by the Church, and the individual joins in not as an isolated individual, but as sharing in the common praise and prayer. The Psalms are not personal religious poems, like many modern hymns: or, if some of them were originally such, they were collected in a Psalter for liturgical use to express the

---

[1] *Die betende Kirche*, p. 177. The same was done with the Introit &c., at the *Semaine liturgique* at Liége in June 1934. See pp. 133–4 *supra*.

[2] See the quotation from St. Augustine on pp. 72–3, *supra*.

common prayer of Israel. As such the Church took them over, and used them as finding their full meaning in Christ.

This use of the Psalms corresponds with the regular interpretation of the Old Testament in the New. The New Testament writers quote the Old Testament continually as a literature which looks forward to the Messiah, and is 'fulfilled' in Him. They do not, like many modern teachers, base the claim of Jesus Christ simply on His moral excellence: they see Him against the background of the Old Testament preparation for His coming. In the New Testament 'Christ' is never used, as we use it, as a proper name: 'Jesus' is His personal name, and 'Christ' means the Messiah, the Lord's Anointed, the promised Deliverer. Thus the term 'Jesus Christ' implies the whole Christian interpretation of the Old Testament; the Old Testament looked forward to Him, and in Him its incompleteness is made complete. 'God who in times past spoke to our fathers in many diverse fragmentary ways, has in these last days spoken to us once for all and inclusively in His Son' (Heb. i. 1).

Here we have the clue to the interpretation of Old Testament prophecy. It is not that the prophets were inspired in a mechanical way to foretell various details of the life of Jesus; it is that the prophets, contemplating God's past and present acts of deliverance, give symbolical and poetical expression to great theological principles, which find their full embodiment in Jesus the Messiah. Thus when in Matt. ii. 15 the Evangelist interprets the word of Hosea 'Out of Egypt have I called my son', of the flight of the infant Jesus into Egypt and His return from there, it is not safe to say that he has in mind only the rather trivial correspondence of detail. It is rather that the God, who of old brought His people out of Egypt by a mighty deliverance, has sent His Son to be the leader

216

of a greater Exodus. In this connexion we think at once of the Paschal Psalm (cxiv), 'When Israel came out of Egypt', which the Church applies to the Resurrection, and of the glorious Paschal Praeconium in the Latin rite for Easter Eve, in which the Exodus and the passage of the Red Sea are used as symbols of the Lord's triumph through death.

The Old Testament finds in Him its fulfilment. Prophets and psalmists say many times that God did not want the merely formal offering of sacrifice: what He really required was the 'sacrifice' of a troubled spirit (Ps. li. 17) and the self-oblation of man to do God's will: 'Lo I come to do thy will, O God' (Ps. xl. 7, 8). The theme of 'Hebrews' is that in the Messiah the true meaning of sacrifice is seen, after which the Old Testament sacrifices were dimly groping: the sacrifices are fulfilled in Him who came to do God's will (Heb. x. 5–10, quoting Ps. xl) and to offer Himself without spot to God. Therefore every reference to sacrifice in the Psalms is to be understood in the light of the sacrifice of Christ.

So it is with the references to 'Jerusalem' and 'Sion'. Isaiah had seen the vision of the future Kingdom of God as an ideal Davidic monarchy (Is. xi. 1. &c.), and had thereby marked out one of the great lines of the Messianic expectation; and the psalmists constantly dwell on the thought of Jerusalem and the Davidic king. Doubtless in many passages of the Old Testament the idea is narrowly nationalistic; but in Jesus the Messiah all this is purged away. Jerusalem is still the centre; Jesus made a triumphal entry into the city, and cleansed the Temple, thereby claiming authority over it: He was crucified outside the gate of Jerusalem, and there He rose from the dead. Jerusalem remains the symbol of His universal and spiritual kingdom, and the New Jerusalem is seen by John the Seer (Rev. xxi. 2) in process of descending from heaven and embodying itself in the Church. It is in the light of all this that we use the Psalms which speak of Jerusalem, such as xlviii ('Great is the Lord, and highly to be praised') or cxxii ('I was glad when they said unto me: We will go into the house of the Lord'). These Psalms are to us poems describing the Church of God, not with the finality of a clear-cut theological exposition, but with the greater richness of meaning that belongs to symbols with such a history.

There are several Psalms which seem to us almost as if written for Jesus the Messiah, such as xxii ('My God, my God, look upon me; why hast thou forsaken me?'), xxiv ('Lift up your heads, O ye gates'), or lxxii, the Psalm of Christ's Kingdom. Many other Psalms, which seem to imply something like self-satisfaction or self-righteousness, can only be rightly used of Him who alone is without sin. It would be exceedingly unhealthy for any person to recite the long Psalm cxix, and apply its expressions of devotion to himself from beginning to end. But it can rightly be used as a description of the mind of Christ; it is also right to use it of the common life of the members of Christ's Body in the world, whose lives are to be governed by obedience to the will of God, as the magnet points to the north.

They are so governed, and yet they are not. The soul of man is ever swaying between the two allegiances, to God and to the self. Thus each Christian finds again and again that he is compelled to interpret the 'ungodly man' of the Psalms as himself, in so far as he has been dominated by the self-willed, proud, contemptuous and irascible ego. But since it is from the dominion of this ego that Christ came to set us free, and bring us into the fellowship of the common life which is in Him, once again we come back to use the Psalms as members of His Body, and join in the common praise and supplication.

They belong to the Church before they belong to us. Joining in the common recitation, we do well if we listen, in spirit, to other people saying them, and hear in them the voice of Him who speaks in all the members of His Body: 'His voice was as the voice of many waters' (Rev. i. 15). The Psalms reflect the trial and conflict and triumph of the whole Body of Christ. Some of them express the new song of the redeemed, praising God for His work of grace: some of them go back to history and tell the story of God's mighty works, like the eucharistic prayer of the Syrian liturgies; some of them call to God in penitence: some of them are written in the midst of oppression and perplexity, 'O God, wherefore art thou absent from us so long.' If we want to pray for the unemployed, the sick, or those in intellectual doubt, we find all that we need in the Psalms.

We may sum up the point in some words of Father Kelly:[1]

'As the Bible is the Word of God, all Bible-reading is a meditation on God's ways. The Bible contains many prayers, that we may see how prayer mingles with life. But in the Psalter we see what prayer and worship are in themselves, since it is the one book drawn up for that purpose. Whatever were the original occasions of the Psalms, it seems that as brought together they were meant to be taken in the person of the Ideal Israel—the People of God—the Kingdom of God. The later Rabbis insisted that God's Purpose was exclusively national; but St. Paul learnt that the Kingdom of God was the family and fellowship for all mankind.

'The Psalter is therefore an epitome of the whole religious history of humanity: its struggle to worship God; its struggle with the powers of evil, as something anti-human and de-humanizing; its recognition that evil is

---

[1] In an unpublished fragment, quoted in *Intercommunion*, p. 101.

yet something in men: its consequent despair over its own
sin and inadequacy, and over the apparent indifference
of things, perhaps even of God. It has been said that
there is no doubt, difficulty or scepticism which human
bitterness has expressed, or its vanity played with, which
the Bible, and especially the Psalms, has not faced far
more frankly, just because they were so sure where an
answer did lie, even when they could not reach it. Evil
was only ungodliness, it lay only in the self-will of men,
the ungodly and the proud; it could have no permanence.

'A meditation upon every phase of man's history, the
Psalms are a meditation upon Christ and His Passion,
since in Christ and His Passion humanity and the history
of man are summed up. But the Psalms are no less
applicable in different ways to any individual, in so far
and in such wise as he enters into and partakes of that
life of humanity which is in Christ.'

The ancient plan of the Divine Office, which is preserved in the Anglican Mattins and Evensong, has for its
staple element the recitation of the Psalms and the reading of the Scriptures in order. As compared with the
Latin Breviary, the Prayer Book has the defect of over-
simplification: antiphons, responds and office-hymns were
ruthlessly cut out, for the reasons given in the Second
Preface to the Prayer Book, 'Concerning the Service of
the Church'. Much that was valuable was thereby lost;
but the solid advantage remains, that the order of Scripture-reading is not interrupted to anything like so serious
an extent by the special lessons for festivals.

It is clear, in the light of what has been said, that we
do wrong if we regard the Old Testament as a series of
moral lessons; the nemesis is that we cannot help seeing
that they are very imperfect moral lessons. Many people
are so shocked by the bloodthirstiness of Jael the wife
of Heber the Kenite, or Saul's destruction of the Amale-

kites, that they would gladly leave the Old Testament lesson out altogether. But then, without the Old Testament we cannot understand the New: and the New Testament freely admits the imperfection of the Old. The Old Testament is the Book of the Church of God under the Old Covenant, in which the Purpose of God is seen working towards its fulfilment in the New Covenant.

In the Church service we read these lessons in order, day after day: we read them as a history, and here all our modern study of the Bible is a help. Some of the lessons about the reigns of the Kings of Israel are not particularly interesting and not at all edifying. The same might be said of large parts of English History. But the Old Testament seeks continually to interpret the events in the light of God's meaning and purpose; we read it in church that we may learn to look for that meaning in all history.

Then again, as we have seen in the case of the Psalms, there is a right use of the old method of mystical interpretation: our Lord uses the Flood as a symbol of world-catastrophe (Luke xvii. 26) and Noah's Ark is an ancient symbol of the Church.[1] More generally, the Scripture lessons constantly acquire new meanings for each person who uses them, as they are found to apply to particular circumstances in his life. The Church constantly suggests such meanings; thus on the Second Evensong for St. James's Day, we read for the first lesson (Jer. xxvi. 1–15) how Jeremiah was once nearly martyred, and the story illustrates both the life of St. James and that of every martyr since. In the second lesson we read of our Lord in the house of Jairus (Mark v. 21–end) not only because St. James was present then, but also because mystically

[1] See 'The Mystical Interpretation of the Old Testament', by Dr. Darwell Stone, in the *New Commentary* (S.P.C.K., 1932), pp. 688–96.

St. James is Jairus's daughter: to His martyr, slain by the sword of Herod, the Lord says 'Talitha cumi'.

A principal of a Theological College, called upon to help newly ordained clergy with their daily meditation, found that they were getting into difficulties because they treated their meditation as something quite separate from their daily Office. He advised them to let the one nourish the other; not to think of the recitation of the Office as a mere duty, after the performance of which they might hope to get down to 'real prayer'; but to treat the Office itself as the main act of devotion, making sure of a few minutes beforehand, if possible, in order to bring their private petitions into it and, when it was over, letting their meditation be helped by what God had shown them in the Psalms and Scriptures for the day. The daily Office, with the eucharistic liturgy, makes up the Church's prayer: the prayer of the individual member of the Body is not something separate from the prayer of the Body, but a part of it. The best way of private prayer is that which trains up the members of the Body in the common life of faith and love by which the Body lives, which unites and does not divide, which kindles in the soul the sense that the object of each soul's faith and devotion is the common treasure of all.

The Sermon is an important element in the liturgy: its function is to save the liturgy from the danger of becoming formalistic. It is the prophetic declaration that the faith which is enshrined in the forms of worship is the living faith of those here present.

Sermons can rightly be of various kinds, not all of which are suitable for the Parish Eucharist. The 'liturgical sermon' is not hortatory, in the usual sense, not theological in the sense of giving a balanced statement of doctrine in the scholastic style, and not devotional in the sense of dealing with 'our spiritual lives' and the ways of indi-

222

vidual prayer. Rather, it gives expression to the common faith of Christians, their common approach to God as children in their Father's House, as members of the Body. Whatever therefore may be the material which it uses, it will use it always as forming part of the act of common worship. It may well analyse the collect for the day, using it to sum up the common intention of the Church's prayer on that day: it may give an exegesis of the Epistle, picturing St. Paul as standing up in the midst of the Church and giving his message: or taking the Gospel for the day, represent Him who healed the deaf and dumb man with the word 'Ephphatha' as the Saviour who is able now to make the dull ears of the soul to hear, and its eyes to see: or it may use the Introit or some words from the fixed prayers of the service.

Such preaching will be 'theological' in the true sense. It will deal with God, God's work of grace, and man's reconciliation with God. It will be helpful to the people in the measure that the priest is himself living the liturgical life, and finding nourishment for himself from the Church's prayer. It will connect the liturgy with private prayer, by bringing the unchanging forms of the service into relation with the 'here' and 'now'. For every sermon that is a good sermon is, so to speak, dated and addressed.

Such is the 'liturgical sermon'. There are other types of sermon, which it is not necessary to analyse here. There is, for instance, the careful and thorough treatment of some particular problem or theme; this, however, will necessarily be too long to be in place at the Parish Eucharist. But two observations may be made: first, that too many sermons occupy themselves wholly with our subjective dispositions and the virtues which we ought to acquire, while failing to dwell on the objective realities on which our faith rests: and second, that much that is heard from the pulpit really belongs to the study-circle.

A friend told me once that he heard two sermons on St. Mary Magdalene's Day, one of which maintained that she was and the other that she was not the sister of Martha and Lazarus. But the pulpit is the place for the word of God.

IV. LITURGICAL TRADITIONS

Liturgical tradition is the continuous life of the Church which expresses itself in liturgical forms, and finds in them a meaning that is partly grasped by the intellect, partly subconscious and unformulated: for that which the forms enshrine is the Christian Mystery and the life of the mystical Body of Christ. The Catholic liturgical tradition, if we use the word 'catholic' in its correct sense, is the worshipping life of the universal Church, the heir of all the ages: the universal tradition is inherited in various degrees by the various local traditions of different countries and periods.

A liturgical tradition is a thing that persists and continues, and is not dependent on the eloquence or personal attractiveness of the priest who happens to be in charge.[1] The Church of England possesses a genuine liturgical tradition. We commonly underrate the liturgical sense which lives in the Anglican laity. Even those queer debates on the Revised Prayer Book in Parliament in 1927 and 1928 testified, by the deep interest which was aroused, to the hold which the Prayer Book has on the affections of the English people.

The Church revival of the nineteenth century effected a great revival of our liturgical tradition. It is easily possible to undervalue the churchmanship of the eighteenth century;[2] but there was as much need for the rebuilding

[1] See Lacey, *The Anglo-Catholic Faith*, pp. 149 ff.
[2] Cf. Frere, *Principles of Religious Ceremonial* (2nd edition, 1928), esp. chaps. XIV, XV.

XIII. THE HÖGALID CHURCH, STOCKHOLM

of the tradition as for the restoration of the fabrics of the churches. In both cases the zeal of the restorer was not always wise, and much that was valuable was obliterated and lost. Well may we regret the replacement by organs and surpliced choirs of the minstrels who once led the music from the west gallery. The warning which this instance contains is still needed. While many unjustified and unintelligent criticisms are made against Anglo-Catholics, there is a sound liturgical sense behind the protest against changes made by those who wrongly assume that the manners and practices of the Counter-Reformation form the only right liturgical model. The Liturgical Movement in the Roman Catholic Church has important lessons for us.

But a more serious danger which threatens the Anglican liturgical tradition is that of the wrong sort of modernization. There is almost everywhere a tendency to cut down the recitation of the Psalms; the laity are losing their old familiarity with them. In Liberal circles we are told that the Prayer Book is out of date: a correspondent of the *Modern Churchman* (March 1934) pleads for 'special services at judicious intervals throughout the Christian year', which 'would do much to arrest the interest and attention of many who simply cannot be brought to see at present the meaning of the ordinary Church services'. He suggests a 'Doctors' Sunday' and a 'Sportsmen's service': stunts, in fact, designed to meet the modern man on his own level. The hymn-book, *Songs of Praise*, especially in its new edition, sets out quite frankly the favourite teachings of Liberal theology, and makes judicious omissions and alterations in many of the familiar hymns which speak of redemption. Hitherto, the hymn-books which have been put into the hands of the people have always been orthodox in intention; but this book presages a corruption and degradation of our liturgical tradition, which is the more serious because the words which the people say or sing make a deeper impression than those which they hear from the pulpit.[1]

The Prayer Book needs revision, but a revision in the same faith in which it was compiled, and a revision in the true liturgical spirit. The forms of prayer which best meet the needs of the modern world are those which are most truly universal: for the needs of the spirit of man are in all ages much the same, and some of the oldest are the most truly modern.[2] They need a modern application; but this is a different thing from the spurious modernity which only succeeds in being trivial and shallow.

If the Anglican liturgical tradition is precious, and to be reverently guarded, so are the corresponding traditions of other parts of Christendom: and here the liturgical way of approach has an important bearing on the problem of Reunion. If the different churches are to understand one another, the mutual study of their liturgical traditions is more important and more fruitful than the discussion of their theological differences. It is not in any way implied that these latter are unimportant: it is that their

---

[1] *Songs of Praise*, enlarged edition, 1931. Words editor, Percy Dearmer. Some instances of 'significant' modifications of the usual version (as given in the first edition, 1925, or in the *English Hymnal*): Alteration of single words and phrases, 70, 72, 160, 271, 279; omission of verses, 129, 131, 260, 274; re-writing of hymns, 130, 273 (both these are unforgivable), 281, 480. For the new idea of sin, cf. 466 with E.H. 72, to the tune of which it is set; for eucharistic doctrine, 262, 274, Pt. ii; among the Advent hymns, 69, which begins:

> 'With Jesus for hero, for teacher and friend,
> The world to the purpose of God shall ascend'.

A good number of orthodox hymns remain untouched; but these instances indicate the trend of the revision. Perhaps we may console ourselves with the reflection that it is by the 'German Christians' that the eyes of the Christians in Germany have been opened to the meaning of their own orthodoxy.

[2] See F. D. Maurice, *The Kingdom of Christ*, Vol. II, p. 19 ff.

meaning is best understood in the light of liturgical practice.[1] To take the extreme instance: The Barthian and
Calvinist on the one hand, and the Eastern Orthodox on
the other, are liable to mean different things by the use
of the same theological terms, such as God, the Incarnation, the Church. But the Barthian doctrine of the Transcendence of God and the radical distinction between the
word of God and the word of man, has for its background
the Reformed type of Church service; the bareness of the
interior of the church building reflects a determination
to seek God by turning away as completely as possible
from visible symbols of His presence, while the doctrine
of the word of God corresponds to a type of service of
which the main element is a sermon which may be or
may fail to be truly prophetic. The Orthodox liturgy, on
the other hand, centres round the conception of God's
coming to man in the Incarnation, His universal presence
mediated through symbols of every kind, and man's
fellowship with God in the communion of saints.

We are not to say that one of these views is 'true' and
the other 'false': rather they seem to be complementary
to one another, and capable therefore of an ultimate
synthesis. But so long as the discussion limits itself to
theological doctrine, it is liable to become a dispute in
which the two sides do not really come within range of
one another. We need to hold conferences which shall
put the exposition and interpretation of liturgical practice
in the first place, and proceed from this to investigate
the doctrinal differences. Such conferences will truly represent the different Churches; for while in every Church
there are different schools of theological thought, in each

[1] From this point of view Dr. Brilioth's account of various eucharistic traditions in *Eucharistic Faith and Practice* is of great value. In
each case he puts the doctrine and the rite side by side. See, e.g.,
his summing up on the Calvinistic rite, pp. 177-9.

case the liturgical practice is common to all the members. This method has been followed in the Anglo-Russian Conferences which have for some years past been held by the Fellowship of St. Alban and St. Sergius, in which the liturgical traditions, Orthodox and Anglican, have been prominently set forth.

Such conferences will show the way to unity: for it is plain that, on the basis of a common faith, as set forth in the Scriptures and the Creeds of the Universal Church, and of a restored unity of order resting on the sacraments and the Episcopal Ministry, which is the necessary symbol and instrument of the unity of the Church, a unity is possible which is not uniformity but unity-in-diversity. Each type has a contribution to bring: there is place within the unity as much for the Calvinistic type of preaching-service as for the orthodox liturgy. Only, before unity can be reached, there must be a great deepening of mutual understanding. Reunion is impossible at present: but it is ultimately possible, and the way to it lies through a mutual understanding of the different types of Church service, which will lead to a desire on the part of each side to share the inheritance of the other. Ultimately, if there is to be Reunion, the Calvinist will have to accept the Episcopal Ministry and the sacramental liturgy, and the Orthodox to find room for the positive elements of the opposite tradition. But the liturgical way of approach opens up the possibility that the reconciliation of the two will be a true synthesis and not a compromise.

When therefore Anglicans and Free Churchmen meet to confer, this is not a fit occasion for 'open communion services'; such services amount to an admission that the actual differences are not real enough to make any difference when it comes to corporate worship. But the differences exist, and are real; and the Lambeth Conferences have clearly affirmed the principle that 'Intercommunion should be the goal of, rather than a means to, the restoration of union'.[1] Therefore the right procedure at such Conferences must surely be for Anglican and Free Church communion services to be held on alternate days, the members of both sides being present at both services and communicating only at one. This has been regularly done at the Anglo-Russian Conferences to which we have referred, with the happiest results. The Reunion to which we look forward is to be a reconciliation of diverse liturgical traditions on the basis of a common faith and restored common order: and Reunion will consist precisely in this, that the separated Churches will once again meet freely in worship.

But liturgical tradition cannot be separated from the wider sense of tradition, as the habits of a common life. From this point of view we may see the importance of missionary work. For the native peoples of South Africa, for instance, the coming of European civilization means the disintegration of their old tribal traditions. In old days the Bantu peoples lived under their tribal chiefs: and though they were the victims of many evils, such as polygamy, witchcraft and tribal war, the old system bound them together in a social life with a strict moral code. In these relatively enlightened days, their condition is worse. They receive modern education, but their social cohesion is broken up and they are becoming a proletariat; morally they have freedom to break every commandment with an impunity that is only limited by the fear of the police, and they become, in fact, the helpless prey of the world, the flesh and the devil. This change is the result of the advent not of the missionary but of the trader, the railway, the cinema and the whole invading host of European civilization. But for the Christian native

[1] *Lambeth Conference Report*, 1930, Resolution 42, p. 52, cf. p. 117; cf. the Encyclical Letter of 1920 (*Report*, pp. 26–9).

the bishop, and in his lower place the priest, step into the place of the tribal chief, and the common life and discipline of the Church binds the people again into a new unity, which is able to resist, as the old tribal life could not resist, the disintegrating influence of civilization.

Even now, to a larger extent than we think, the Church is fulfilling a similar function in England. In the midst of the levelling, disintegrating, and de-humanizing influences of the modern social system, the Church even now creates a true social life: the modern man, isolated among a multitude of strangers in the modern suburb, is drawn out of his loneliness into the fellowship of a spiritual family.

V. COMMON ACTION

We cannot escape from the need of saying something, of however tentative a character, about the problem of government; for we must not leave the impression that the contribution of the Church to a true social life consists solely in a sentiment or spirit. It includes a firm upholding of certain institutions, above all that of Marriage according to the Divine law, as the basis of society. It includes also a radical criticism, in general, of the Liberal-democratic theory of government, namely that the best form of government is that of an assembly in which various interests meet in conflict, and the vote of the majority prevails.

We shall only be able here to discuss the principle in the simplest forms in which it can be studied; we cannot enter on the very complicated problems raised in the government of the modern State. It is, however, necessary to note in passing that in the British Constitution the Liberal-democratic principle is deeply modified by the presence of the Crown and the House of Lords side by side with the House of Commons. The Opposition is 'His Majesty's Opposition'. The ceremony of the Coronation of the King in Westminster Abbey is far more than an antique and picturesque ceremonial; it has the deepest meaning for the life of the whole nation.

The typical form of government in the Church is that of the Bishop with his Synod. It appears to embody two principles: first, that there is reality of responsibility, since one man is given the work to do and made responsible for it; and second, the co-operation of the members of the body in free consultation, in order to form a common mind. That these principles have been very systematically neglected in the actual government of the Church is obvious enough, and it is not necessary to give instances. Yet they are there; and, wherever the Church is true to herself, they find expression in some form or other.

Perhaps the point is best made clear by contrast. The liberal principle is expressed on a small scale in the usual type of committee-government, in so far as they are dominated by the vicious principle of the majority-vote. There is a chairman, but he is not responsible for what is done in the sense that a bishop is responsible in his sphere; the committee as a whole is responsible, and the fact that the members are corporately responsible means that no one is actually responsible. At the meetings the members have their opinions to maintain, or their party points of view to urge; and the fact that the matter is determined by the vote of the majority means that the course of action which is taken is the resultant of the various opposing forces. The body is leaderless. It is the common saying that 'a committee has neither a body to be kicked nor a soul to be damned', and that a committee habitually does things which any one of its members would not take the responsibility of doing.

Not all committees, however, exhibit these vices. There are committees which make a practice of taking no action which is not unanimous; in other words, they go on discussing till they reach a common mind. This is the principle which properly belongs to the Church, which is by nature, and is seen in its worship to be, a body with a common faith. It is the denial of the principle of government by the majority-vote, and the affirmation of the principle that many minds should co-operate in free discussion, till a solution is found which embodies on a higher level the positive principles for which the different sides have contended. The classical instance of such a solution is the Council of Jerusalem in the *Acts of the Apostles* in which, after the matter had been fully aired, an agreed solution was reached which St. James could sum up with the words, 'It seemed good to the Holy Ghost and to us'.

The history of Religious Orders has had many ugly pages, and it may surprise some readers that a Religious Community should be presented as a laboratory in which principles of government can be worked out: nevertheless, a member of such a Community may be allowed to give his testimony that such can be the case. Here the principle of the majority-vote is excluded by the fact that the Superior is responsible. But he cannot in practice receive willing obedience unless the Chapter is with him: and the Chapter has its defined rights of free discussion. Some remarkable instances could be given of the solution of perplexing difficulties, when the formula finally agreed upon by all was different from any of the proposed solutions, and yet combined the positive elements of them all, not by way of compromise but by that of synthesis.

Such is the true principle alike of the rule of the Bishop with his Synod and of the Parish Priest with his Parochial Church Council. The bishop and the priest in their several spheres have a burden of responsibility which they alone have to bear: but they cannot govern without the goodwill of the governed, or lead except as leaders of a team. Colonial bishops in the Anglican Communion have their synods. But episcopacy in England is a misrepresentation of the principle of episcopacy, because the bishop is in law an autocrat. But episcopal autocracy is inconsistent with the nature of the Church as a Body: and therefore it can be a duty to disobey a bishop when he acts as if he were an autocrat, and seeks to enforce his own private opinions. The English bishops are for the most part making noble efforts to rule their unwieldy dioceses with the co-operation of their clergy and people, but lacking the help of properly constituted Synods.

At the present time the Church of England is in serious danger through the fact that the Church Assembly is modelled not on the Church's own methods of constitutional government, but on the pattern of the secular Parliament: hence it is in danger of all the evils of the party system, lobbying and vote-catching. The Parochial Church Councils are in danger of the same evil spirit: they often model themselves upon committees, and behave as if they were committees.

But this is impossible if and in so far as the P.C.C. acts as the Council *of the Church*: for the Church is a worshipping body, and worships as a body. If the P.C.C. behaves like a committee, it is denying in act what the common worship of the Church affirms: and the nature of the Church, expressed in its worship, must, in so far as it is actualized, deliver the P.C.C. from this evil secularizing influence. In so far as it acts as the Council of the Church, it must work to attain a common mind and embody the reality of the unity which exists.

Here then we have a principle which is radically opposed to the democratic principle according to which every one, wise or foolish, can claim the right to make his voice heard. It is that those whose opinions are worth hearing have, not the right, but the duty to contribute them to help form the common mind. The opinions of the majority ought not to prevail unless they are right; and both the majority and the minority have the duty of bringing in their opinions to the common stock. All alike have a responsibility to the truth.

It should be needless to add that in thus criticizing the democratic principle we are in no way decrying freedom of speech, and have no desire to see autocracy substituted for it. We criticize it precisely because freedom of speech does not fully come into its rights; the majority-vote comes in to stop free discussion before the matter has been fully discussed and a common mind reached. But the Church is by nature a Body, and is thus impelled, in so far as it is true to itself, to seek a common mind; and this is possible because the Church's existence is based on a common faith. It is thus that the Church has the power to create a social life, not through mere organization but through the actualization of the organic life of the Body. Can anything but this common faith and this organic life re-create our secular politics?

VI. WHAT I LEARNT IN THE HOUSE OF GOD

'What is your name?'
'Who gave you this name?'

I was born into a family, and into a nation;
The head of the family was my father,
The head of the nation is the king.
But where could I find the eternal Father, the universal King,
 Claiming the allegiance of my spirit?
Where were the signs of His Family and His Kingdom?

At my baptism I received my Christian name.
There I was born anew,
 a child of an unseen Father,
 a member of a spiritual Family,
  the Church, the Body of Christ,
 an inheritor of an eternal Kingdom.
God had a meaning for my life.

My father and my mother
  had become man and wife before God's altar:
A new family had come into being;
God had a meaning for that family.

The king of England was crowned before God's altar,
  by the Archbishop, the Primate of the Church:
The kingship is a sacred office;
God has a meaning for common life and labour.

The Church exists to bear witness
that there is an universal King and Father of all mankind.

Her Bible tells
  of Abraham the father of a family,
  of David the king of a nation,
    both confessing the universal Father and King.
It tells also of other kings, as Nebuchadnezzar,
    making men their slaves,
    claiming the title of the Man-god.
It tells of the GOD-MAN, Jesus Christ,
  of the seed of Abraham,
  of the line of David,
    who came to proclaim the Kingdom of God,
    to reconcile all nations and families into one,
    having slain the enmity
      by the suffering of the Cross,
      by the Resurrection-victory.

Into this faith the Church baptizes us,
  faith in the eternal Father and King,
      in Jesus Christ the Reconciler,
      in the Holy Spirit, the Life of her life.
The Church is a Family and a Kingdom;
The head of the Family, in each place,
  is the Bishop, consecrated before God's altar
  as the successor of the Apostles of Jesus Christ,
    to be Father-in-God to God's people,
      Shepherd of Christ's flock,
      Priest, in Christ's Name.

The Church meets on the Lord's Day to offer the Holy
    Sacrifice,
  using universal symbols, bread and wine,
  proclaiming therewith God's redeeming love in Christ:
    'This is My Body which is given for you; take, eat.'
    'This is My Blood of the Covenant; drink ye all of this.'

235

In eating and drinking at the Table of the Lord
    the brethren of the family, my neighbour and I,
    are shown as reconciled with Him
        and in Him with one another:
God has a meaning for our lives, singly and all together:
    'What I do thou knowest not now, but thou shalt know
        hereafter.'

Here we see that the root of all evil is godlessness,
    practical godlessness,
    the exaltation of the self,
    the claim of the self to live as it pleases without God.
Here we see the root of all evil in ourselves,
    and confess and are absolved:
    'Thou hast broken my bonds in sunder.'

Thanks be to Him who has redeemed us and continues to
      save us
    out of this godlessness,
    into the common life which is in Him,
    into the universal spiritual Family and Kingdom,
And has promised the perfecting of this salvation and
    fellowship in the life everlasting.
    Glory be to God for all things. Amen.

'But who is blind, but My servant?
    'Or deaf, as My messenger that I send?
'Who is blind as he that is at peace with Me,
    'And blind as the LORD's servant?'

CHAPTER X

CHRISTIANITY AND ART

*

I. THE EXPRESSION OF A SPIRIT

The problems which we have been discussing touch at so many points the nature of Art, that we are compelled to include a discussion of this subject. It will give an opportunity to sum up much that we have had to say about the Liturgy, dogma, the Bible and religious symbolism in general, and in particular to say something about modern church architecture, which is already providing an outward expression for the new spirit in the Church: and, because the new church buildings are built on the street, they attract the attention of the man in the street. One of the greatest expressions in poetry of the new spirit, *The Rock*, by Mr. Eliot, is written round the theme of church-building, and was produced in aid of a church-building scheme.[1]

The starting-point that we want is given us by Dr. Herwegen:

'Christianity is in its essence not a doctrine but life, the life of Christ in the baptized. Wherever Christianity sheds its light, powerful impulses of life arise, which soon make themselves visible as creative or transforming forces in the outward world of phenomena. Modern investi-

---

[1] *The Rock*, by T. S. Eliot (Faber & Faber, 1934), a pageant play written for performance at Sadlers' Wells Theatre, 28 May–9 June 1934, on behalf of the Forty-five Churches Fund of the Diocese of London.

gation shows with increasing clearness what an inward transformation was wrought in the ancient world by the Christian soul. The style of Augustine the rhetorician changes under the slowly transforming influence of Christianity into that of the sermons of the Bishop of Hippo. Hymns and music produce under Christian inspiration new manifestations of spiritual power. Even plastic art soon shows traces of the immanent power of the new view of life.

'From the multitude of detailed observations the conclusion emerges that the Christian conception of art worked a radical change, in contrast with the purely formal art of [late] antiquity, by assigning primary importance to the meaning (*Inhalt*) of artistic work. In place of merely sensuous beauty, the Christian made the spiritual quality of the formative idea the creative principle of art. In all the life-expression of the Christian, and therefore also in his art, there is seen the utterance of "the word", in the double sense of the Christian idea, and of its relation to the Divine Word—the Logos.' [1]

Evidently, then, the term 'Christian art' can by no means be limited to what we call religious art; it must cover the whole expression of the Christian spirit in life.

What then is the Christian spirit? We speak of Christianity as 'supernatural'; but according to the principle of the Incarnation the supernatural is the redemption of the natural. Thus when our Lord lays down the principle of Christian Marriage, He goes back to the story of the Creation: 'From the beginning of the creation God made them male and female' (Mark x. 6). Human perversity and sin have obscured the true nature of marriage: hence the permission for divorce in the Jewish Law (vss. 3–5); but in Christian Marriage, in the Kingdom of God, the true and original nature of marriage is restored.

[1] *Christliche Kunst und Mysterium*, pp. 7, 8.

On this basis we may say that the ordinary implements of daily life, or works of engineering, may achieve beauty simply in fulfilling the function which they are intended to serve. The Forth Bridge is beautiful just because it makes no conscious effort to be beautiful by adding need-less ornament to its construction, but simply in solving the practical problem of carrying trains weighing several hundred tons over a mile of sea at a height of two hundred feet above the water-level.

This is a simple instance: the Forth Bridge solves a problem in mathematics and mechanics. The architec-ture of domestic and public buildings raises more compli-cated issues, for here the design expresses the spirit of a period and a civilization. Eighteenth-century Bath has a beauty which is very different from that of fifteenth-century Lübeck. Sin likewise expresses itself in ugliness: the meanness and sordidness of modern commercialism has stamped its image on the parts of Bristol and Birming-ham seen by the traveller approaching by rail from the east. The impression given by the most recent buildings is harder to sum up. There is much that is very good; but the main impression is that of lack of unity. The diversity of style reflects the strange confusion of ideas in the present age and its lack of a common mind.

The Church equally is forced to express herself in the church-buildings which she erects. The Puritan spirit, in its strength and simplicity, and also in its bareness and lack of imagination, has expressed itself in the older type of chapel which is scattered all over England, a type which contrasts favourably with the pretentiousness of many of the more modern Free Church buildings. The churches similarly tell their own tale. It was a bad sign that churches in the Victorian period were built in Gothic: the fact that churches were being built in a different style from public buildings and dwelling-houses seemed to say that the Church was following a false romanticism, seeking to escape from the present and live in a particular period of the past. It was really preposterous that the architect called upon to design a church should first of all have to sit down and consider which period he should imitate, instead of applying himself at once to the solution of the problem of building a church for a particular congregation. The Gothic revival was thus a symptom that the Church was failing to meet the modern world and give its message in the language of the day.

But we must add that in another sense the Gothic revival was healthy, and perhaps even necessary: for it signified that the Church was making a great effort to recover her hold on her own tradition and her own history. An interesting example of the positive value of tradition may be seen in the new St. Giles' suburb of Lincoln, where a large and admirably planned estate of modern houses has grown up, and the eighteenth-century church of St. Peter-at-Arches, which till last year stood in the main street of the old city near the Stonebow, has been re-erected in their midst. Not all the old material has been used, but the features of the old church have been preserved, and it stands in the new district as an exceedingly valuable link with history and tradition.

The fact that few Gothic churches are now being built is a healthy sign that the Church is setting herself in earnest to speak to the modern world. But in doing so it is vital that she should retain her hold on her own past: and the best modern churches are those which unite modern design and construction with a sense of tradition.[1] There are some, especially on the Continent, which succeed only in being odd and bizarre. They are not to be

[1] We are happy to be able to include illustrations of some modern churches which may truly be said to fulfil this ideal. See Illustrations Nos. X–XVI.

XIV. ST. NICHOLAS' CHURCH, BURNAGE

criticized for being too daringly modern, but because they do not look like churches: they are unfaithful to the past.

It is for the church architect to express the Church's mind; and there have been some happy instances of co-operation between architect and congregation, in which the architect has felt that a quasi-priestly function is assigned to him, in interpreting the faith of the Church and of this congregation, and the people have responded. In one such instance the congregation seems to have adopted the architect, as it were, into the family: and on Sunday mornings, while the new church was in building, the congregation used to troop across in a body after the service in the old mission room, to see how the building was going on. And this was a 'modern' church, in some respects very daring.[1]

In general, the tragedy of modern art is the divorce between art and the people. There is no popular art, because there is no common faith and therefore no common mind. The artist is driven to express his own ideas; and these ideas, divorced from a common tradition, become eccentricities or fads. They attract circles of 'fans' among minds that are, or that would be, like the artist's own. But they do not speak to the people. The people of England are artistically almost inarticulate. There remains in them only a vague preference for what is established and what is usual, for the familiar forms of sham Gothic and sham Renaissance.

The solution begins to come when the artist is a Christian living the Church's life; for the Church still has something of a tradition and a common mind. He can strive to express in brick and concrete the faith which he and the congregation share. And when he has succeeded, the Christian people instinctively recognize that what he has given them is theirs as well as his.

[1] See Illustration No. XIV.

And if churches, why not also railway stations, post offices and banks? It is not that these should be made to look like churches, it is that they should become themselves, and be seen to be products of the common life of the people of the town. When this begins to happen, art has begun to come into its own.

II. SYMBOLIC ART

So far we have been speaking of an art which can be called utilitarian, in so far as it is concerned with things needed for use, in whose form some spirit, or some tradition, or the lack of it, finds expression. But music, painting and sculpture are instances of things which are not necessary, as buildings are necessary, for the supply of bodily needs: they exist solely in order to express ideas and emotions which are common to men. These ideas are always universal ideas: even when art is drawn into the service of the patriotism of particular nations, the war-memorials of enemy nations express the same themes.

Christian symbolic art is concerned with these same universal ideas: its symbols are all universal symbols, because they represent in one aspect or another the manifestation of God, the Universal, in the flesh. Thus St. Mary with the Holy Child in her arms is the symbol not only of the human birth of the Son of God, but of universal human motherhood also, as transformed and hallowed thereby. We may even say that a pagan artist in depicting Motherhood is depicting St. Mary, or rather, that which finds in her its fulfilment: we might say the same of an Egyptian figure of Isis and Horus, as an expression of an universal idea to which the historical fact of the Incarnation gives an eternal meaning. We may speak of the Incarnation, in Platonic terms, as the manifestation in the flesh of the Idea of the Good: and the Idea, in the Platonic sense, is just that which the artist is seeking.

242

Thus in early times Christians could even be content to take over pagan works of art and re-interpret them, seeing in a drawing of a city in the formal antique style a likeness of the heavenly Jerusalem, in a shepherd-idyll the favourite image of the Good Shepherd, and even in a representation of Orpheus a symbol of Christ who with the Cross as His lute overcame the powers of death and hell.[1]

This gives the clue to the art of the early Christians. The aim of the paintings in the Catacombs is not to help to visualize the actuality of the Gospel story, in the manner with which modern paintings have made us familiar: it is to represent ideas, above all the idea of redemption, the same Christian Mystery which the Liturgy set forth in a sacramental manner. The favourite subjects of the catacomb paintings are given by Dr. Herwegen as follows:[2] Noah's Ark, the Sacrifice of Isaac, Moses bringing water from the rock, the story of Jonah, the burning fiery furnace, Daniel in the Lions' Den, the Adoration of the Magi, the healing of the paralytic, the Good Shepherd, the raising of Lazarus. The first, second and fifth of these occur among the lessons read on Easter Eve according to the Roman Rite (see p. 66 above); 'and here the reference to the resurrection of Christ and the resurrection of the Christian to life through Baptism has still a living meaning for us'. The story of Moses and the rock is a minor episode in the Bible story: but it finds its meaning as an illustration of the Christian Mystery, signifying the Water of Baptism and the life-giving drink in the Eucharist, and it is already so used by St. Paul in 1 Cor-inthians x. 3–4. The story of Jonah and the Whale is a

[1] *Christliche Kunst und Mysterium*, pp. 10–11.

[2] *ibid.*, pp. 14 ff.; he takes the list from Paul Styger, *Altchristliche Grabkunst* (Munich, 1927). Several of the subjects mentioned here occur in Illustration No. IV.

symbol of death and resurrection, as in Matthew xii. 40. Daniel is depicted in these paintings, not sitting, as in the Bible story, but standing with his arms stretched out, a type of crucified Saviour: the lions are the powers of death and hell over which He has prevailed.[1] The Adoration of the Magi may be called a liturgical subject. In the church of St. Apolinare Nuovo at Ravenna, the mosaics above the arcading on the side walls represent on the one side a procession of male saints bearing crowns, on the other a procession of female saints, headed by the Magi, offering their gifts to the infant Saviour. Beneath in the church, at the time of the Liturgy, there was to be seen a similar procession of men and women bearing their gifts of bread and wine to the altar at the offertory. Thus the theme of the mosaic is the unity of the earthly offering with the heavenly.[2]

The symbolic art of the early Church has survived in the Ikons of the Orthodox Eastern Churches, which here as elsewhere have preserved ancient traditions which the West has partly forgotten. The figures in the Ikons, solemn, austere, noble, with a background of golden light, make no attempt at realism. They represent the eternal, the other-worldly, the mystery of faith, in a manner which recalls the great figure of Christ in glory which dominated the basilica-churches from the semi-spherical apse above the altar.

Thus the classical tradition of Christian art illustrates the liturgical use of the Scriptures, according to which a Gospel story, such as that of Christ healing the blind man, is read both as an historical story and as a symbol of the continuing activity of the living Saviour. Modern critical study of the Bible seeks to disentangle the historical order

---

[1] *Christliche Kunst und Mysterium*, pp. 16 ff.
[2] Herwegen, *Kirche und Seele*, p. 35. Pictures of the mosaic at Ravenna in Diehl, *Manuel d'art byzantin*, pp. 187, 212.

of events and the development of doctrine, aiming at what we might call a photographically accurate record. We have insisted repeatedly that the critical study of the Bible is right and is necessary, because Christianity appeals to history and must stand by that appeal. But a photograph is different from a painting; and the modern scholar, with his keen historical sense, is at his weakest in the interpretation of the eternal meaning of that which he describes. This is not to say merely that the critical study of the Bible needs to be supplemented by devotional study, by the use of the Bible for the nourishment of the spiritual life of the individual. The true balance is that which is given when the Bible is seen in the context of the Liturgy, and the symbols which it gives are seen as symbols of the eternal facts of the Christian Mystery. And this is the interpretation of the Bible alike in the Bible itself and in the classical tradition of Christian art.

The modern development of critical study corresponds with the medieval and modern development of Western art in the direction of realistic historical representation. We noted in an earlier chapter the contrast between the catacomb-paintings of the Last Supper, where the emphasis is on the sacrament, and the great picture by Leonardo da Vinci, where the interest is psychological, and the parallel development of the crucifix into a realistic representation of a human sufferer. The older type gave the idea of *Christus Victor*, and we might even say that earlier still, when Christians wished to represent the crucifix, they drew Daniel in the lions' den. But the modern development of realism, both in art and in historical study, has not been in vain. A modern crucifix by a great sculptor has succeeded in combining a thorough realism—even to the use of a saddle to support the body and ropes to secure it—with the identical pose of the old triumphal crucifixes, with the arms extended straight. It is the living, not the dead Christ, and His eyes are open, looking upon God.[1]

The Bible and the Liturgy do not merely provide symbols of which art can make use: they themselves partake of the nature of art. There is no need to enlarge on the literary quality of the Bible: but it is worth while to draw attention to the artistic aspect of Liturgy.[2] Always in art there is a certain fitness and inevitableness, and each detail has to be just right; and so it is in Liturgy. The Christian Liturgy at its best moves on the level of supreme art, as does the story of the Resurrection in the twentieth chapter of St. John; as instances we might give the eucharistic prayer in the Liturgy of St. Basil, the Mass in the Roman rite for the Saturday after Pentecost, or the Anglican form for the Ordination of Priests. It is not merely the text that is to be taken into account, for liturgical forms, like drama, are composed in order to be acted; and again, they differ from drama, in that there is no audience, and all those present share in the action; if any one is present merely as an onlooker, he misses all the meaning that matters.

Just because Liturgy has its own exacting standards, much liturgical composition must be condemned as bad: some, not all, of the new collects and prayers in the Revised Prayer Book of 1928; in older times, much, very much, of the Gallican rites which were superseded in the West by the Roman rite in the early Middle Ages. For the same reason the choice of hymns for a service requires a high liturgical tact and sense of fitness. The genius of Liturgy is nowhere better exemplified than in the old Roman collects, and Cranmer's English translations which fall little short of the originals.

[1] See Illustration No. XV.
[2] Cf. Dr. Herwegen's pamphlet, *Das Kunstprincip der Liturgie* (Paderborn, 1929).

246

XV. THE ROOD AT KELHAM

Christian Dogma likewise has a certain affinity to art. Dogma is concerned with the 'inevitable' relation of the redeeming God to humanity as seen by a higher vision than that of the mere logician. To say this is to affirm and in nowise to deny that dogma expresses absolute truth: for it is a matter of God's truth, not man's. The preparation for the Gospel, alike in the Old Covenant and the Prophets of Israel, and in the mystery-cults of Egypt, Syria and Greece, and in Plato and the tragic poets, had sketched out a rude picture, a rough outline, which nevertheless seemed to have a certain inevitability. Salvation, when it came, must be by way of suffering, by the blood of a dying God, by the revelation of a Son. Christ came, Christ the Fulfiller; He came, not to destroy, but to fulfil: He wrought out the salvation of men in terms of human life, which must therefore be expressed in the universal forms drawn from elemental human things, fatherhood, sonship, sacrifice, redemption, reconciliation. It is these elemental forms which make the stuff out of which Christian dogma is woven.

The truth which dogma presents in a reasoned form is presented by Apocalyptic in a pictorial form. Therefore, to interpret our Lord's prophecies of the Second Advent 'literally', and to try to determine the day and the hour (as He warned us not to do), is to make nonsense of them. They are symbolic pictures of Divine truth, of the background of eternity against which our lives are lived, of the rock of reality by which we shall be judged at the last, because we are being judged by it now.[1]

It is in this way that we are to understand the profound teaching of the Book of the Revelation. Here we have

---

[1] On this subject see Gore, *Belief in Christ* (Murray, 1922), chap. V, on 'The Apocalyptic Teaching of Jesus'; von Hügel, *Essays and Addresses on the Philosophy of Religion* (Dent, 1921), pp. 109–43; *New Commentary* (S.P.C.K., 1932), on St. Matt. xxiv, pp. 193–4.

dogma in pictorial form. The figure of the glorified Christ in the first chapter (vss. 10–20) is not a figure that could be painted: the details are incongruous; it is evidently not a transcription of something apprehended in a manner analogous to bodily sight. On the other hand, it is not an artificial construction, a patchwork of intellectual conceptions: it is clearly something which has been *given* to the seer. It has been apprehended as a theological-mystical apprehension of spiritual reality: real, external to the observer, seen with the mind rather than with the eye: an intellectual vision of symbolism. The incongruities of such a vision are necessary to its completeness. He is seen in the midst of the seven golden candlesticks, and He holds seven stars in His right hand: then we are told that the seven stars are the angels of the seven churches, and the candlesticks are the churches. Christ is in the midst of the Church, and He holds the Church in His hand.[1]

We are in a region of supreme art, akin to poetry and akin to the Liturgy. The vision of the heavenly worship in Revelation chs. iv and v is a liturgical vision: its background is the eucharistic worship of the Church, and we can see already the lines of the Church Liturgy. There is the throne, and (as in the Church the presbyters sat in the apse on either side of the bishop, so here) round about the throne there are four and twenty presbyters sitting, clothed in white robes. There are lights burning before the throne; and the song which the living creatures sing is the *Sanctus*. After this, in the Liturgy, comes the eucharistic memorial of Christ's sacrifice: here we read how the Lion that is of the tribe of Judah hath overcome, and how in the midst is the Lamb slain, not lying dead, but standing as it had been slain, the object of adoration. Then follows the communion anthem of the redeemed: 'Worthy art

[1] See Carrington, *The Meaning of the Revelation* (S.P.C.K., 1931), pp. 78–86.

thou, to take the book and to open the seals thereof, for thou wast slain, and hast redeemed us to God by thy blood out of every kindred and tongue and people and nation.'

This liturgical note runs throughout the book. As God's judgements proceed, we hear from time to time a sort of chorus of liturgical voices, of angels or of men, glorifying Him. As a rule we are told the words of their song, but not always: when the Lamb is seen 'standing on Mount Zion and with Him a hundred and forty and four thousand, having His name and the name of His Father written on their foreheads', they sing 'as it were a new song before the throne and before the four living creatures and the presbyters: but no one could learn the song save the hundred and forty and four thousand which were redeemed from the earth' (xiv. 1, 3).

And when Babylon the great city has fallen amid cosmic terrors, while men 'blaspheme God because of the hail' (xvi. 21); when her merchandise has all come to ruin—'merchandise of gold and silver and precious stones and pearls and fine linen and purple and silk and scarlet and all thyine wood and every vessel of ivory and every vessel made of most precious wood and of brass and iron and marble and cinnamon and spice and incense and ointment and frankincense and wine and oil and fine flour and wheat and cattle and sheep and merchandise of horses and chariots and slaves and souls of men'—and the merchants from their ships on the sea look from afar on the smoke of her burning, saying 'Woe, woe, the great city', lamenting her ruin and theirs—again are heard the liturgical voices, singing:

'Alleluia.
Salvation and glory and honour belong to our God:
For He hath judged the great harlot
Which did corrupt the earth with her fornications,
And He hath avenged the blood of His servants at her hand.
Alleluia.' [1]

---

[1] Rev. xviii. 12, 13; xix. 1, 2.

The fall of Rome did not take place for more than three centuries after St. John wrote. But his prophecy is not mere prediction. It expresses the judgement of God which is continually being pronounced on every godless civilization, and which from time to time takes shape in terrible catastrophes. But amid the judgement, and after the catastrophe has happened, there are still heard the liturgical voices praising Him whose kingdom cannot be shaken.

A God whom our limited minds could demonstrate and comprehend would thereby be proved not to be the true God. Because His ways are not as our ways, nor His thoughts as our thoughts, our thoughts of Him must work with symbols, images and rituals; it is through a glass darkly that now we see. But we can believe that these are symbols and images of truth and rituals having contact with reality, because they are subject to and controlled by the fact of the coming of God in the flesh, in history.

CHAPTER XI
AFTER LIBERALISM

*

It was characteristic of Liberalism that it looked with hope towards the future, rejoicing that the superstitions of the Middle Ages had been left behind, and desiring to see Christianity emancipated from bondage to past modes of thought, and to exhibit it as a moral and rational religion suited to the modern world. It is characteristic of the modern world that it is looking back with something of admiration and regret to the Middle Ages, as to a time when Europe lived by a common faith. There are very many who envy the men of those days the privilege of living in an age which had a common faith, and heartily wish that it were possible to put the clock back five centuries; but it is not possible, for the civilization of the Middle Ages is dead and gone. They would compare the present age with its dying civilization to the age of Augustus; the religious movements of this age, in particular the Anglo-Catholic Movement, seem to them to be parallel to the endeavours of that age to galvanize the state religion into life, or alternatively to find a personal religious satisfaction in the mystery-cults: it may be that when the present age has passed and a new age has come, some new religion will appear which every one will be able to believe, much as Christianity appeared in the ancient world and brought to it new life. In any case the Church seems to such people to be a reactionary institution, whose modes of thought and life are survivals

251

from an age that is gone. They are waiting for something: waiting for it, even while they do not know what it is to be.

Such people, if this book falls into their hands, will want to ask how it is that we, who evidently desire to ask the questions which the modern world is asking, and who evidently repudiate the Liberal answers, can yet be associated in the Church with people whose modes of thought are reactionary: with people who shrink back from asking the modern questions precisely because they abhor the Liberal answers. Yet we profess an enthusiastic faith in the Church, and do not appear to be greatly troubled over what (as it seems to them) must be an uneasy association with the people who do not ask questions; we are evidently much more uneasy over our association in the Church with those who still hold to the Liberal theology. What are we to reply to this question?

This: that the Christians whose modes of thought seem to be reactionary are nevertheless living by a faith in a truth which is not of man or from man, a faith which is a common faith, embodied in the Church's worship and life; and we believe that this faith holds the answer to the perplexities of the modern world, and contains that for which men are waiting. Certainly it is necessary to ask questions: in the words of a revered Christian teacher, 'Be sceptical, and with all thy learning learn scepticism'. It is necessary then, first, to test and try the foundations of faith, that the things which are not shaken may remain; in other words, mankind needs a *Weltanschauung* which can stand the test of truth. And second, it must be a common faith, for it is for lack of a common faith that civilization is falling to pieces. No purely personal construction of belief can satisfy, no belief which is merely 'our own -doxy': we cannot really believe that which does not find its echo in the conscience of mankind. What we long for but do not yet see is a whole social order grounded on a common faith. Can we find a foothold anywhere, can we find a light of faith sufficient at least to walk by?

When we apply these two tests, it is plain that there is no help to be found in those who would confine the things of the spirit to the imaginative world: in Mr. Middleton Murry's dissociation of the spiritual and ethical from the material and scientific: in Mr. I. A. Richards, with his clear distinction between 'emotive' and 'scientific' beliefs: in Bertrand Russell, desiring to cherish 'the lofty thoughts that ennoble our little day',[1] but admitting that these lofty thoughts have nothing to do with truth. Such an attitude is really a survival of Liberalism, and recalls the distinction of the Ritschlian theology between 'judgements of fact' and 'judgements of value', *Seinsurteile* and *Werturteile*.

D. H. Lawrence cannot be called a concealed Liberal, and at times he is prophetic. Having long since shaken himself free of all Christian belief, and having seen the falsity not only of contemporary civilization, but also of all attempts of communists and others to impose their own ideas upon it for its amelioration, he writes thus in *Kangaroo*:

'But he kicked against the pricks. He did not yet submit to the fact which he *half* knew: that before mankind would accept any man for a king, and before Harriet would even accept him, Richard Lovat, as a lord and master, he, this self-same Richard who was so strong on kingship, must open the doors of his soul and let in a dark Lord and Master for himself, the dark god he had sensed outside the door.'

And again:

'Any more love is a hopeless thing, till we have found

[1] See Dawson, *Progress and Religion*, p. 21, where the whole passage is quoted.

again, each one for himself, the great dark god who alone will sustain us in our loving one another. Till then, best not play with more fire.'

These utterances, however, speak of a hope rather than a faith. They are prophetic, but prophetic of what?

Mighty national movements in several countries, such as the Nazi movement in Germany, or the religious militarism of Japan, appear to provide those nations with a common faith. These movements are messianic in character: but plainly they have in view the welfare of one nation at the expense of the rest, and in spite of the Nordic myth of the Chosen Race, it must be hard for any one who asks questions really to believe that God is a German. These national movements fail to face the problem of truth, and fall short of the promise of coherence and intellectual integrity that is offered, however fallaciously, by Marxian materialism.

Marxism seeks to elaborate a world-view which claims to be universally true, on a basis of pure materialism. Thereby it starves those sides of human nature which cannot be satisfied with mathematics and mechanics. Yet (and here is the incongruity) Russian Communism lives by its religious fervour, by its messianic hope of a good time coming, which inevitably introduces an element of 'emotive' belief into materialism.[1] There is a fundamental contradiction in a religion which denies God and a messianic movement whose formal belief is the denial that man has a soul.[2]

Elsewhere the longing for a revived common culture has given birth to American Humanism, once led by Irving Babbitt and Paul Elmer More. Now that some

---

[1] See an article by Christopher Dawson, 'The Catholic Interpretation of History', in *Christendom*, Sept. 1934, esp. pp. 182 ff.

[2] Berdyaev, *The Russian Revolution* ('Essays in Order', Sheed and Ward), pp. 40–8.

people in all countries are able to study the sacred books of all cultures, this movement hoped for a revived common order on the basis of a combination of what is best in many religions. But such a combination is essentially eclectic. The religions of the past have differed from one another, but have all lived in virtue of some kind of a living belief; any attempt to combine them can only succeed in combining certain outward features, while missing that which is really dynamic in each. The cultured cosmopolitan intellectual cannot provide a common faith for all. And in fact the American Humanist movement has practically collapsed. Irving Babbitt is dead; Paul Elmer More and T. S. Eliot have become orthodox Christians.

Are we then to sit still and wait for the 'second religiousness' of our exhausted 'Faustian Civilization', foretold by Spengler—perhaps some form of Nazism, in some cosmopolitan shape which has not yet appeared, or some form of Communism? There may be hope here of a common faith, when it appears: but what happens to the need for a real answer to the question of truth, the need for a trustworthy belief about the ultimate meaning of the world and our life in it? We have here the old Stoic doctrine of 'cycles of civilization', each of which in turn has its rise and maturity and decay; and can we regard each in turn as anything more than another cycle of vanity and striving after wind? Or is there a real meaning in history?

If we can dare at least to hope that history has a real meaning and coherence—that what past seers have seen in the ages behind us was not all illusion, but part illusion and part light, and the light was a true light—we must at least acknowledge Christianity to have been the inheritor and transmitter of the ancient wisdom of Western Asia and Europe. We may go on to see that the main features of that ancient wisdom, which the Christian Gospel developed and transformed, are universal—the conception of the union of the divine and human, as in the ancient kingship, the instinct of sacrifice, the symbol of the dying god, the desire for re-birth and for immortality. This is to acknowledge a real authority and a real truth in the tradition out of which we ourselves have been born: and it cannot be denied that this tradition has been summed up in the Christianity which was the common faith of the ages behind us and which has claimed to be true.

To go so far as this is not necessarily to accept orthodox Christianity. There are many who feel the acceptance of Christianity and the Church to be impossible for them because it seems to involve belief in the ultimate validity of the forms of thought of a past age, of the monumental scholastic system of Christian doctrine, under the shadow of which we still live. But, as we tried to show in Chapter IV, Christianity cannot be equated with any such system; it is not only that Christianity existed long before scholasticism was thought of, but much more that the centre of Christian dogma is not belief in any such system but in the personal revelation of God Himself through Christ. The Creeds and the definitions of the Councils were shaped, not in order to create a speculative system, but in order to guard this faith in God and His real action. Liberal theology in our day, accepting the false assumption that Christianity is a system of beliefs, seeks to replace the old beliefs by a new system, which must become out of date in its turn, and indeed is out of date already. But Christianity cannot be equated with any such system, medieval or modern; and as St. John's Gospel states in the clearest terms, it has at its base the conception of a TRUTH, not of man nor from man, the truth of God which makes men free.

XVI. ST. SAVIOUR'S CHURCH, ELTHAM

It is exactly this which is the stumbling-block. The critic of Christianity is found again and again to be assuming that Christianity is a doctrine or a belief: but his sense that it is something more than this is shown by the fact that people who are tolerant and fair-minded in everything else become prickly and irritated when they come against the absolute claim of Christian dogma. It is, in fact, a claim that here is a truth which will not allow us to sit in judgement on it—if we could be allowed either to approve it or reject it we would not mind; what is maddening is that it claims to sit in judgement on us. Faith in God is the acceptance of this judgement on the self, the practical acknowledgement that God, and not man, is sovereign.

So we come to the demand for conversion. A common presentation of Christianity puts this and this alone in the forefront. 'Are you saved?' cries the evangelical preacher. So presented, Christianity seems to be a way of personal piety sustained by a hope of a future reward in heaven. Such personal religiousness is often in danger of becoming a way of escape from the world, the seeking of a refuge from the troubles of life, and so an 'emotive belief'. But, as we have seen in Chapters V and VI, Christianity cannot be equated with a way of personal religion; it is not the New Testament and the early Church, but the medievals and moderns who lay exaggerated emphasis on personal piety, tending to lose the redemption of the body and of social life in a one-sided stress on individual salvation. No Christian may evade the question 'Are you saved?'; but Christianity is not to be thus limited. It is essentially the Gospel of the coming of God in the flesh for the redemption to God of the whole man and of common life (Chapter VIII).

This emphasis on personal religion makes it easy for Christianity to be regarded as if it were one among many religions. If it were, one would expect that in time it would become outworn and cease to be, like the others. But it is essential to Christianity that it takes a whole view of history as a continuous process, rejecting the old pagan doctrine of cycles of civilization: it affirms a Divine purpose which gathers up, as in a drag-net, first the heritage of Israel and then those of Greek philosophy and the pagan mystery-religions and the tribal cults that formed unities of social life in primitive society. Looking backwards, Christ is thus seen as the Fulfiller: looking forwards, the Church has for its function to gather in the riches of all nations and cultures, through Christ the Head of the Ages (Chapter II).

But if Christianity finds its fulfilment in the life of the Church, as Christ's mystical Body, those who believe in the Church cannot seek to impose on the Church a programme of their own. They must look to God to fulfil His own purpose through the Church in which there is one Spirit but diversities of gifts. The nature of the Church is seen most clearly in her sacramental order and her common worship (Chapter III): if this be so, we shall expect to learn in the actual visible Church of today (Chapter VII) and in the worship and life of our own parish church (Chapter IX) the secret of God's meaning both for His world and for our little lives.

Are we demonstrating to our own satisfaction, after the manner of apologetic, that Christianity is true? Does the claim stand in view of the seeming fact that Christianity has failed, and that a civilization which grew up under the aegis of the Church is in process of collapse? Any one who wishes may point out the Church's failure, and criticize her shortcomings. Only let him beware lest his criticism of the Church's sins be, in fact, a psychological self-defence to save him from confessing his own; lest, in picking holes in the Church's doctrines, he should be seeking

to hide from himself his own unpreparedness to respond
to Truth.

Of course the actual Church is imperfect and unworthy.
But did He even lead us to anticipate anything else?

'So is the Kingdom of God
  As if a man should cast seed upon the earth,
  And should sleep and rise, night and day,
  And the seed should spring up and grow, he knoweth not
    how:
  The earth beareth fruit of itself
    First the blade,
    Then the ear,
    Then the full corn in the ear.
  But when the fruit is ripe,
  Straightway he putteth forth the sickle, because the harvest
    is come.'

(Mark iv. 26-9.)

The Church is imperfect, immature; the time of perfection is not yet. The present stage is that of growth,
through trial and conflict, and of the weakness and limitation which He took upon Himself in becoming man, and
in which He endured His Passion. In the present stage
of growth, faith for us is hope:

'By hope we are saved. But hope that is seen is not
hope; for who hopeth for that which he seeth? But if we
hope for that which we see not, then do we with patience
wait for it.'

Through His Passion Christ went to His Resurrection.
The principle of life-through-death, through defeat the
victory that is beyond defeat, is set forth once for all in
the One Son, that it may be fulfilled in the many sons.
For us also, present imperfection and conflict are shot
through with the triumph that is still future.

Therefore the Church in this world does not stand
as something complete, finished and perfect. When the
Church seeks to present herself as if she had already
attained, she is deeply false to herself. She lives by faith

259   R*

and hope in the eternal, in the future, in things not seen, of which only a foretaste is actualized in the present.

In these days of anxiety and fear and impending tribulation, Christians have their witness to bear, of the reality of God as the owner of His world and the Master in His own house; of the real manifestation of God in the flesh, for the redemption of all human life to God; of the dignity of man, called to be a child of God, so that the bodily life even of the lowest has an eternal meaning; and of the vocation of the Church to express in her worship and the common life of her members the pattern of the Foundations of the City of God.

'When these things begin to come to pass, then look up and lift up your heads, for your redemption draweth nigh.' It is not unlikely that in days to come the Church will have to lose her temporalities, vested interests, and privileges. Only let her be manifested as the Body of Christ, and find her life through losing it, that the world may believe that God has sent Him; and so may she bring to birth the civilization of the future, on the basis of a common faith. Now in the present, let Christians be Christians, and let the Church be the Church:

'I say unto you: *Make perfect your will.*
I say: take no thought of the harvest,
But only of proper sowing.' [1]

---

[1] *The Rock*, p. 9.

BIBLIOGRAPHY

This list includes the books referred to in the footnotes, and all quotations made in the text. Titles of books are in some instances given here in an abbreviated form.

Acts of the Apostles, 104, 232
Amos, 202
Apuleius, 62
Architect, The, 26
Architecture Illustrated, 26
Atchley, *Ordo Romanus Primus,* 74
Augustine, St., 238
　City of God, 78
　On the Psalms, 72
　Sermons, 78, 79, 85
Aulén, G., *Christus Victor,* 35, 97, 186

Baruch, 66
Beauduin, Dom. L., *La piété de l'Eglise,* 128
Bede Frost, the Rev., *The Art of Mental Prayer,* 121
Berdyaev, N., *The Russian Revolution,* 203, 254
Bevan, E., *Christianity,* 124
Bevan, G. M., *Early Christians of Rome,* 24, 66
Birkbeck, W. J., *Russia and the English Church,* 147
Book of Common Prayer, 41, 46, 157, 163, 173, 215, 220, 224–6, 246

Brightman, W. E., *Liturgies Eastern and Western,* 76
Brilioth, Y., *Eucharistic Faith and Practice,* 48, 67, 81, 82, 103, 116, 123, 125, 171, 211, 227
Browe, P., *De frequenti communione,* 81

Cabrol, Abbot, *Liturgical Prayer,* 75, 128
Caronti, Abbot, 128
Carpenter, S. C., *Church and People,* 145
Carrington, P., *The Meaning of the Revelation,* 248
Catholic Encyclopaedia, 127
Christopherson, Bp., 173
Church Times, 190
Colossians, 95
1 *Corinthians,* 91, 104, 151, 153, 206, 243
Cutts, E. L., *Priests and People in the Middle Ages,* 116

Daniel, 66, 93
Dawson, Christopher, *Christianity and the New Age,* 34
　Progress and Religion, 31, 253

261

Inge, W. R., *Outspoken Essays, second series*, 31

Innocent I, Pope, *Ad Decentium*, 76

Isaiah, 52, 58, 66, 217

Jacks, L. P., *Two Letters*, 35

James, E. O., *Christian Myth and Ritual*, 46, 47, 56, 59, 62

James, W., *The Varieties of Religious Experience*, 113

Jeremiah, 221

Joad, C. E. M., 33

John, Gospel according to, 47, 58, 61, 103, 106, 109–10, 141, 152, 208, 246

1 *John*, 110, 141

Jonah, 66

Kelly, H. H., 88, 89, 144, 171, 219

Khomiakoff, A. S., 147, 148

Kirk, K. E., *Conscience and its Problems*, 209

Lacey, T. A., *Anglo-Catholic Faith*, 213, 224

Lambeth Conference Reports, 229

Laporta, Dom., G., *Piété eucharistique*, 118

Lawrence, D. H., *Kangaroo*, 253–4

Lebe mit der Kirche, 129

Liturgical Press, Collegeville, Minnesota, U.S.A., 128

Liturgische Zeitschrift, 131

Liturgy of St. James, 67, 79

Liturgy of St. Mark, 76, 80

Luke, Gospel according to, 200, 221

Mackay, H. F. B., *Paul of Tarsus*, 55

Mahoney, E. J., 128

Mark, Gospel according to, 54, 60, 93, 106, 130, 221, 238, 259

Matthew, Gospel according to, 15, 60, 66, 91, 94, 105, 216, 244

Maurice, F. D., *Kingdom of Christ*, 108, 109, 153, 189–90, 226

The Church a Family, 40–1

Mersch, Emil, *Le corps mystique du Christ*, 78, 126

Middleton Murry, J., *The Necessity of Communism*, 166, 253

Modern Churchman, The, 34, 225

More, P. E., *Anglicanism* (ed.) 175

The Catholic Faith, 140

The Sceptical Approach to Religion, 101

Mozarabic rite, 68

Muller, J. A., *Letters of Stephen Gardiner*, 173

Mysterium Christi, 48

Nairne, A., *Faith of the New Testament*, 33

Narsai, Homilies of, 68

Nehemiah, 167

New Commentary (S.P.C.K.), 54, 221, 247

New Statesman, 34, 185

Nygren, A., *Agape and Eros* 91, 140 ff.

Oecumenica, 169, 179

Pascal, *Provincial Letters*, 119
Philippians, 81, 142
Pius X., Pope, 105, 126, 213
Plotinus, 140
Psalms, The, 54, 72–5, 136, 167, 214–20
Psalms of Solomon, 93

Questions liturgiques et paroissiales, 118, 129, 133
Quick, O. C., *The Christian Sacraments*, 35, 57
The Ground of Faith and the Chaos of Thought, 191

Rashdall, H., *Idea of Atonement*, 33
Raven, C. E., 35
Reckitt, M. B., *Faith and Society*, 204
Redfern, Dr., 32
Renaudot, *Liturgiarum Orientalium Collectio*, 70
Revelation, Book of the, 152, 164, 217, 219, 247–9
Roman Missal, 59, 65, 66, 74, 76, 77, 135, 243
Romans, 61, 80, 81, 141, 151, 164
Russell, Bertrand, 253

S.S.M. Quarterly, 15, 89, 171
Sassé, H., 48
Sidgwick, H., 114
Similitudes of Enoch, 93
Söderblom, N., *Mystery of the Cross*, 56–7, 94, 201
Songs of Praise, 225–6
Sparrow Simpson, W. J., *Non-communicating Attendance*, 81
Spencer, H., 31
Stone, Dr. Darwell, 221

Theology, 75, 80, 118, 144, 185
Thomas à Kempis, *De Imitatione*, 112, 125
Thomas Aquinas, *Summa Theologica*, 91, 99, 170
Thomson, J. A., *Introduction to Science*, 110
Turner, C. H., 37, 54

Universe, The, 128, 133

Virgil, *Aeneid*, 114
von Hügel, F., 112, 247

Williams, N. P., *Northern Catholicism*, 181
Wordsworth, C., 173

A SELECT INDEX OF SUBJECTS